LIES, DAMNED LIES, AND
DRUG WAR STATISTICS

Lies, Damned Lies, and Drug War Statistics

A Critical Analysis of Claims Made by the Office of National Drug Control Policy

Matthew B. Robinson
Renee G. Scherlen

STATE UNIVERSITY OF NEW YORK PRESS

Published by
State University of New York Press, Albany

© 2007 State University of New York

For information, address State University of New York Press,
194 Washington Avenue, Suite 305, Albany, NY 12210-2384

Production by Michael Haggett
Marketing by Susan M. Petrie

Library of Congress Cataloging-in-Publication Data
Robinson, Matthew B.
  Lies, damned lies, and drug war statistics : a critical analysis of claims made by the office of National Drug Control Policy / Matthew B. Robinson, Renee G. Scherlen.
     p.   cm.
  Includes bibliographical references and index.
  ISBN-13: 978-0-7914-6975-0 (hardcover : alk. paper)
  ISBN-13: 978-0-7914-6976-7 (pbk. : alk. paper)
  1. United States. Office of National Drug Control Policy.
  2. Drug control—United States. 3. Drug control—United States—Statistics.
  4. Drug abuse—Government policy—United States.
  5. Drug abuse—United States—Statistics.
  I. Scherlen, Renee G., 1962- II. Title.
  HV5825.R63 2007
  363.450973—dc22   2006007115

10 9 8 7 6 5 4 3 2 1

CONTENTS

———————————

Contents

List of Figures and Tables

FIGURES

TABLES

Preface

There are three kinds of lies: lies, damned lies, and statistics.

—Mark Twain

Actually, it is not fair to say that statistics are lies (as Mark Twain claimed[1]), or that statistics lie (as so many others often claim). It is more accurate to say that statistics can be used to lie. That is, they can be manipulated to support any argument, including a knowingly false argument.

Here's a fictional example: If a thousand people were in a room with Microsoft magnate Bill Gates, the average worth of all the people in the room would be at least one million dollars. This is a statistical fact, if the average in this case refers to the *mean*. The mean is equal to the total worth of everyone in the room divided by the total number of people in the room. Since Bill Gates is worth more than one billion dollars[2] (not to mention whatever the other one thousand people are worth), it is safe to conclude that the average worth (or mean) of all the people in the room would be at least one million dollars because one billion divided by one thousand equals one million.

Although the mean statistic in this example is accurate, it is still misleading. It is misleading because saying that the average worth of Bill Gates and one thousand other people is one million dollars implies that each person in the room is worth somewhere in the vicinity of one million dollars, which would be highly unlikely (at least not if the other thousand people are average, everyday citizens).

A more useful and less misleading statistic would be the *median* wealth. The median is equal to the middle wealth of the people in the room, where half of the values for wealth are above the median and half are below the median. In 2000, the median household worth in the United States was $55,000.[3] Since half of all American households are worth more than $55,000 (including Bill Gates) and half are worth less, this gives us a better sense of what the average worth would be if Bill Gates was in a room with a thousand average people, each of which is worth $55,000 if they are the representatives of their households.

Here's another example, this time real. President George W. Bush used statistics in a similarly misleading way on at least one notable occasion. On February 19, 2004, President Bush told the American people that the average tax cut he signed into law was $1,089, suggesting that the typical person would pay approximately one thousand dollars less in taxes.[4]

In fact, President Bush was also talking about the mean rather than the median. In this case, the mean is also misleading because it is inflated due to the huge tax cuts given to the very small number of extremely wealthy Americans. The median tax cut—that's the statistic that tells us the middle tax cut or the value for which half the people in the United States who received a tax cut received more than this and the other half received less than this—was only $470.

The larger mean figure owes itself to the fact that households that earned more than one million dollars got an average tax cut of nearly $113,000![5] When President Bush reported the $1,089 tax cut average, he implied that the average American family could expect to pay about $1,000 less in taxes, which is not true.

It should be noted that neither of these examples involved a lie. Instead, the statistics, though factual, were misleading.

Simply stated, this matters. Actually, it matters a lot. People use and read statistics everyday, and, from them, we get our sense of the world and everything in it. When people use statistics to mislead, we often get a false sense of the world and the many things in it.

This book is about drug war statistics. It is about how the federal agency responsible for leading the fight in America's so-called war on drugs—the Office of the National Drug Control Policy (ONDCP)—regularly uses statistics to mislead the American people, thereby giving us a false sense of the drug war and our successes and failures in it.[6]

Every year, ONDCP publishes its *National Drug Control Strategy* that "directs the Nation's anti-drug efforts and establishes a program, a budget, and guidelines for cooperation among Federal, State, and local entities."[7] The National Drug Control Strategy (or, simply, the Strategy) is the primary mechanism through which the White House and the federal agencies involved in the war on drugs communicate with the American people about the drug war.

In this book, we present a study of six years of the Strategy (2000–2005) and the main claims contained therein. We are primarily interested in how ONDCP uses statistics to make claims about the nation's drug war, and whether these claims are accurate, honest, transparent, and justifiable. Since ONDCP regularly presents graphs and figures to depict important drug war statistics, we also critically analyze how it chooses to present the data visually.

Although the word *lie* appears in the book's title (twice), we do not claim that ONDCP knowingly lies to the American people about the drug war. Rather, the findings of this book suggest that either: (1) ONDCP knowingly uses statistics to mislead about the drug war; or (2) the authors of its annual

Strategy need some basic instruction about the nature of basic statistics (including how to use them, how not to use them, and how to visually depict them in graphs and figures). We leave it to readers to decide for themselves which is most likely.

OVERVIEW OF THE BOOK

This book is divided into three main parts. In Part One, we introduce the main issues of the book and provide a solid yet brief background on the major issues pertaining to America's war on drugs. In chapter 1, we discuss the role of ideology and claims-making in policy formation and the drug war, and end with an examination of policy analysis. Here, we provide the tools needed to understand our study of claims-making by the Office of National Drug Control Policy (ONDCP) and the tools needed to evaluate any government policy. In chapter 2, we briefly trace the history of America's drug war at home and abroad, noting the establishment of major drug war agencies, identifying key laws, and discussing significant events. We also provide an important foundation through a brief discussion of issues such as the goals of the drug war, the agencies that fight the drug war, and the drug war budget. Here we provide some background and context for America's drug war.

In Part Two, we offer the methodology and findings of our study of claims-making by ONDCP. Chapter 3 describes the study's methodology, telling what we did, how we did it, and why. Chapters 4 through 6 contain the findings of our study. Throughout this part of the book, we illustrate how ONDCP misuses statistics and visual graphs based on these statistics to justify American's drug war.

In chapter 4, we discuss ONDCP claims regarding efforts to reduce drug use. We find that ONDCP generally claims success in reducing drug use, both when it is warranted and when it is not. Among other things, ONDCP focuses almost exclusively on the good news with regard to drug use trends, downplays or totally ignores the bad news about drug use trends, and "spins the data" by selectively presenting certain statistics while ignoring others to show positive results.

In chapter 5, we discuss ONDCP claims regarding efforts to heal drug users and disrupt drug markets. We find that ONDCP does not generally claim success in healing drug users, largely because the statistics so clearly point to failure. For example, the vast majority of people who need drug treatment do not receive it.

We also find that ONDCP does not generally claim success in disrupting drug markets. Nevertheless, ONDCP continues to stress the importance of its eradication, interdiction, and foreign intervention efforts, despite the relevant statistics showing that these efforts are failing.

In chapter 6, we discuss how ONDCP deals with the costs of drug use and abuse, and attempt to cull out from the costs those that can actually be attributed to drug use and abuse itself and those that are better characterized as drug war costs. We find that economic costs are rising, and that deaths attributable to illicit drugs and emergency room mentions of illicit drug use are consistently increasing.

In Part Three, we provide a fair assessment of America's drug war, including both the costs and the benefits. We also offer conclusions from the study and suggest policy implications.

In chapter 7 we offer a fair assessment of America's drug war, focusing on the years 1989 through 1998. Since ONDCP was created in November 1988, we begin our analysis in 1989 and continue it only through 1998 because this is the last year for which all statistics on drug use trends are comparable (due to methodological changes in one household survey of drug users). Here, we provide an empirical assessment of the nation's drug war during a ten-year period. This represents the first time that ONDCP goals have been systematically evaluated over any period. We find that statistics readily available to ONDCP suggest that illicit drug use was not down during this period, that the need for drug treatment was up, that deaths attributable to illicit drugs and emergency room mentions of illicit drugs were up, that illicit drugs were still widely available, that prices of illicit drugs were down, and that illicit drug purity was up. None of these outcomes is consistent with the drug war goals of ONDCP. Thus, it is safe to conclude that the first ten years of the drug war under ONDCP were not successful. We also find that the costs of the drug war are simultaneously enormous and ignored by ONDCP, whereas the benefits of the drug war are modest.

In chapter 8 we conclude the book by summarizing the study and our analysis of the drug war. We also provide policy recommendations to change how ONDCP uses, presents, and discusses statistics, as well as fights the nation's drug war.

The postscript of the book contains commentary related to the 2006 strategy, which was released after completion of our study.

Finally, in the Appendix, we describe a brief response to our findings that ONDCP is ineffective from ONDCP Director John Walters.

Acknowledgments

We would like to thank the following people who reviewed this study and offered comments and/or arranged to have it reviewed by other experts in the field. The book is surely stronger as a result of their generous contributions. We, however, remain responsible for any errors or flaws in logic.

- Paul Armentano, NORML | NORML Foundation
- Chuck Armsbury, November Coalition and Senior Editor of *The Razor Wire*
- Brian Bennett, Former U.S. Intelligence analyst and author of *Truth: The Anti-Drugwar*
- Michael Braswell, Anderson Publishing
- Matt Briggs, Drug Policy Alliance
- Nora Callahan, November Coalition
- John Chase, November Coalition
- Jack Cole, Executive Director, Law Enforcement Against Prohibition
- Robert Field, Common Sense for Drug Policy
- Mike Gray, author of *Drug Crazy* and Chairman, Common Sense for Drug Policy
- Ethan Nadelmann, author of *Cops Across Borders* and Executive Director, Drug Policy Alliance
- Ed Parsons, Cambridge University Press
- Michael Rinella, State University of New York Press
- Leah Rorvig, Publications Associate, Drug Policy Alliance
- Ruth Ann Strickland, Department of Political Science and Criminal Justice, Appalachian State University
- Alex Tabarrok, Department of Economics, George Mason University and Director of Research, The Independent Institute
- Mike Wendling, Taylor & Francis Group
- Joseph White, Change the Climate

We also sincerely appreciate the important work done by the many people at SUNY Press that made the final product a reality.

Finally, we acknowledge the love and support of our families who stood by us and provided needed encouragement as we completed the book. Our hope is that the research in this book demonstrates to our children an allegiance to truth, which an informed citizenry depends on to participate in a functional democracy.

Part One

Chapter One

Introduction

In this chapter, we explain how our study of the Office of National Drug Control Policy (ONDCP) came about. In so doing, we provide a few examples of inappropriate uses of statistics by ONDCP. We also introduce the most significant literature important to our study of ONDCP's drug war claims, that which deals with ideology, claims-making and moral panics, and policy analysis.

In preparing for and teaching a class titled "The War on Drugs" at our university, we relied heavily on U.S. government agencies involved in fighting the nation's drug war for data on types of drugs and their effects, the nature and extent of drug use and production in America and abroad, drug use trends, goals of the drug war, drug war spending, and so forth. One primary agency we relied on was ONDCP. As noted on its Web site, ONDCP was established by the Anti-Drug Abuse Act of 1988. Its principal purpose is to

> establish policies, priorities, and objectives for the Nation's drug control program. The goals of the program are to reduce illicit drug use, manufacturing, and trafficking, drug-related crime and violence, and drug-related health consequences. To achieve these goals, the Director of ONDCP is charged with producing the National Drug Control Strategy. The Strategy directs the Nation's anti-drug efforts and establishes a program, a budget, and guidelines for cooperation among Federal, State, and local entities.[1]

The National Drug Control Strategy (the Strategy) is published each year by ONDCP. Along with it, ONDCP also publishes separate statistical

3

supplements and occasionally creates visual presentations that depict various trends in data. We acquired as much information as we could to better inform the materials for our class.

In our searches, we found an online PowerPoint© presentation prepared by ONDCP called "The Drug War Today: Goals, Means, Concerns, and Strategies."[2] We printed up the slides and used many of them in class when discussing the war on drugs.

When we got to our unit on drug use trends in the United States, we discovered something striking about some of the figures created by ONDCP. For example, the titles of some of the slides did not seem to match the data depicted in the figures. At other times, we found the initial dates of the figures very interesting. For example, one ONDCP slide claimed: "Since 1985, all major drugs show a substantial decline in the level of current use." We've reproduced it here as Figure 1.1.

Given that ONDCP was not created until November 1988, we found it strange that it would begin a figure with 1985 data. If one looked at the data beginning in 1988 when ONDCP was created, there has been virtually no change in drug use in the United States. This would require a new title to the slide—perhaps: "Since 1988, current drug use is virtually unchanged."

Clearly, the two titles send different messages. Read them both and consider:

- "Since 1985, all major drugs show a substantial decline in the level of current use" (ONDCP title).
- "Since 1988, current drug use is virtually unchanged" (alternative title).

Interestingly, both titles are equally true. Since 1985, current drug use is down (although "a substantial decline" may not be accurate, depending on what this means), but since 1988, current drug use is stagnant, steady, unchanged. Why would ONDCP choose to characterize this trend as a substantial decline rather than an unchanging trend? The answer may be obvious to the reader: Since ONDCP is in the business of the drug war—in fact, it is the agency responsible for leading the fight in the drug war[3]—of course it would accentuate the positive. This justifies continuing the drug war even though during the period from its establishment to 1999 (the end date in the ONDCP figure), current drug use was not being reduced in line with ONDCP goals.

Yet, is it right that ONDCP used statistics this way, to create a false impression in consumers of its data? Don't American citizens deserve more from their own government? Couldn't ONDCP just tell it like it is by letting the actual data speak for itself?

Here is the title we would have chosen for the ONDCP figure: "Between 1985 and 1988, the level of current drug use declined, but since 1988, the level of current drug use is unchanged." This alternate title captures both

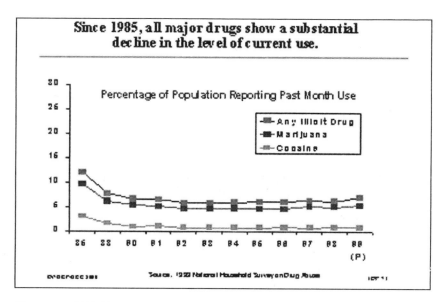

FIGURE 1.1   ONDCP Claims Success in Reducing Current Drug Use (NHSDA) with 1985 as Starting Point, 2000 Strategy

of the above claims (that drug use is down and that it is unchanged). And this title is the most accurate because it tells the full story. Perhaps ONDCP did not choose such a title because then it might be required to explain why drug use rates declined from 1985 to 1988 but remained unchanged since ONDCP was created.

Another ONDCP figure from the same slide show claimed: "Since 1979, current drug use is down substantially." We've reproduced it here as Figure 1.2.

We found it odd that ONDCP would begin the figure with 1979 data, for 1979 was the peak of drug use for most forms of illicit drugs. For example, in the 2001 National Household Survey on Drug Abuse (NHSDA), the U.S. Department Health and Human Services explains:

Prior to the increase in youth illicit drug use in the early to mid-1990s, there had been a period of significant decline in drug use among both youths and adults. This occurred from *1979, the peak year for illicit drug use prevalence among adults and youths,* until 1992. During that period, the number of past month illicit drug users dropped from 25 million to 12 million. The rate of use dropped from 14.1 to 5.8 percent of the population aged 12 or older. Among youths aged 12 to 17, the rate fell from 16.3 to 5.3 percent. Thus, although the rate of illicit drug use among youths in 2001 is approximately twice the rate in 1992, it is still

significantly below *the peak rate that occurred in 1979*. Similarly, the
overall number and rate of use in the population are roughly half of
what they were in 1979. . . . Prior to *1979, the peak year for illicit drug
use*, there had been a steady increase in use occurring throughout the
1970s. . . . Although the first national survey to estimate the prevalence of illicit drug use was conducted in 1971, estimates of illicit drug
initiation, based on retrospective reports of first-time use, suggest that
the increase had begun in the early or mid-1960s. . . . These incidence
estimates suggest that illicit drug use prevalence had been very low
during the early 1960s, but began to increase during the mid-1960s as
substantial numbers of young people initiated the use of marijuana.[4]

Not only has the U.S. Department of Health and Human Services shown
that 1979 was the peak in drug use, they have provided some better understanding of long-term drug use trends in the United States. Knowing that illicit
drug use rose from the mid-1960s until 1979, declined until 1988, and then remained relatively constant since, suggests either that something about the drug
war has changed or something other factors that affect drug use has
changed. That is, no longer are we seeing large increases or declines in most
forms of drug use; instead, statistics show that relatively little seems to be happening with illicit drug use trends. This seems like an important topic for

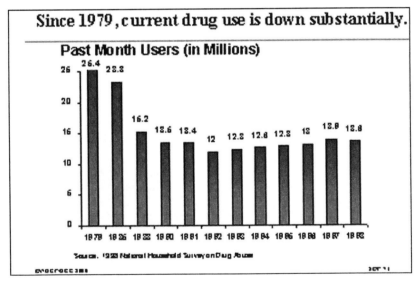

FIGURE 1.2   ONDCP Claims Success in Reducing Current Drug Use (NHSDA) with 1979 as
Starting Point, 2000 Strategy

ONDCP to consider. Yet, the authors of the slide show fail to explore this issue (as do the authors of the annual versions of the Strategy). ONDCP is, instead, attempting to focus mostly on its successes.

If ONDCP began its examination from 1988, a different title to the slide would have to be created—perhaps: "Since 1988, current drug use is virtually unchanged."

The two titles clearly send different messages. Read them both and consider:

- "Since 1979, current drug use is down substantially" (ONDCP title).
- "Since 1988, current drug use is virtually unchanged" (alternative title).

Again, both claims—the original and the alternative—are equally true. Since 1979, current drug use is down (and even "substantially"), but since 1988, current drug use has almost not changed.

Here is the title we would have chosen for the ONDCP figure: "Between 1979 and 1988, the level of current drug use declined, but since 1988, the level of current drug use is virtually unchanged." This alternate title also captures both of the above claims (that drug use is down and that it is unchanged), and it also is the most accurate because it tells the full story.

Why did ONDCP begin the figure with data from 1979, the peak of drug use in the United States? One possible reason is so that ONDCP could show a successful drug war. This is problematic. The stated purpose of the Strategy is *not* to showcase ONDCP. Rather, it is to direct policy. A well-designed policy requires a clear understanding of the problem it is meant to address.

Another ONDCP slide stated: "While drug use is still unacceptably high, 2000 is the fourth year without significant changes in current use of 'Any Illicit Drug'." We've reproduced it here as Figure 1.3.

Although the claim by ONDCP is a true statement, the same figure also shows clear increases in drug use by eighth, tenth, and twelfth graders since 1991. Perhaps a more fitting title would be: "Since 1991, drug use by young people has increased."

A more accurate title for this slide that would still capture what ONDCP said is "Current drug use by eighth, tenth, and twelfth graders increased from 1992 until 1997, but then remained steady through 2000." Such a title was not chosen by ONDCP, we presume, because it runs counter to its goal of reducing drug use among young people.

According to notable drug policy experts: "Accurate description of trends and cross-sectional patterns in drug use, prices, and other relevant variables [are] essential to informed development of drug control policy."[5] Our own analysis of drug use trends during the course of the semester led us to believe that ONDCP was not accurately describing patterns in drug use. Thus, we arrived at different conclusions from those of ONDCP. Of course, we are not in

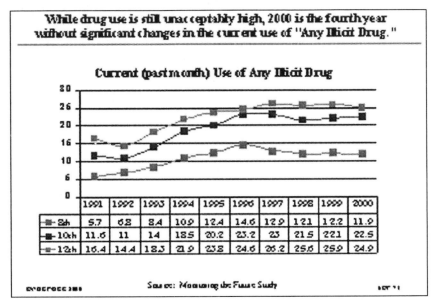

Figure 1.3 ONDCP Fails to Acknowledge Increasing Drug Use Among Students (MTF), 2000 Strategy

the business of defending the government's war on drugs policy—instead, the goal of our course was to arrive at some truths about the drug war. We wondered, is such misrepresentation and inappropriate use of statistics common by ONDCP? And if ONDCP regularly misuses statistics for its own benefit, is this for the purpose of maintaining its own ideology?

IDEOLOGY

Ideology is generally understood to mean the beliefs, values, and attitudes of a people, and often includes a prescription for the proper role of government in our lives. More specifically, it can be understood to mean a coherent set of beliefs about the political world—about desirable political goals and the best way to achieve them.[6] In modern American society, dominant ideologies emerge in part because powerful groups and individuals own and control the dominant means of communication—most notably, the mass media.[7]

Dominant ideologies arise from government activities, as well, both domestic and international.[8] The war on drugs—which is being fought within our borders and beyond—both depends on and maintains a dominant ideology. There are four key components to this drug war ideology. Government agencies, most notably ONDCP, use various claims-making activities to assure the public that (illegal) drugs are: (1) always bad; (2) never acceptable; (3) supply-driven; and (4) must be fought through an ongoing war.

This can be understood as the prevailing ideology of the federal government, including ONDCP, when it comes to illicit drugs. Words similar to ideology include outlook, philosophy, and view.[9] Even a superficial review of its rhetoric makes it clear that the dominant outlook, philosophy, and view of ONDCP is that illicit drug use is bad, never acceptable, supply-driven, and must be fought through an ongoing war. The value of the drug war ideology is that it "lulls us into assuming a number of properties about drugs. We refer to certain drugs . . . as if they were little demons committing crimes." Further, waging war on drugs, "as if the drugs themselves constitute our 'drug problem'," assures that we will not examine the underlying reasons why people use the drugs: "The language of ideology fools us into thinking that we're waging war against drugs themselves, not real people."[10]

The term *war* is obviously an important part of the drug war. Declaring war is a dramatic event that calls on "society to rally behind a single policy, against a common foe." Once a declaration of war is made, mass media attention increases, and the "enemy . . . has no one speaking on its behalf. There is the sense that society is united behind the war effort. Declaring war seizes the moral high ground."[11] War is also inherently punitive, with casualties and high costs that must be accepted in order to triumph.

Given that ONDCP is the official mouthpiece of the federal government when it comes to the war on drugs, it is the agency that logically plays the most important role in creating and maintaining the dominant ideology of America's drug war. In this book, we typify the dominant drug war ideology and demonstrate ways in which it is—simply stated—false. As it turns out, ONDCP uses statistics in several inappropriate ways to present a misleading picture of the nation's drug war. This misuse of statistics helps to justify the dominant ideology. This process is most clear in the claims-making aspects of the Strategy, which serve to uphold moral panics that sustain the drug war and hinder rational policy analysis. We examine claims-making, moral panics, and policy analysis next.

CLAIMS-MAKING AND MORAL PANICS

Several models of claims-making activities have been put forth in the literature. Scholars in disciplines such as political science and sociology have explained how social movements begin, how policies are created, and how government agencies engage in claims-making. Some assert that social movements and changes to public policy grow out of the objective condition of social problems. This is the "objectivist model." One example is when groups operating at the grassroots level are born in response to perceptions of social problems. According to this model, social movements occur in five stages: incipiency; coalescence; institutionalization; fragmentation; and demise.[12]

Incipiency represents the beginning of a social movement. At this stage, there is no strong leadership and no organized membership.[13] Coalescence refers to when "formal and informal organizations develop out of segments of the sympathetic public that have become the most aroused by perceived threats to the preservation or realization of their interests."[14] Institutionalization occurs "when the government and other traditional institutions take official notice of a problem or movement and work out a series of standard coping mechanisms to manage it."[15] Fragmentation occurs when the coalition that forced the emergence of the movement breaks apart or weakens due to the co-opting of the issue by the government. Finally, demise occurs when claims-makers lose interest in the issue.[16]

Such stages may be relevant for understanding how drug wars begin, and possibly for how they might end. Yet, the modern drug war has already been institutionalized. That is, there is already strong leadership and an organized membership involved in the war on drugs—represented best by ONDCP.

Others suggest that social movements and changes to public policies occur after powerful elites construct or create social problems from objective social conditions.[17] This is the "constructionist model."

When an objective social problem is blown out of proportion, the result can be a "moral panic." Moral panics occur when:

> A condition, episode, person or group of persons emerges to become defined as a threat to societal values and interests; its nature is presented in a stylized and stereotypical fashion by the mass media; the moral barricades are manned by editors, bishops, politicians, and other right-thinking people; socially accredited experts pronounce their diagnoses and solutions.[18]

Because moral panics "typically involve an exaggeration of a social phenomenon, the public response also is often exaggerated and can create its own long lasting repercussions for society in terms of drastic changes in laws and social policy."[19]

The United States has witnessed several moral panics when it comes to drugs—for example, dealing with crack cocaine and "crack babies" in the 1980s.[20] This does not mean that illegal drug use (and especially drug abuse) is not problematic. Moral panics over drugs can emerge from the general public if the objective threats posed by drug use and abuse are viewed as significant enough to warrant legitimate concerns.

The danger of moral panics is that they often lead to unnecessary changes in existing public policies or entirely new policies that are based on exaggerated threats. Misguided drug policies result from at least three factors: political opportunism; media profit maximization; and desire among criminal justice professionals to increase their spheres of influence.[21] Following this logic, politicians create concern about drug use in order to gain personally from such claims in the form of election and reelection; they achieve this largely by using the media as their own mouthpiece. After media coverage of drugs increases, so does public concern. Indeed, research shows that public concern about drugs increases after drug threats have been hyped in the mass media.[22] Finally, criminal justice professionals and government institutions (e.g., ONDCP) agree to fight the war, not only because they see drug-related behaviors (such as use, possession, manufacturing, sales) as crimes, but also because it assures them continued resources, clients, and thus bureaucratic survival.

Concern over drugs typically occurs in a cycle whereby some government entity claims the existence of an undesirable condition and then legitimizes the concern, garnering public support through the media by using "constructors" who provide evidence of the problem. Claims-makers then "typify" the drug problem by characterizing its nature.[23] For example, illicit drugs are typified as "harmful" even when used responsibly or recreationally. They are characterized as "bad" regardless of the context in which they are being used. Any illicit drug use is wrong even if it is not abuse.[24] Finally, illicit drugs are connected to other social problems to make them seem even worse. Recently, illicit drugs have been tied to acts of terrorism in television commercials and print ads created by ONDCP, paid for by taxpayers.[25]

Several myths about drugs exemplify this typification. For example, the "dope fiend mythology" promulgated by the U.S. government in the early 1900s that pertained to users of heroin, cocaine, and other then legally available drugs contained these elements: "the drug addict is a violent criminal, the addict is a moral degenerate (e.g., a liar, thief, etc.), drug peddlers and addicts want to convert others into addicts, and the addict takes drugs because of an abnormal personality."[26]

Another example is the typification of the use of marijuana, as indicated in a pamphlet circulated by the Bureau of Narcotics in the 1930s:

> Prolonged use of Marihuana frequently develops a delirious rage which sometimes leads to high crimes, such as assault and murder. Hence Marihuana has been called the "killer drug." The habitual use of this narcotic poison always causes a marked deterioration and sometimes produces insanity. . . . While the Marihuana habit leads to physical wreckage and mental decay, its effects upon character and

morality are even more devastating. The victim frequently undergoes such moral degeneracy that he will lie and steal without scruple.[27]

The propaganda circulated by the Bureau of Narcotics included the story of a "murder of a Florida family and their pet dog by a wayward son who had taken one toke of marijuana."[28]

Empirical evidence about the relative harmlessness of marijuana was ignored. Dozens of other similar stories were printed in papers across the country, including the *New York Times*. Such storied both instituted and maintained moral panics.

One possible reason why empirical evidence concerning marijuana was ignored in favor of dramatic (and nonsensical) characterizations and stories such as those above, is that several of the individuals involved in creating concern over marijuana use had ulterior motives for their actions. In 1930, the Bureau of Narcotics was formed within the U.S. Treasury Department. Harry Anslinger was appointed director by the Secretary of the Treasury, Andrew Mellon, who also happened to be Anslinger's uncle (by marriage) and owner of the Mellon Bank. Mellon Bank was one of the DuPont Corporation's banks. DuPont was a major timber and paper company. These players also had close links to William Randolph Hearst, another timber and paper mogul who published several large newspapers. Hearst used his newspapers to crusade against marijuana and this benefited its paper manufacturing division and Hearst's plans for widespread use of polyester, both of which were threatened by hemp. DuPont also had just developed nylon, which also was threatened by hemp.

Hearst and Anslinger also held racist attitudes toward Mexicans, Chinese, and African Americans.[29] For these reasons, they launched a campaign against the "killer weed" and "assassin of youth" (marijuana).[30] One result was the Marijuana Tax Act of 1937, which required a tax stamp to sell marijuana, established laborious procedures to prescribe the drug, and put forth very tough sentences for law violations (such as "life" for selling to a minor). The Bureau of Narcotics also wrote a sample bill banning pot that was eventually adopted by forty states.

It has been alleged that the reason marijuana was criminalized was due not to its harmful nature but instead to efforts by these men to protect their economic interests. According to the constructionist model, economic interest plays a large role in determining the dominant ideology.

Many scholars claim that wars on drugs as inanimate objects "tend to be concerned less with the drugs they purportedly target than with those who are perceived to be the primary users of the drugs."[31] For example:

- The war on opium in the late 1800s and early 1900s was focused on Chinese laborers who represented unwanted labor competition. Thus, laws passed in the late nineteenth century, which forbade importation and manufacture of opium by Chinese, excluded the Chinese in America from participating fully in the labor market.[32]

- The war on marijuana in the 1930s was grounded in racism against Mexican immigrants, who were characterized as "drug-crazed criminals" taking jobs away from Americans during the Great Depression.[33]
- Crack cocaine use by the urban poor was demonized by political leaders in the 1980s to divert attention from serious social and economic problems.[34]

Each of these drug scares blamed all sorts of societal evils on "outsiders"[35] — poor minority groups — and crime and drug problems were typified as "'underclass' problems resulting from insufficient social control."[36]

In the 1980s, all sorts of societal problems were blamed on crack cocaine, largely because media portrayals of crack cocaine were highly inaccurate.[37] This doubtlessly served to create a moral panic. The scare began in late 1985, when the *New York Times* ran a cover story announcing the arrival of crack to the city. In 1986, *Time* and *Newsweek* ran five cover stories each on crack cocaine. *Newsweek* and *Time* called crack the largest issue of the year.[38] In the second half of 1986, NBC News featured 400 stories on the drug. In July 1986 alone, the three major networks ran 74 drug stories on their nightly newscasts.[39] Drug-related stories in the *New York Times* increased from 43 in the second half of 1985 to 92 and 220 in the first and second halves of 1986, respectively,[40] and thousands of stories about crack appeared in magazines and newspapers.[41]

After the *New York Times* coverage, CBS produced a two-hour show called *48 Hours on Crack Street,* and NBC followed with *Cocaine Country.* In April 1986, the National Institute on Drug Abuse (NIDA) released a report called "Cocaine: The Big Lie," and 13 public service announcements that aired between 1,500 and 2,500 times on 75 local networks. In November 1986, approximately 1,000 stories appeared about crack in national magazines, where crack was called "the biggest story since Vietnam," a "plague," and a "national epidemic."[42]

As media coverage of drugs increased, people began paying attention. Not surprisingly, citizens were more likely to recognize drugs as the "most important problem" in response to the notable attention in the national news. Drug coverage in the media was more extensive in the 1980s than at other times. For example, the CBS program *48 Hours on Crack Street* obtained the highest rating of any news show of this type in the 1980s.[43] Public concern over drug use peaked in the 1980s, evolving into a full-fledged moral panic.

Once the media and public were all stirred up, laws were passed that aimed at toughening sentences for crack cocaine. For example, the Anti-Drug Abuse Act of 1986 created a 100:1 disparity for crack and powder cocaine (5 grams of crack would mandate a five-year prison sentence, versus 500 grams of powder cocaine). The U.S. Sentencing Commission recommended to Congress that this disparity be eliminated, yet Congress rejected the recommendation (which was the first time Congress ever rejected the Commission). Additionally, the Anti-Drug Abuse Act of 1988 lengthened sentences for drug offenses and created the Office of National Drug Control Policy (ONDCP).

The intense media coverage of crack cocaine is problematic because it was inaccurate and dishonest. News coverage did not reflect reality, as crack cocaine use was actually quite rare during this period;[44] in fact, cocaine use was declining at this time. According to NIDA, most drug use peaks occurred between 1979 and 1982, except for cocaine which peaked between 1982 and 1985.[45] Media coverage of cocaine use increased in the late 1980s even after drug use had already begun to decline. For example, new users of cocaine numbered 1.2 million in 1980, grew to 1.5 million by 1983, and fell to 994,000 by 1986. Although in 1987, the number grew to 1 million, each subsequent year saw declines in the numbers of new users of cocaine so that by 1990, there were 587,000 new users.[46]

New users of crack cocaine did rise for seven consecutive years between 1980 and 1986, from 65,000 to 271,000. The number then fell in 1987 to 262,000 and rose again until 1989, when the number was 377,000 new users.[47]

This coverage of drugs in the media typified social problems as stemming from the *psychopharmacological* properties of drugs such as crack cocaine (e.g., when a user becomes violent because of the effects of the drug on the brain), when in reality most of the associated violence stemmed from volatile crack cocaine markets.[48] Most of the violence associated with the illicit drug trade was *systemic* (e.g., drug dealers killed rival drug dealers) and *economic compulsive* (e.g., people robbed others to get money to buy drugs). News stories were also generally inaccurate or misleading in the way they characterized addiction to crack cocaine as "instantaneous," as if everyone who tried crack would become addicted immediately.[49]

The crack war was thus based on fallacies and the media reported those fallacies. The crack crisis also served to construct an atmosphere conducive to getting tough on crime and maintaining status quo (drug war) approaches to fighting drugs. As the data show, the public was not concerned about drugs until after the media coverage captured their attention. President Ronald Reagan's re-declaration of war against drugs in August 1986 created an "orgy" of media coverage of crack cocaine, and public opinion about the seriousness of the "drug problem" changed as a result.[50] In mid-August 1986, drugs became the most important problem facing the nation in public opinion polls.[51] Compare this to June 2004, when only 1% of Americans said that drugs are the most important problem facing the country.[52]

Not surprisingly, this chronology bolsters opinions about the constructed nature of the drug problem. Scholars suggest that drug control policies growing out of problems like the crack wars of the 1980s (including the toughening of sentences for crack cocaine versus powder cocaine in 1986 and even the creation of ONDCP in 1988) generally do not arise out of the objective nature of drug use per se, but instead tend to develop out of moral panics created and promoted by actors in the political realm. With crack cocaine, concerns did not arise out of the public health domain, but instead were prompted by politicians who decided to seize on an easy issue to promote drugs as the cause of so many social problems.[53]

If drug war efforts grow not out of objective conditions of drug use but rather moral panics, then claims-making by government agencies fighting the war will tend to reinforce symbols related to drugs and drug use[54] and expand state power by increasing resources of agencies responsible for arresting and punishing drug criminals rather than accurately describe the situation.[55] In the case of ONDCP—which specifically was created in the wake of the moral panic about crack cocaine in the 1980s—its claims probably thus serve as a primary source of justifications for the drug war regardless of its degree of efficacy.

When policies are developed to eradicate problems that are relatively minor, based on hyped accounts of the dangers they cause, one possible outcome is policies that do more harm than good. A growing number of scholars characterize drug war policies on these grounds.[56] So, too, do many drug reform groups.[57]

Groups that seek to end or modify the nation's drug war have the ability through claims-making and the promotion of their own ideologies to influence public opinion to some degree.[58] One means of achieving their goals is countering or refuting claims-making activities of the agencies involved in the war on drugs, including ONDCP. In the 2003 Strategy, ONDCP characterizes the efforts of some of these "well-funded legalization groups" as dishonest "misinformation":

> [These groups] have even insinuated to young people that drug use is an adolescent rite of passage and that adults who tell them otherwise are seeking to limit opportunities for personal growth that are rightfully theirs. . . . Operating with the benefit of slick ad campaigns, with virtually no opposition, and making outlandish claims that deceive well-meaning citizens, campaign proponents have tallied up an impressive string of victories.[59]

This characterization is not accurate. ONDCP has far more power and reach than any (and probably all) anti-drug war groups combined. First, ONDCP has enormous government resources to lead the war on drugs, whereas the anti-drug war groups rely on nongovernment donations. Second, ONDCP has launched massive public advertising campaigns on television, radio, in print, and on the Internet, whereas drug reform groups above do most of their publicizing through their respective Web sites. Third, ONDCP claims are likely seen as more legitimate since they represent the official word of not just the federal government but specifically the president of the United States, whereas at least some anti-drug war groups are likely seen as being left-wing or fringe groups with radical ideas.[60]

Given the power of ONDCP to promote its drug war ideology and its far-reaching influence on the people of the United States, it is critical to determine if ONDCP claims-making is accurate, honest, transparent, and justifiable. That is, does ONDCP justify the continuation of the war on drugs based on its established successes or does ONDCP attempt to defend the drug war even when the relevant statistics do not warrant it?

Citizens would likely hope that all government agencies (including ONDCP) would evaluate their policies (including the drug war) using the basic tenets of policy analysis, a technique employed by social scientists and policy-makers to determine if a policy is effective.

Policy Analysis

Traditionally, the policy process has been divided into different stages.[61] These are agenda setting, policy formation and legitimation, policy implementation, and policy evaluation. *Agenda setting* refers to the rise (either deliberate or not) of a topic as a policy issue. *Policy formation and legitimation* is that phase when the state deliberates and constructs the preferred response to the issue. *Policy implementation*, as the name suggests, is that stage when the state administers the policy. Finally, the process turns to *policy evaluation*. This is the stage of assessment when data collected during the existence of the policy are considered.

Each period raises its own questions for an analyst. For instance, an exploration of agenda setting usually encompasses questions of how problems are structured, publics are mobilized, and methods by which issues are placed on (or kept off) the agenda.

It is the latter part of the process — evaluation — that most heavily depends on government claims-making. During evaluation, one must determine the lens through which one will examine a policy such as the war on drugs. For example, will one examine its empirical or its moral effectiveness? A group of experts on data and research for drug war policy conclude that "adequate data and research are essential to judge the effectiveness of the nation's efforts to cope with its illegal drug problem . . . there is a pressing need for the nation to assess the existing portfolio of data and research."[62] That is, to determine if any policy is effective, we must have quality data on which to base our judgments.

We concur that the best approach to evaluate any policy, including the war on drugs, is to use empirical evidence — data — to determine if the policy is effective. Yet, when it comes to policies such as the war on drugs, significant moral issues may become important to decision-making. Issues such as whether it is moral for people to use drugs, to alter their consciousness, and to break the law, as well as whether it is moral for the government to interfere with the privacy and civil liberties of citizens, may become relevant for which drug control policies we should pursue, if any. Here, "data and research cannot resolve disagreements about the morality of drug use, but they may be able to narrow the divergence of views on the effectiveness of drug control policy today and contribute to the formation of more effective policy tomorrow."[63]

Assuming that one evaluates a policy based on empirical evidence, one can use a variety of standards to assess a policy, which is the core of policy evaluation. One common method of assessment is goal-oriented. Two drug policy experts assert that: "Any assessment of U.S. drug policy must consider its stated objectives."[64] If statistics indicate that a policy is achieving desired goals, then this would lead to a positive evaluation. In contrast, under a goals-oriented perspective, if statistics from the policy implementation phase indicate failure to achieve policy objectives, then one might expect a negative evaluation of the policy. Both outcomes, of course, assume the presence of an honest evaluation process using accurate information.

Drug policy experts note that: "Drug use policy cannot . . . be evaluated solely on the basis of whether it has achieved its stated aims. It has had side effects, both good and bad."[65] With this in mind, another method of assessment is cost-benefit analysis. Increasingly practiced in a variety of public policy arenas, cost-benefit analysis involves a deliberate comparison of the costs of a policy as compared to the benefits derived from the policy. Methodologically, costs and benefits should have comparable measures, thus ensuring the validity of the comparison. In practice, this can entail placing a monetary value on such benefits as saving lives or reducing drug use. Thus, this approach is not without its problems.[66] However, mechanisms can be adopted that allow for qualitative as well as quantitative assessments of costs and benefits.[67] Policies in which benefits outweigh costs typically have a positive evaluation. Conversely, when costs outweigh benefits, a negative evaluation would be forthcoming. Again, this assumes honesty in evaluating the policies using truthful data.

Claims by the government about policy outcomes are key ingredients in cost-benefit analysis. While an accurate cost-benefit analysis requires accurate data, truthful government claims with regard to the data are also essential for accurate policy evaluation. Unless government agencies are honest about their claims, and unless their claims are based on appropriate statistics, policy evaluations will not be reliable or useful.

Ideally, the policy process is cyclical. Policy evaluation should influence agenda setting. One would expect that a positive evaluation would result in an agenda for continuation of the policy; similarly, a negative evaluation would lead to an agenda for policy change. Thus, the claims of the government are central to evaluation and (by extension) to policy support or termination. Therefore, the veracity of government claims about the impact of our drug war policy is critical. An accurate picture of the impact of the war on drugs is crucial if the government and the public are to make informed decisions about whether or not to continue the policy.

Chapter Two

About America's Drug War

In this chapter, we briefly outline many key facts of and key events in America's drug war. Our goal is to provide some perspective to our analysis of claims-making by ONDCP. Whereas ONDCP was created in 1988 in the wake of one drug war (the crack war of the 1980s), America has been fighting drugs and drug users for longer than a couple of decades. We identify and discuss key events in the history of our drug war and attempt to identify key lessons of America's experience in the drug war. We also discuss the goals of the drug war, identify agencies that fight the drug war, and dissect the drug war budget.

Key Historical Events in the Drug War

Though local, state, and federal governments in the United States have fought drug wars since their existence, it was not until the late nineteenth and twentieth centuries that Congress passed laws banning particular drugs and their use. The first anti-drug law in the United States was passed at the city level, in San Francisco, California, in 1875. This law "prohibited the smoking or possession of opium, the operation of opium dens, or the possession of opium pipes."[1] More than twenty states, mostly in the West, then passed laws banning opium. In the 1880s, cities such as New York banned opium parlors, which were mostly inhabited by Chinese immigrants.

One writer claims America's war on drugs began "in November 1880 when an 'absolute prohibition' on the shipment of opium between the United States and China was agreed to in treaty negotiations between the two countries."[2] In the 1880s, Congress also acted: "Congress passed legislation in 1883 raising the tariff on opium imports . . . and then in 1887 prohibited the importation of the low-potency opium favored by smokers. The 1887 law also contained a prohibition on opium importation by Chinese; only U.S. nationals were allowed to bring in the drug."[3]

Yet, other forms of opiates besides smoking opium "were as accessible during the nineteenth century as aspirin is today. Physicians dispensed morphine and heroin directly to patients and wrote prescriptions for these drugs, pharmacies sold opiates over the counter without prescriptions, even grocery stores and mail order houses sold opiates."[4] There is no disagreement that these early laws were thus not about opium. In fact, opium had been used in America since at least the early 1700s, when Dover's Powder was introduced. It contained opium, ipecac, licorice, saltpeter, tartar, and wine.[5] By the late 1700s, "patent medicines containing opium were readily available throughout the urban and rural United States . . . advertised as painkillers, cough mixtures, soothing syrups, consumption cures, and women's friends . . . [for] diarrhea, dysentry, colds, fever, teething, cholera, rheumaism, pelvic disorders, athlete's foot, and even baldness and cancer."[6]

Historians agree that efforts to limit opium *smoking* grew out of an effort to control Chinese immigrants and their influence on (white) Americans. Of serious concern to legislators at the time were stories of white women frequenting opium dens occupied by Chinese men.

These anti-drug laws must be kept in the context of efforts to restrict Chinese immigration to the United States. In 1880, the United States was empowered to "regulate, limit, or suspend" it, and, in 1882, the Chinese Exclusion Act prohibited immigration for ten years.[7]

Additionally, "from the early 1880s until about 1905, there were no criminal prohibitions against either the sale or use of [cocaine or heroin], as indeed there were no regulations governing the use and distribution of any psychoactive substances, except for alcohol."[8] Further, "between about 1890 and 1920, it was possible in many states to purchase heroin or cocaine legally, though the sale of alcoholic beverages and cigarettes was prohibited."[9]

There are important lessons here. First, drug laws at times are not really about drugs, but instead about who is using them. Second, it is doubtful that many Americans would stand for the prohibition of alcohol and tobacco products today, yet these substances were also once banned. Modern Americans would hardly be willing to allow doctors to sell "hard drugs" such as cocaine and heroin. This suggests that it is not the nature of the drug that determines its legal or criminal status.

In 1906, the Food and Drug Act became law. The law was partially in response to Upton Sinclair's book, *The Jungle,* which detailed the horrendous conditions related to the production of America's food. It also grew out of abuses in the patent medicine industry. The law required truthful and complete labeling of all products, including the drugs being sold by the patent medicine industry. This law did not ban anything. The only issue resolved by this law was "whether a product was misbranded or adulterated."[10]

Later amendments to the law "required the labels to contain accurate information about the strength of the drugs and to state that federal purity standards had been met." One notable judge called this "the most effective law dealing with psychotropic substances in United States history."[11] Yet, the drugs were still available for use: "As long as they were clearly and accurately labeled on their packages, drugs such as morphine, cocaine, heroin, and opium could be legally sold."[12]

According to many experts, the nation's first major drug problem — addiction to opiates and cocaine — was brought about as a result of doctors, pharmacists, and unregulated marketing of legal substances that contained amounts of various drugs.[13] For example, with cocaine "[t]he medical profession lost control of the provisions of cocaine by the end of the 1890s. The market continued to grow, largely through the efforts of manufacturers, who publicized selective medical opinion to promote the drug and created their own popular market by ignoring the guidelines of standard medical practice."[14] Under this system of unregulated manufacturing, distribution, and use, the nature of use changed: "Now it was clearly a vice, not simply a powerful medicine whose misuse under medical supervision could lead unfortunate victims to a career of addiction."[15] This was America's first notable drug problem, although cocaine consumption then was not as high as it is today.[16]

Several notable examples show how available some (now illegal) drugs were. For example:

- Vin Coca Mariani was widely available in the 1880s, a drink made with an extract from coca leaves and wine.
- John Styth Pemerton, who had already marketed various patent medicines, created French Wine Cola-Ideal Nerve and Tonic Stimulant. In 1886, "he added an additional ingredient, changed it to a soft drink, and renamed it Coca-Cola."[17]
- After cocaine was isolated in 1859, it was added to patent medicines in the 1890s and none other than Sigmund Freud called it a magical drug.[18]
- In the 1897 edition of the Sears Roebuck catalog, hypodermic kits were available. They included syringes, needles, vials, and carrying case for delivery of morphine.[19]
- Around 1898, Bayer and Company was selling heroin as a sedative for coughs.[20]
- By 1905, there were more than 28,000 patent medicines, also called elixirs or snake oils.[21]

Here's another important lesson. In a capitalistic marketplace where drugs are advertised and sold freely to willing users, use grows and becomes problematic. Modern day proponents of legalization ought to carefully consider the possibility that true legalization would significantly increase drug use and consequently drug abuse.[22]

The 1906 Food and Drug Act virtually put an end to the patent medicine industry. Three years later, in 1909, the Opium Exclusion Act became law. This law banned smoking opium and was aimed exclusively at Chinese immigrants. This should not be surprising, for even the anti-opium laws of the late 1800s were "clearly racist in intent."[23]

From the early 1900s to about 1920, the United States was engaged in a series of efforts to impose restrictions on the opium trade into China (and the Philippines, which America controlled). One result of these efforts was the passage of the Harrison Narcotics Control Act in 1914. This law required registration with the Treasury Department to import, manufacture, sell, or dispense cocaine and opiates. It also levied a prohibitive tax and allowed physicians to prescribe and dispense the drugs for legitimate medical purposes in the course of professional practice (but not to maintain addicts).

According to historians, this law "was passed primarily for reasons other than controlling domestic opiate problems."[24] American officials were attempting to control opium production in China for reasons that were in part humanitarian and also selfish—namely, American control over the Phillippines that meant America was responsible for dealing with large numbers of Chinese inhabitants, some of which smoked opium.

American leaders participated in The Shanghai Commission that aimed at creating international controls on the opium market. Reportedly, the major thrust for the Harrison Act "was the necessity of avoiding embarrassment in dealings with other nations by having the U.S. adopt legislation consistent with the Shanghai Commission."[25] The Shanghai Commission was held in 1908, after President Theodore Roosevelt requested it. This meeting did not yield much, but led to the Hague International Opium Conference of 1912 that "passed a resolution calling for international control over opiates."[26] The result at home was the Harrison Act.

There is also a major lesson here. America's drug laws are not necessarily in place to reduce illicit drug use for the sake of reducing drug use. Ulterior motives—some related to foreign policy—also operate.

Ironically, the Harrison Act did not actually prohibit use of opiates. In fact, "the Harrison Act contained no actual reference to drug users at all. Disallowing neither use nor distribution of narcotics, it was concerned more with the authority of medical personnel than with public health."[27]

The law was merely "for the orderly marketing of opium, morphine, heroin, and other drugs. . . . It is unlikely that a single legislator realized . . . that the law . . . would later be deemed a prohibition law."[28] In fact, it was officials with the Treasury Department's Narcotics Division who interpreted the Harrison Act to be prohibitory. The law permitted a doctor to prescribe drugs "in the course of his professional practice, only"; Treasury officials decided administering drugs to addicts was not a normal part of "legitimate medical purposes."

Once the Harrison Act was law, "the criminalization process began in earnest."[29] In 1919, the Treasury Department began arresting doctors who wrote opiate prescriptions for addicts. "The courts were often in agreement with the law enforcement position, and in a series of decisions during the next three years (1919-1922), the Supreme Court effectively prohibited physicians from prescribing narcotics to addicts."[30] One of the decisions, *Webb v. United States* (1919), "held that it was illegal for doctors to dispense prescription drugs to alleviate the symptoms of narcotics withdrawal [and] inaugurated the Drug Prohibition era in which we still live."[31] In another, *U.S. v. Behrman* (1922), the Court held that "a narcotic prescription for an addict was unlawful, even if the drugs were prescribed as part of a cure program." This was reversed in the case of *Linder v U.S.* (1925) when the Court held that "addicts . . . were entitled to medical care like other patients." The latter ruling meant little since "physicians were unwilling to treat drug-dependent patients under any circumstances, and a well-developed, illegal drug marketplace had emerged had emerged to cater to the needs of the narcotic-using population."[32]

Here's another lesson of history—prohibition produces a black market that can survive and even thrive, despite the best efforts of criminal justice agencies to deny the opportunities. The most well-known prohibition effort in the early 1900s dealt with a drug that is currently legally available in the United States—alcohol. In 1917, the 18th Amendment prohibited alcohol, and it was ratified by the states in 1920. The period of alcohol prohibition lasted until 1933, when the 21st Amendment repealed prohibition.

Alcohol prohibition has been widely studied and possibly offers several lessons for America's current drug war. First, we know that prohibition was promoted by several ideological groups, including the Women's Christian Temperance Union (WCTU). The WCTU was motivated not only by concern over alcohol consumption but also by anti-immigrant fever.

Researcher Jeffrey Miron's analysis of the benefits and costs of prohibition offers another lesson. He suggests that prohibition reduced cirrhosis death rates by 10 to 20%.[33] Conceivably then, prohibition saved some people from killing themselves by drinking too much. Yet, Miron's figures also show that cirrhosis death rates were already falling before prohibition and that no large increases were seen after repeal. Additionally, a state-by-state analysis shows more pronounced declines in cirrhosis death rates in the 1920s in states that served alcohol than those that had adopted prohibition.

Most important to the relevance for current drug prohibition, Miron finds that alcohol prohibition only reduced alcohol use by a modest amount. Simultaneously, it resulted in great costs. These included corrupted enforcement, overly aggressive enforcement, increases in organized crime, increases in homicide, an enormous increase in opportunities for illegal profiting through crime and violence, and an expansion of criminal justice.[34]

An example of criminal justice expansion is provided by the Jones Act, passed into law in 1929. It levied extremely tough sentences for even first-time alcohol offenses. For example, a first-time offender could receive five years imprisonment and a ten thousand dollar fine.[35] A fair assessment of alcohol prohibition would weigh its modest benefits against its large costs and conclude, as most scholars do, that is was a significant failure.

Congress made significant efforts during alcohol prohibition to address other "drug problems," too. For example, the 1922 Jones-Miller Act outlawed possession of "any illegally obtained narcotic" and increased penalties for dealing such drugs. In the same year, the Narcotics Drugs Import and Export Act "restricted the import of opium and coca leaves to medicinal uses." And in 1924, Congress passed the Heroin Act which "limited the manufacture and possession of heroin to research sponsored and controlled by government."[36]

In 1930, the Bureau of Narcotics was formed within the Treasury Department. As noted in chapter 1, Harry Anslinger, nephew (by marriage) of the Secretary of the Treasury, Andrew Mellon, was appointed director. Anslinger, a racist and inventor of tall tales with regard to drugs such as marijuana, sought to assure the bureaucratic survival of the Bureau of Narcotics by bringing about a ban on marijuana use. His campaign against the drug — in which he claimed it led users to murder and rape, and that the drug was as strong as heroin and more harmful than opium — has received widespread coverage in the academic literature. One result: "Through the 1930s, state after state enacted antimarijuana laws, usually instigated by lurid newspaper articles depicting the madness and horror attributed to the drug's use."[37]

The culmination of Anslinger's crusade was the passage of the 1937 Marijuana Tax Act. As noted earlier, the law required a tax stamp to sell the drug, established laborious procedures to prescribe the drug, and mandated very tough sentences for breaking the law. For example, a life sentence was imposed for selling to a minor.

This law "specifically recognized marijuana's medical utility and provided for medical doctors and others to prescribe it, druggists to dispense it, and others to grow, import, and manufacture it, as long as each of those parties paid a small licensing fee. It was only the non-medicinal and unlicensed possession or sale of marijuana that was prohibited. But that was enough."[38] And just as early anti-opium laws were anti-Chinese, this law was clearly influenced by anti-Mexican sentiment:

it was Mexican immigrants (and other marginalized groups such as Caribbeans and blacks) who were the targets of claimsmakers. Seen as a threat to American culture and the American way of life, Mexican immigrants were negatively portrayed as drug-crazed criminals— made immoral and violent by their use of marijuana—who were responsible for the moral collapse of many communities throughout the West and southwest.[39]

Without question, many of America's drug wars have been inspired by racist sentiment or ethnocentrism. This is another lesson of our drug war history.

The only doctor who testified to Congress did so against the 1937 Marijuana Tax Act, saying he thought marijuana had legitimate medicinal uses. The American Medical Association (AMA) also urged Congress not to vote for the bill. Yet, the bill became law. This is still another important lesson— often empirical evidence and expert opinion have mattered less than politics in the nation's drug war. The harms attributed to marijuana were almost entirely invented for political purposes. Yet, states passed laws against the drug, largely due to the scare tactics of Harry Anslinger and the Bureau of Narcotics.

The criminalization of marijuana, a relatively benign drug, emboldened Congress to expand the drug war further. In 1951, the Boggs Act became law, quadrupling penalties for marijuana offenses and calling for mandatory death sentences for selling to a minor. This law was the first to include "marijuana in the same category of drugs as heroin and cocaine."[40] Similarly, in 1956, the Narcotic Drug Control Act was signed into law, providing possible death sentences for selling heroin to minors, as well as mandatory sentences of incarceration and no parole for second or subsequent drug violations.

In 1961, the United States signed the Single Convention of Narcotics Drugs "which said in effect that there was only one way to attack the drug menace, and that was *our* way."[41] Fifty-four nations signed the treaty, which read, in small part:

> The parties shall take such legislative and administrative measures as may be necessary:
>
> a. To give effect to and carry out the provisions of this Convention within their own territories;
> b. To co-operate with other States in the execution of the provisions of this Convention; and
> c. Subject to the provisions of this Convention, to limit exclusively to medical and scientific purposes the production, manufacture, export, import, distribution of, trade in, use and possession of drugs.[42]

This was followed with the 1971 Convention on Psychotropic Substances and later with the United Nations Convention Against Illicit Traffic in Narcotics Drugs and Psychotropic Substances in 1988. According to the International Narcotics Control Board: "Each successive treaty brought complementary regulations and advances in international law. From the beginning, the basic aim of the international drug control treaties has been to limit the use of drugs to medical and scientific purposes only."[43]

In 1966, the Bureau of Drug Abuse Control (BADC) was formed within the Food and Drug Administration. The BADC enforced the Drug Abuse Control Amendments of 1965 regulating stimulants and sedatives. In 1968, the Bureau of Narcotics and Dangerous Drugs (BNDD) was formed within the Justice Department. It combined the Bureau of Narcotics (from the Treasury Department) and the Bureau of Drug Abuse Control (from the Department of Health, Education, and Welfare).

In 1969, Operation Intercept was launched, requiring a three-minute search of vehicles crossing the Mexican border. The operation was a major failure, essentially shutting down the border for two weeks. This is an important event in drug war history for it reminds citizens that drug control efforts often interfere with other priorities of American government—in this case, mobility, immigration and emigration, tourism, free trade, and the movement of goods and services inherent in a capitalist economy.

In 1970, the Narcotics Treatment Administration was formed by President Nixon. Dr. Robert Dupont, a leading expert in drug abuse treatment, was appointed director. This was spurred by the realization that a large number of American military personnel were coming back from Vietnam hooked on heroin. And it was the only time in drug war history when treatment actually received the majority of funding in the drug war.

Also in 1970, the Comprehensive Drub Abuse Prevention and Control Act was created. The Controlled Substances Act (CSA), Title II of the Comprehensive Drug Abuse Prevention and Control Act of 1970, consolidated many laws regulating the manufacture and distribution of narcotics, stimulants, depressants, hallucinogens, steroids and chemicals used in the illicit production of controlled substances. It established five drug schedules through its Controlled Substances Act. These are shown in Table 2.1.

Note that marijuana is categorized as a Schedule I drug. This means it has a high potential for abuse and no recognized medical benefits. Several drug experts assert this is simply not true on either count. Most people who use marijuana do so recreationally, and its dependence rates are lower than "hard drugs" like cocaine and heroin, and even lower than alcohol and tobacco. Marijuana also has several widely recognized medicinal uses.[44]

This 1970 law has been called the "the most far-reaching federal statute in American history, since it asserts federal jurisdiction over every drug offense in

Table 2.1 Drug Schedules of the 1970 Controlled Substances Act

- Schedule I—the drug or other substance has a high potential for abuse and has no currently accepted medical use in treatment in the United States. There is a lack of accepted safety for use of the drug or other substance under medical supervision. Examples include heroin, LSD, marijuana, and metaqualone.
- Schedule II—the drug or other substance has a high potential for abuse but has a currently accepted medical use in treatment in the United States or a currently accepted medical use with severe restrictions. Abuse of the drug or other substance may lead to severe psychological or physical dependence. Examples include morphine, PCP, cocaine, methadone, and methamphetamine.
- Schedule III—the drug has a potential for abuse less than the drugs or other substances in Schedules I and II and has a currently accepted medical use in treatment in the United States. Abuse of the drug or other substance may lead to moderate or low physical dependence or high psychological dependence. Examples include anabolic steroids, codeine and hydrocodone with aspirin or Tylenol, and some barbituates.
- Schedule IV—the drug has a low potential for abuse relative to the drugs or other substances in Schedule III and has a currently accepted medical use in treatment in the United States. Abuse of the drug or other substance may lead to limited physical dependence or psychological dependence relative to the drugs or other substances in Schedule III. Examples include Darvon, Talwin, Equanil, Valium, and Xanax.
- Schedule V—the drug or other substance has a low potential for abuse relative to the drugs or other substances in Schedule IV and has a currently accepted medical use in treatment in the United States. Abuse of the drug or other substances may lead to limited physical dependence or psychological dependence relative to the drugs or other substances in Schedule IV. Over-the-counter cough medicines with codeine are classified in Schedule V.

Note: The higher the level drugs (nearer to Schedule I), the more vigorously they are pursued.

the United States, no matter how small of local in scope."[45] According to the National Academy of Sciences' Committee on Data and Research for Policy and Illegal Drugs: "Until the 1970s, the primary instrument of national drug policy was enforcement of state and federal drug laws, and the federal role was relatively minor."[46]

On June 17, 1971, President Richard Nixon declared a war on drugs.[47] Nixon announced "a new, all-out offensive" against drugs, which he said were "America's public enemy number one."[48] This launched what some call the modern drug war. Since then, the United States has spent an ever-increasing amount of time and money attempting to combat drug use and drug abuse. To a lesser or greater degree, every presidential administration—regardless of its party affiliation—has pursued this drug war. Consisting of both domestic and foreign policy components, America's drug war policy has had a tremendous impact on the lives of millions of people both inside and outside of the United States.

Motivated in part by a realization that a large portion of military personnel returning from Vietnam were addicted to heroin, President Nixon also set up the Special Action Office for Drug Abuse Prevention (SAODAP), headed by Dr. Jerome Jaffe, a methadone treatment expert. In 1972, the Office of Drug Abuse and Law Enforcement (ODALE) was formed under President Nixon. Miles Ambrose, a former Customs Director, was appointed director. ODALE consisted of coordinated task forces to reduce drugs and crime and represented a quick shift toward a law enforcement approach that is still with us today.

In 1973, the first National Drug Control Strategy was produced. The call in this document for greater information about illicit drugs in the United States was partly responsible for the creation of the main sources of drug use, including the National Household Survey on Drug Abuse (NHSDA) and Monitoring the Future (MTF), each of which is discussed in chapter 3.

Also in 1973, the Drug Enforcement Administration (DEA) was formed, an idea of Miles Ambrose. The DEA is now the primary federal agency involved in drug seizures and federal drug busts. It also assists in the development of interdiction and eradication measures. The creation of the DEA signaled a major shift in the drug war from treatment to a law and order approach. Nixon, concerned with winning reelection, made an effort to secure support of a wider base by focusing on law enforcement and other punitive measures to fight the drug war. The DEA operates within the United States and abroad.

Soon thereafter, more and more tools were created for the drug war. For example, in 1978, the Comprehensive Drub Abuse Prevention and Control Act was amended, allowing for asset forfeiture. This is a technique that has been widely used in America's drug war. Enforcement officers are permitted to seize the assets (money, property, real estate, etc.) of suspected drug dealers, even based on the tips of convicted criminals who alert law enforcement to suspects for monetary or other reward.

The focus of the United States was not exclusively domestic. In 1978, the United States used Agent Orange in Mexico, a highly toxic defoliant first utilized in the Vietnam War. This was the initial method of eradication of poppy fields in that country.

In 1981, the United States and Colombia ratified a treaty allowing extradition of cocaine traffickers from Colombia to the United States. Extradition was also pursued in Mexico. This was seen as an effective tool in the drug war, since it offered harsh sentencing against criminals deemed critical to drug enterprises. Extradition proved to be very controversial in Latin America. In both Colombia and Mexico, the United States had to battle strong forces within those countries to enact extradition. In the case of Colombia, this led to the "extradition wars" during which drug cartels attacked the government in an effort to get the 1981 extradition treaty overturned. Extradition was banned in 1991 by the new Colombian Constitution, but has since been reinstated and used by American officials to extradite Colombians to the United States. It is still strongly opposed by groups within Colombia.

The drug war abroad led to changes in US domestic law. In 1981, the Reagan administration pushed for modification of the principle of *posse comitatus*. The prohibition against using military forces for domestic policing had been a central tenet of the US legal system. However, the 1981 legislation allowed for the use of the military in international drug interdiction. Subsequently, *posse comitatus* has been further eroded.[49]

In 1983, Drug Abuse Resistance Education (DARE) was founded, in Los Angeles, California. Since then, "the DARE curriculum has rapidly spread from the Los Angeles area to schools across the country. In fact, more than half of all schools in the United States currently use the program; almost 20 million schoolkids a year are visited at least once by a DARE instructor."[50] Unfortunately, almost every analysis of the program finds that it does not work. One scholar summarizes: "DARE is very popular with students, school administrators, police, and the general public. This, in spite of the fact that research over the decades has repeatedly demonstrated that *DARE is not only ineffective, but also sometimes counterproductive.* That is, students who graduate from DARE are sometimes more likely than others to drink or do drugs."[51]

In 1985, First Lady Nancy Reagan started the "Just Say No" to drugs campaign. Mrs. Reagan appeared on television promoting personal responsibility and denouncing drug use. Her simple message, distributed on television and on radio, as well as in print in popular magazines, on T-shirts, buttons, and bumper stickers, was "Just Say No." This campaign is largely viewed as a failure, except by federal drug control agencies who still celebrate it.

Despite DARE and "Just Say No," the drug war in the 1980s became even more punitive. For example, the Comprehensive Crime Control Act of 1984 lengthened sentences for drug offenders and increased bail amounts for those accused of drug crimes. It also justified and encouraged asset forfeiture in drug cases and promoted money laundering investigations in an effort to disrupt illicit drug markets.

The Anti-Drug Abuse Act of 1986 called for mandatory sentencing for drug offenses and for "mandatory life sentences for 'principals' convicted of conducting a continuing criminal enterprise."[52] The law also established a 100:1 sentencing disparity for crack versus powder cocaine. Additionally, the law

> also made it a federal offense to distribute drugs within 1,000 feet of a school and required the president to evaluate annually the performance of drug-producing and drug-transit countries and to certify those that were 'cooperating' as anti-drug allies. Decertified countries were to lose foreign aid, face possible trade sanctions, and suffer U.S. opposition to loans from international financial institutions.[53]

The Anti-Drug Abuse Act of 1988 created the Office of National Drug Control Policy (ONDCP) to lead the war on drugs, and William Bennett was appointed director. It "further expanded federal offenses to include the distribution of drugs within one hundred feet of playgrounds, parks, youth centers, swimming pools, and video arcades."[54] The 1988 law also allowed judges at the federal and state level to deny more than 400 types of benefits to people convicted of drug offenses (including possession).[55]

When the law was amended in 1990, it required "public housing authorities to include lease provisions providing that drug-related activity on or near the premises is cause of termination of the lease . . . and . . . made lease holders subject to forfeiture for drug-related activity." Later, in 1997, the Department of Housing and Urban Development (HUD) adopted a rule that allowed a resident's tenancy to be terminated for "any drug-related activity on or near the premises."[56]

The 1988 Anti-Drug Abuse Act also required that the director of ONDCP "transmit a consolidated National Drug Control Program (Program) budget proposal" and "submit to the Congress annual reports on a National Drug Control Strategy." Further, the law provided "for coordination among executive branch departments and agencies, including a requirement that the head of a Program agency notify the Director in writing of any proposed policy changes relating to Program activities" and required "the Director to respond promptly as to whether the change is consistent with the National Drug Control Strategy." The law also instructed "the Director to report to the President and to the Congress concerning the need for coordinating, consolidating, or otherwise reorganizing agencies and functions of the Federal Government involved in drug supply reduction and demand reduction." The law entitled ONDCP to be in existence for only five years.[57]

The 1988 law that created ONDCP stated: "It is the declared policy of the United States Government to create a Drug-Free America by 1995."[58] Clearly, this objective was not achieved, and ONDCP's existence was extended for another five years in 1994, then again for another five years by the Office of National Drug Control Policy Reauthorization Act of 1998, and then again by the

Office of National Drug Control Policy Reauthorization Act of 2003. Table 2.2 details many key laws and executive orders pertaining to the mission of ONDCP.[59]

Prior to the establishment of ONDCP, no one agency was responsible for coordinating all drug control agencies to achieve drug war goals. Instead, numerous agencies operated independently of one another, with little coordination, to achieve their own functions and goals. These included agencies in various federal departments (each with its own drug control budget).

One might wonder how there was no accountable agency in the nation's drug war, prior to ONDCP, given the requirements of policy analysis identified in chapter 1. Which agencies then set the agenda for the drug war prior to ONDCP? Who decided what policies to pursue? Were the policies aimed at some specific goals? Was there ever an evaluation of any drug war policy? As it turns out, many agencies pursued their own policies, with little or no coordination with others and with few or no clear goals. The lesson here is that the drug war, prior to 1988 when ONDCP was created, was not a clearly formulated and carefully planned policy of the U.S. government. Further, there has never been a complete evaluation of the drug war.

The moral panic that produced the Anti-Drug Abuse Act of 1988 clearly facilitated one of the more extreme policy responses to the drug problem. In 1989, for the first time, the United States invaded another country to pursue its drug war policy. While there were several reasons (stated and unstated) for the US operation, President George H. W. Bush highlighted the drug war aspect when he announced the invasion to the American public:

> Fellow citizens, last night I ordered U.S. military forces to Panama. . . .
> The goals of the United States have been to safeguard the lives of Americans, to defend democracy in Panama, *to combat drug trafficking*, and to protect the integrity of the Panama Canal Treaty. Many attempts have been made to resolve the crisis through diplomacy and negotiations. All were rejected by the dictator of Panama, General Manuel A. Noriega, *an indicted drug trafficker*.[60]

"Operation Just Cause," the invasion of Panama, had as a primary objective the extraction of Manuel Noriega from Panama. The US military seized him in order to bring him to the United States where he could stand trial for drug crimes. He would be convicted and imprisoned in the United States.

In 1993, the North American Free Trade Agreement (NAFTA) was passed, making thorough inspections of cargo coming into the country impossible. While not explicitly part of the war on drugs, this agreement and others like it have made it more difficult for law enforcement and customs officials to search vehicles and seize drugs coming into the country. The important lesson

Table 2.2 Laws Pertaining to the Mission of ONDCP

The Anti-Drug Abuse Act of 1988 established the creation of a drug-free America as a policy goal. A key provision of that act was the establishment of the Office of National Drug Control Policy (ONDCP) to set priorities, implement a national strategy, and certify federal drug-control budgets. The law specified that the strategy must be comprehensive and research-based; contain long-range goals and measurable objectives; and seek to reduce drug abuse, trafficking, and their consequences. Specifically, drug abuse is to be curbed by preventing young people from using illegal drugs, reducing the number of users, and decreasing drug availability.

The Violent Crime Control and Law Enforcement Act of 1994 extended ONDCP's mission to assessing budgets and resources related to the National Drug Control Strategy. It also established specific reporting requirements in the areas of drug use, availability, consequences, and treatment.

Executive Order No. 12880 (1993) and *Executive Orders Nos. 12992 and 13023* (1996) assigned ONDCP responsibility within the executive branch of government for leading drug-control policy and developing an outcome-measurement system [Performance Measures of Effectiveness]. The executive orders also chartered the President's Drug Policy Council and established the ONDCP director as the president's chief spokesman for drug control.

The Drug-Free Communities Act of 1997 authorized the Office of National Drug Control Policy to carry out a national initiative that awards federal grants directly to community coalitions in the United States. Such coalitions work to reduce substance among adolescents, strengthen collaboration among organizations and agencies in both the private and public sectors, and serve as catalysts for increased citizen participation in strategic planning to reduce drug use over time.

The Media Campaign Act of 1998 directed ONDCP to conduct a national media campaign for the purpose of reducing and preventing drug abuse among young people in the United States.

The Office of National Drug Control Policy Reauthorization Act of 1998 expanded ONDCP's mandate and authority. It set forth additional reporting requirements and expectations, including:
    Development of a long-term national drug strategy
    Implementation of a robust performance-measurement system Commitment to a
        five-year national drug-control program budget
    Permanent authority granted to the High Intensity Drug Trafficking Areas
        (HIDTA) program along with improvements in HIDTA management
    Greater demand-reduction responsibilities given to the Counter-Drug Technology
        Assessment Center (CTAC)
    Statutory authority for the President's Council on Counter-Narcotics
    Increased reporting to Congress on drug-control activities
    Reorganization of ONDCP to allow more effective national leadership
    Improved coordination among national drug control program agencies
    Establishment of a Parents' Advisory Council on Drug Abuse

here is that often one priority of government (e.g., free trade) takes precedence over another (e.g., drug control), and even interferes with it. An early contradiction is even starker. During the 1960s, the CIA set up "Air America" to fly raw opium from Burma and Laos. Helping allies of the U.S. in the fight against Vietnam was more important than stopping the flow of illegal drugs.

A more recent example of this is the toppling of the Taliban government in Afghanistan. America's goal of destroying a regime that sponsored terrorism, successfully carried out by America's invasion of the country in 2002, led to an explosion in opium production in Afghanistan. The Taliban had been extremely effective at eradicating the crop; the Northern Alliance—the US ally against the Taliban—was heavily involved in poppy cultivation and smuggling. Yet again, a foreign policy security concern conflicted with a drug war objective.

While the United States did not officially participate in Taliban efforts to eradicate poppy cultivation, it was significantly involved in Latin America in the 1990s. The United States worked diligently to attack the supply of cocaine through interdiction and eradication. In Latin America, it pursued an aggressive policy of eradication that included aerial fumigation. Despite health concerns and opposition from groups within Bolivia, Colombia, and Peru, this program continues to this day.

In the area of interdiction, the United States established an air brigade that sought to disrupt illicit air traffic between Peru (a producing country) and Colombia (a processing country). Utilizing intelligence as well as equipment from the United States, the air brigade targeted suspicious flights. These airplanes would be forced down—shot down, if deemed necessary. While the air brigade generated quite a lot of anger in Latin America, it took the deaths of American citizens (missionaries in one plane shot down) for the United States to end this program.[61]

Foreigners were not the only ones bearing the brunt of an increasingly punitive drug war. President Bill Clinton signed into law his first major crime bill in the Violent Crime Control and Law Enforcement Act of 1994, which called for the death penalty for killers involved in the drug trade. The law also "instituted 'criminal enterprise' statutes that called for mandatory sentences of from twenty years to life" for some drug offenders.[62]

In 1995, the U.S. Sentencing Commission recommended reversing mandatory minimum sentences for crack cocaine, but was rejected by Congress. As noted in chapter 1, this was the first time Congress ever rejected the Commission.

In 1996, the Personal Responsibility and Work Opportunity Reconciliation Act allowed recipients of food stamps and cash assistance to be denied these benefits upon conviction of a drug felony. This was another effort to remove welfare benefits from those ensnared in drug abuse.

In 1998, Congress passed the Drug-Free Media Campaign Act. The law called on the Director of ONDCP to "conduct a national media campaign . . . for the purpose of reducing and preventing drug abuse among young people in the United States."[63] In conjunction with the Partnership for a Drug Free America, ONDCP develops advertisements to be broadcast in a wide variety of media. The law required broadcasters to give the government a two-for-one deal, whereby broadcasters received funds to broadcast an advertisement once and then they provided an additional broadcast for free. Media outlets have also been able to substitute their own anti-drug content in lieu of the second ad.

Interestingly, studies show that this ad program does not work. For example, an assessment published in 2002 found:

> There is little evidence of direct favorable Campaign effects on youth. There is no statistically significant decline in marijuana use to date, and some evidence for an increase in use from 2000 to 2001. Nor are there improvements in beliefs and attitudes about marijuana use between 2000 and the first half of 2002. Contrarily, there are some unfavorable trends in youth anti-marijuana beliefs. Also there is no tendency for those reporting more exposure to Campaign messages to hold more desirable beliefs.[64]

Given the relative unimportance of empirical evidence in our nation's drug war, the media campaign continues to this day.

From the late 1990s to the present, drug war laws have gotten tougher and tougher. One writer of the Congressional Research Service claims: "In recent years, Congress has taken an increasingly punitive stance toward drug addicts and casual users alike."[65] One example is the Higher Education Act, passed in 1998. This law amended the 1968 Higher Education Act to ban students from receiving financial aid from the federal government upon a conviction of a drug offense. There is no such law banning college financial assistance for those convicted of an alcohol offense (the most widely used drug on college campuses), or is there even a law for banning assistance to those convicted of violent crimes like murder, assault, and rape.

In 2000, the U.S. government stepped up its war on drugs abroad with Plan Colombia, a $1.3 billion "military-assistance-focused initiative to provide emergency supplemental narcotics assistance to Colombia."[66] This plan placed hundreds of U.S. military personnel in Colombia, all of whom were involved in efforts to inhibit coca cultivation to help reduce cocaine use in the United States. Much of the money budgeted for the plan went to the Colombian military for the purchase of equipment, supplies, weapons, and so forth. A small portion of funds was also provided for "strengthening democratic institutions; protecting human rights; and providing humanitarian assistance."[67] As witnessed in other situations previously noted, the pursuit of one policy frequently conflicts with another. In this case, the drug war often collides with promotion of human rights — with drug war concerns triumphing.

In 2001, Plan Colombia was rolled into the Andean Regional Initiative. This plan entailed additional focus beyond Colombia to other countries that historically experienced "spillover" effects from America's efforts in Colombia. Nearly half of the funds were appropriated for Colombia, but money was also provided for Bolivia, Brazil, Ecuador, Panama, Peru, and Venezuela.

The Illicit Drug Anti-Proliferation Act of 2003 aimed at increasing controls of club drugs such as Ecstasy. Although the bill was originally introduced to Congress as a separate bill, it did not get out of committee. Consequently, it was attached as a provision of the Child Abduction Protect Act (a bill that set up so-called Amber Alerts when children go missing and are presumed kidnapped). The Illicit Drug Anti-Proliferation Act amended a section of the Controlled Substances Act, "known as the 'crack house statute,' to more directly target the producers of dance events, or 'raves,' at which drugs such as MDMA (Ecstasy) are often used." This "shifts the statute's emphasis from punishing those who establish places where drugs are made and consumed, such as crack houses, to those who knowingly maintain 'drug-involved premises,' including outdoor events such as rock concerts."[68]

Perhaps the one issue that most clearly illustrates how the federal government's drug war has become more and more punitive concerns medical marijuana. The state of California, in 1996, became the first to approve the use of marijuana under prescription and supervision of a medical doctor—hence the term "medical marijuana." Since then, at least ten other states have passed similar laws allowing seriously and terminally ill patients to smoke marijuana under the orders of a medical doctor. These include Alaska, Colorado, Hawaii, Maine, Maryland, Montana, Nevada, Oregon, Vermont, and Washington.

Yet, the federal government does not approve. In 1998, the U.S. House of Representatives passed a resolution condemning medical marijuana. Additionally, "DEA agents have raided and shut down medical marijuana providers in several states, backed by a 2001 U.S. Supreme Court ruling affirming that federal drug laws take precedence over state laws and barring doctors from prescribing illegal drugs."[69] The decision affected distributors of the drug and did not overturn any state laws. In 2005, in the case of *Gonzales v. Raich*, the U.S. Supreme Court settled the issue of federal prohibition of medical marijuana versus states rights to allow it. It ruled 6–3 that medical doctors can be stopped by federal agents from prescribing marijuana for patients being treated with marijuana as a pain killer.

More than 150 other drug policy reforms were passed by at least forty-six states between 1996 and 2002 that

> address a broad range of issues relating to racial justice, drug treatment, property rights, HIV/AIDS and more. They allow people to grow and use marijuana for medical purposes; reduce . . . long and

costly prison sentences for nonviolent drug offenders; increase legal
access to sterile syringes to reduce the spread of HIV/AIDS; restore
the rights and duties of citizenship to those with a felony conviction
in their past; curtail . . . asset forfeiture by government agencies; and
so on.[70]

In the last two years, two major issues before the American people pertained to the links between drugs and terrorism and mandatory drug testing
in schools. ONDCP linked drug use, even low-level recreational experimen-
tation by juveniles, to acts of terrorism. Additionally, it called for and has promoted mandatory drug testing for students interested in participating in
after-school activities. Whether the policy is effective at reducing drug use
seems to be irrelevant.

Plainly, this review of America's drug war history shows that the underlying purpose of US drug war policy has been to reduce drug use. However, over
the years, the explicit goals of the government have varied.

GOALS OF THE DRUG WAR

According to ONDCP's 2005 National Drug Control Strategy, the goals of the
drug war are to:

1. Stop use before it starts through education and community action.
2. Heal America's drug users by getting treatment resources where they
   are needed.
3. Disrupt the market by attacking the economic basis of the drug
   trade.[71]

It should be noted that no explicit drug war goals related to reducing
harms—even the adverse consequences of drug use such as "overdoses, lost productivity, and HIV infection"—are stated by ONDCP.[72] Although it might
seem like reducing drug use would reduce consequences of drug use, drug use is
not a good indicator of drug use consequences. This is because: (1) most users
are "light users"; and (2) adverse consequences are most associated with "heavy
users" and drug abusers.[73] Two drug policy experts assert that "some of the failures of current policies may be as much the consequence of inadequate or misguided goals as of approaches to achieving them."[74] For example, the overall
goal of current American drug war policy is to reduce the prevalence of drug use
(the percentage of Americans who use drugs). This has little to do with "the
negative consequences of drug use, such as the societal cost of lost productivity,

health care, and crime attributable to drugs." In fact, as drug use declined in the 1980s, harms associated with drug use "rose enormously."[75] We revisit this issue in chapter 6.

ONDCP's drug war goals have shifted over the years. In the 2000 and 2001 versions of the Strategy, the ONDCP stated five goals. These included:

1. Educate and enable America's youth to reject illegal drugs as well as tobacco and alcohol.
2. Increase the safety of America's citizens by substantially reducing drug-related crime and violence.
3. Reduce health and social costs to the public of illegal drug use.
4. Shield America's air, land, and sea frontiers from the drug threat.
5. Break foreign and domestic drug sources of supply.

These goals were first stated in 1996. Recall that the ONDCP was created in 1988, suggesting the possibility of different goals (or no clearly stated goals) between 1988 and 1996. For example, in the 1995 Strategy, ONDCP presented fourteen goals in the areas of demand reduction, domestic law enforcement, and international activities. Its overreaching goal is stated as "Reduce the number of drug users in America."[76]

In the 1996 Strategy, ONDCP also stated measurable objectives. The objectives were in the areas of teaching about the dangers of drugs through education, prevention, advertising, promoting zero-tolerance drug policies, strengthening law enforcement, improving the ability of High Intensity Drug Trafficking Areas to counter drug trafficking, promoting and providing treatment to drug abusers, reducing drug-related health problems including infectious disease, promoting drug-free workplaces, supporting research into drug treatment, conducting useful operations at the borders of the country and within it to seize drugs, improving law enforcement coordination, improving cooperation with Mexico, reducing worldwide production of drugs, disrupting drug trafficking organizations, deterring money laundering, and using asset forfeiture to seize drug-related goods and money. Some of these objectives included time frames by which they should be achieved. For example, the 1998 National Drug Control Strategy, subtitled, *A Ten Year Plan*, stated goals to be achieved by 2007. Two of its objectives were to reduce drug use and drug availability by 50 percent by 2007.[77]

Planned change through the creation of policies and programs requires clearly stated goals and testable objectives. When a policy's goals are changed after its implementation—particularly on more than one occasion and years after the policy has been in place—it is likely that the policy was not well planned. Poorly planned policies are based on supposition rather than sound theory and scientific evidence, are created by moral entrepreneurs and politicians rather than by experts, and are generally not carefully considered. They are also far less likely to succeed.[78]

We cannot claim that the war on drugs is unplanned and therefore destined to fail simply because its goals have shifted over the years, but it raises the real possibility that the ONDCP's Strategy is not well thought out. In the 2000 Strategy, for example, the ONDCP claims: "The *1996 Strategy* established five goals and thirty-two supporting objectives as the basis for a coherent, long-term national effort. These goals remain the heart of the *1999 Strategy* and will guide federal drug control agencies over the next five years."[79] One thus presumes that the Strategy goals from 1996 would be in effect at least until 2003 or 2004, yet this is not the case.

Given the long history of America's drug war, what is truly amazing and suggestive of poor planning is that even after one hundred years of fighting drugs, the U.S. government still cannot settle on the goals of the drug war. Further, the agencies that fight the drug war are numerous and still uncoordinated.

AGENCIES THAT FIGHT THE DRUG WAR

The drug war is "fought" through the following agencies:

- Department of Defense
- Department of Education
- Department of Health & Human Services (National Institute on Drug Abuse, Substance Abuse and Mental Health Administrative Services)
- Department of Homeland Security (Border and Transportation Security, US Coast Guard)
- Department of Justice (Bureau of Prisons, Drug Enforcement Administration, Interagency Crime and Drug Enforcement, Office of Justice Programs)
- Department of State (Bureau of International Narcotics and Law Enforcement Affairs)
- Department of Veterans Affairs (Veterans Health Administration)
- The Office of National Drug Control Policy

The Department of Defense (DoD) spends most of its drug war resources on interdiction activities, followed by intelligence gathering and prevention activities. As noted in ONDCP's FY 2005 Budget Summary, DoD is "the single lead federal agency to detect and monitor the aerial and maritime transit of illegal drugs toward the U.S." It also analyzes and disseminates "intelligence on drug activity" and provides "training for U.S. and foreign drug law enforcement agencies and foreign military forces with drug enforcement responsibilities."[80] DoD also administers drug tests to military personnel and Pentagon employees, promotes a drug-free workplace, and provides drug treatment for its personnel.

The Department of Education spends all of its drug war resources on prevention efforts, most notably through its Safe and Drug-Free Schools and Communities State Grants.

The National Institute on Drug Abuse (NIDA), part of the Department of Health and Human Services, spends most of its drug war resources on treatment research and prevention research. NIDA runs its own clinical treatment trials and tailors some of the prevention efforts to specific communities.

The Substance Abuse and Mental Health Administrative Services, also part of the Department of Health and Human Services, spends the largest share of its drug war resources on treatment research, followed by prevention research. Its official function is "to build resilience and facilitate recovery for people with or at risk for substance abuse and mental illness."[81]

Customs and Border Protection, part of the Department of Homeland Security, spends the great bulk of its drug war resources on interdiction, followed by intelligence. It detects and apprehends "illegal entrants between the ports-of-entry along the 8,000 miles of the United States borders" including "alien and drug smugglers, potential terrorists, wanted criminals, and persons seeking to avoid inspection at the designated ports-of-entry."[82] Its goal is to "interdict and disrupt the flow of narcotics and ill-gotten gains across out nation's borders and dismantle the related smuggling organizations."[83]

Immigration and Customs Enforcement, also part of the Department of Homeland Security, spends most of its drug war resources on investigations and interdiction. It is aimed at enforcing drug laws and discovering and disrupting money laundering.

The U.S. Coast Guard, also part of the Department of Homeland Security, spends all of its drug war resources on interdiction activities. Though it "does not have a specific appropriation for drug interdiction activities" it provides maritime drug interdiction.[84]

The Bureau of Prisons, part of the Department of Justice, spends all of its drug war resources on treatment for inmates housed in its correctional facilities. This includes "screening and assessment; drug abuse education; non-residential drug abuse counseling services; residential drug abuse programs; and community transitional drug abuse treatment."[85]

The Drug Enforcement Administration (DEA), also part of the Department of Justice, spends the great bulk of its drug war resources on investigations, followed by international efforts and intelligence. The DEA provides both domestic and international enforcement of drug laws, and offers assistance to state and local governments, in order to attack "drug supply and money laundering organizations operating at the international, national, regional, and local levels having a significant impact upon drug availability in America."[86]

Interagency Crime and Drug Enforcement, also part of the Department of Justice, spends most of its drug war resources on investigations and prosecutions. Units involved in this group include the Drug Enforcement Administration, the Federal Bureau of Investigation, the U.S. Marshals Service, Immigration and Customs Enforcement, the Internal Revenue Service, the Bureau of Alcohol, Tobacco, Firearms, and Explosives, the U.S. Coast Guard, and the U.S. Attorneys Office (Criminal Division and Tax Division). This is "a multi-agency partnership among federal, state and local law enforcement officers and prosecutors, working side by side, to identify, dismantle and disrupt sophisticated national and international drug trafficking and money laundering organizations."[87]

The Office of Justice Programs, also part of the Department of Justice, spends most of its drug war resources on treatment and state & local assistance. Some of its budget is directed toward residential substance abuse treatment and drug courts programs. It also "supports a variety of prevention programs, which discourage the first-time use of controlled substances and encourage those who have begun to use illicit drugs to cease their use. These activities include programs that promote effective prevention efforts to parents, schools and community groups and assistance to state, local and tribal criminal justice agencies" to "investigate, arrest, prosecute, incarcerate drug offenders, or otherwise reduce the supply of illegal drugs."[88]

The Bureau of International Narcotics and Law Enforcement Affairs, part of the Department of State, spends the great bulk of its drug war resources on international programs. Its goal is "to develop, implement and monitor U.S. Government international counternarcotics control strategies and foreign assistance programs" and to "advance international cooperation in order to reduce the foreign production and trafficking of illicit coca, opium poppy, marijuana and other illegal drugs."[89]

The Veterans Health Administration, part of the Department of Veterans Affairs, spends almost all of its drug war resources on treatment. This includes specialized treatment for veterans with substance abuse problems.

Finally, as noted earlier, the Office of National Drug Control Policy (ONDCP) establishes policies, priorities, and objectives for America's drug war. It produces the National Drug Control Strategy that directs drug war efforts and establishes a program, a budget, and guidelines for cooperation among agencies at various levels of government. The largest share of its drug war resources are intended for prevention education, state and local assistance, treatment, and interdiction and international spending. Whereas ONDCP does not "fight" the drug war on the streets of American and the fields of foreign countries, it is the single agency responsible for setting drug war policy and "selling" the drug war.

Drug War Budgets

Table 2.3 shows the official ONDCP drug war budget, with dollar figures for each agency listed in ONDCP's budget.

Of these dollar figures, the amount of money budgeted for each agency involved in the drug war is shown in Table 2.4.

Fiscal year 2005 funding requests for the drug war were $12.6 billion. Of these dollars, ONDCP claims that 55% are for supply reduction and 45% are for demand reduction (which consists of treatment and prevention). More specifically, 29.4% is for treatment (with research), 25.3% is for domestic law enforcement, 20.6 percent is for interdiction, 15.6% is for prevention (with research), and 9.1% is for international spending.[90]

Fiscal year 2006 funding requests for the drug war were $12.4 billion. Of these dollars, 26.2% is for treatment (with research), 27% is for domestic law enforcement, 23.2% is for interdiction, 12.6% is for prevention (with research), and 11% is for international spending. Note that of the FY 2006 budget requests, only 38.7% of funds are for demand reduction, whereas 61.3% is for supply reduction efforts.[91] As noted in chapter 1, part of the prevailing ideology of America's drug war is that drug use is supply-driven and thus must be attacked with supply-side policies. The budget priorities of ONDCP are consistent with their ideology.

ONDCP's budget figures do not accurately represent government spending on the drug war, for at least two reasons. First, the numbers do not include expenses incurred by states, cities, and counties. Virtually every law enforcement agency has a drug budget, including almost every federal agency, three out of four state level agencies, and more than nine out of ten local agencies.[92] The actual amount of federal dollars spent on the drug war is actually higher when criminal justice costs (law enforcement, courts, and corrections) stemming from the war on drugs are added. Through 2002, such costs were included in the National Drug Control Strategy. Looking at the budget from the 2002 Strategy gives us a better idea of the true federal drug control budget. In 2002, the federal drug control budget was $19.2 billion.

Table 2.3 The Drug War Budget, by Function, FY 2006

Function	Request (in billions)
Domestic law enforcement	$3.36 (27%)
Treatment (with research)	$3.25 (26%)
Interdiction	$2.88 (23%)
Prevention (with research)	$1.56 (13%)
International	$1.37 (11%)
TOTAL	$12.4

Table 2.4 The Drug War Budget, by Agency, FY 2006

	FY 2005 Enacted	FY 2006 Request
Department of Health and Human Services	$3.5 billion	$3.5 billion
Department of Justice	$2.7 billion	$2.9 billion
Department of Homeland Security	$2.4 billion	$2.5 billion
Department of State	$899 million	$1.1 billion
Department of Defense	$906 million	$896 million
Department of Veteran Affairs	$457 million	$533 million
Department of Education	$593 million	$233 million
ONDCP	$507 million	$267 million
Other Presidential Priorities	$1 million	$2.5 million
TOTAL	$12.2 billion	$12.4 billion

Second, beginning only with the 2003 National Drug Control Strategy, ONDCP removed from the budget those dollars spent related to the war on drugs unless they related directly to judgments about drug policy. Thus, billions of dollars spent by law enforcement to arrest drug offenders, by courts to convict them, and by corrections to punish them, are no longer included in the ONDCP's Strategy; such costs are now reported separately. Given that careful policy analysis requires consideration of the costs and benefits of the policy, separating out the costs may hinder fair and complete assessments of the effectiveness of the war on drugs in a policy evaluation.

ONDCP openly admitted it changed its budget format. For example, in the 2002 Strategy, ONDCP noted that the federal drug budget would be restructured beginning with the 2003 Strategy: "Only agencies with a primary drug law enforcement or demand reduction mission would be displayed in the drug budget. This change would limit the budget to those agencies or accounts that have been, or should be, the principal focus of drug control policy."[93] Further explanation is offered in the 2003 Strategy:

> the budget reflects only those expenditures aimed at reducing drug use rather than, as in the past, those associated with the consequences of drug use. (The latter are reported periodically in *The Economic Costs of Drug Abuse in the United States*.) . . . Now that the drug control budget has been narrowed in scope and presented in terms of actual expenditures, it will serve as a more useful tool for policymakers.[94]

In the 2002 Strategy, ONDCP predicts that: "Application of these principles is likely to reduce dramatically federal resources deemed to represent drug control funding, without affecting the overall federal commitment to reducing drug use."[95] The federal budget allocated to fight the drug war does indeed shrink, as predicted by ONDCP.

ONDCP acknowledges: "The drug control budget includes close to 50 budget accounts totaling over $19 billion for 2003." Yet, it then presents a revised budget for 2003, in line with its new accounting principles, in the amount of only $11.4 billion. This is a manipulation of statistics. The fact is that the government spent at least another $8 billion because of the war on drugs (in the form of increased arrests, convictions, and incarcerations). And federal drug control spending has generally increased over time.

Readers of the ONDCP Strategy reports may wonder how such a change provides a more honest accounting of how the government spends taxpayer money to reduce drug use, especially since we are still spending the rest of the money that is no longer represented in the budget.

The Drug Policy Alliance (DPA) explains that, beginning with the 2002 Strategy, ONDCP distorts the true costs of the drug war by "not counting drug war expenditures by many law enforcement agencies" even though the agencies will continue to be on the front lines of the drug war. In essence, ONDCP was able to reduce the amount it says is spent on the nation's drug war by eliminating the economic costs associated with the drug war (such as policing and increased incarcerations). The net effect of this change is to increase the percentage of the Strategy's stated budget that is intended for treatment.[96]

The DPA characterizes the new budget as "fuzzy math" and claims the budget "conceals billions of dollars spent on incarcerating drug offenders and certain law enforcement efforts by excluding these categories from the budget and including inflated expenditures on treatment services." The DPA claims ONDCP did this to bring its "enforcement to treatment ratios more into line with public sentiment" that tends to favor treatment over punishment for non-violent drug offenders: "Last year [2002 Strategy], the Office stated it spent 33% of the drug war budget on drug treatment and prevention activities while 67% went to law enforcement and interdiction. This year [2003 Strategy], despite making no substantive spending changes, the Office claims to be spending 47% on drug treatment and only 53% on law enforcement activities."[97]

According to the DPA:

Although ONDCP stops counting many law enforcement expenses, it appears to continue counting many 'drug treatment and prevention' expenses for agencies not actually involved in drug war efforts. It may also fraudulently increase the amount of federal drug treatment expenditures reported to Congress and the public by counting money spent reducing alcohol abuse, even though ONDCP's charter specifically excludes alcohol from its scope of responsibilities.[98]

Fiscal Year 2006 Drug Budget

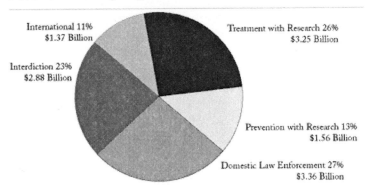

FIGURE 2.1   ONDCP Claims a Balanced Drug War, FY 2006

The truth remains that, although about 70 percent of federal drug war spending has been on supply reduction activities through police, prisons, and the military, ONDCP now claims a more balanced National Drug Control Strategy and a more compassionate and reasonable drug war. Strangely, in its own National Drug Control Strategy FY 2006 Budget Summary, ONDCP provides a figure depicting the portion of its requested budget that goes toward disrupting the market, healing users, and stopping use.[99] We've recreated it here in Figure 2.1.

The reader can clearly see that the majority of ONDCP's budget each year goes toward market reduction. That is, the drug war is mostly aimed at supply-side strategies such as eradication of drugs and interdiction in foreign countries. Far less goes toward stopping use and healing drug users.

Drug policy experts note that the drug war budget is clearly tilted toward law enforcement.[100] A review of ONDCP budget data shows that enforcement has historically received the bulk of the drug war budget—typically about two-thirds.[101] Meanwhile, "treatment expenditures have always been substantially larger than those for prevention."[102] The problem with this, according to the experts, is that the effectiveness of enforcement has diminishing returns and money spent on enforcement is better spent on areas that are more effective, such as treatment and prevention.[103] Although treatment and prevention may "proceed by small degrees" and thus take more time to be effective than enforcement, which may work faster and have more direct effects, treatment and prevention are more effective in the long run.[104] We'll return to the issues of effectiveness of enforcement and treatment in chapters 4 and 5, respectively.

ONDCP achieves its so-called balanced and compassionate drug war by manipulating its budget format to present misleading statistics about spending on the drug war. Because of these and other serious problems, two drug policy experts assert that the federal drug control budget is "peculiar," "highly questionable," and "deeply flawed.[105] As it turns out, this is only one of the potentially misleading uses and presentations of statistics of ONDCP in its National Drug Control Strategy.

Part Two

Chapter Three

Methodology

In this chapter, we outline the methodology underlying our study of ONDCP's National Drug Control Strategy claims regarding its efforts to reduce drug use, heal drug users, and disrupt markets. We discuss what we did and how we did it. We also identify our sources of data and discuss limitations of the data.

While others have challenged claims by ONDCP, no research to date has systematically evaluated claims-making activities of ONDCP.[1] Therefore, we chose six of the most recent editions of the National Drug Control Strategy (2000–2005) to examine ONDCP claims-making activities. Originally, we analyzed the Strategy reports through 2004, yet as we progressed on the study, the 2005 Strategy was released. Therefore, we added it to our analysis as well. Comments regarding the 2006 strategy are contained in the Postscript.

We chose to analyze the National Drug Control Strategy for three primary reasons. First, the Strategy is the primary means of communicating the goals and outcomes of the drug war to government agencies and American citizens. It is the document prepared each year by ONDCP that is required by law. Second, the Strategy represents the main source of information whereby statistics related to the goals of the war on drugs are presented graphically and evaluated. It is here where ONDCP consistently makes claims related to its goals of reducing drug use, healing drug users, and disrupting drug markets. Third, the Strategy is easily accessible, either in print or online. The Strategy is located on the front page of the official Web site of ONDCP, and this is likely viewed by thousands of people every year. The last four versions (2002, 2003, 2004, 2005) of the Strategy appeared on the ONDCP Web site, whereas the previous two versions (2000 and 2001) were obtained from the Web site of the National Criminal Justice Reference Service.[2]

Since the ONDCP budget changes were implemented in the 2003 Strategy, this means that the first three versions of the Strategy (2000–2002) we analyzed were calculated and written under the old drug budget (when the social and criminal justice costs were included) and the last three versions of the Strategy (2003–2005) were calculated and written under the new drug budget (when such costs were not included). This itself raises at least one interesting question that we attempt to answer.

As noted in chapter 1, the differential in the drug war budget under the new budget format is $8 billion less than under the original budget format. ONDCP made no effort to hide the budget changes by leaving the 2002 Strategy report off of its Web site. So there must be another reason why the 2000–2001 versions of the Strategy are not included on the ONDCP Web site. Perhaps one explanation is a format change to the Strategy. In 2002, ONDCP significantly altered the format of the Strategy in 2002, eliminating many useful figures related to trends in drug use, drug prices, drug availability, drug purity, and costs associated with drug use, drug abuse, and the drug war.

Beginning in 2002, readers of the annual Strategy can no longer find any data whatsoever — not even any mention of any statistics of any kind — on what is happening to drug price trends. Nor is there any data or mention of statistics on drug purity trends. Nor is there any data or mention of statistics on drug availability trends. The 2002 Strategy contains only three figures and none of them relates to such trends. The 2003, 2004, and 2005 versions of the Strategy contain more figures, but none of them describe price and availability and only selected figures relate to use.

Therefore, to obtain answers to such questions as Are drugs more or less expensive over the years? Are drugs harder or easier to obtain over the years? Are drugs more or less pure over the years? readers must look elsewhere to find answers.[3] Yet, the answers to these questions are essential for policy evaluation and analysis.

Further, all data and statistics related to costs of drug use, drug abuse, and the drug war itself are no longer included in the annual Strategy reports. Instead, after only being briefly mentioned in one box in the 2002 Strategy, they were completely removed from the 2003, 2004, and 2005 Strategy reports and are separately included in the ONDCP report, *The Economic Costs of Drug Abuse in the United States 1992–1998*.[4]

The implications of this for sound policy analysis are discussed later in the book (see chapter 8). For now, it is important to note that there were important differences in the five annual reports of the National Drug Control Strategy from 2000 to 2005. This did not affect our ability to locate and analyze ONDCP claims related to reducing drug use, healing drug users, or disrupting drug markets. Essentially, there were far fewer claims made in the later versions of the Strategy than in earlier versions.

WHAT WE DID

Rather than analyzing every claim made by ONDCP in its National Drug Control Strategy over six years, we isolated and evaluated the types of claims regularly made by ONDCP. We looked for patterns of claims or consistently made claims in each version of the Strategy. We wanted to be able to answer how ONDCP generally treated the many topics it considers each year in its annual reports.

To assess the effectiveness of the drug war, based on the stated goals of ONDCP, we examine the following types of claims:

1. Claims of success in reducing drug use
2. Claims of success in healing America's drug users
3. Claims of success in disrupting drug markets

Because the primary goal of the drug war is to reduce drug use, drug use trends are the most important indicators of success or failure. Therefore, the largest portion of our analysis deals with evaluation of claims about reducing drug use. As explained by ONDCP, all its goals are really related to reducing drug use:

> Focusing the efforts of the Federal Government on the single goal of reducing drug use is a useful reminder of the singular purpose of drug control efforts. When Americans teach young people about the dangers of drug use, when treatment specialists help free the addicted, when communities unite to drive out drug dealers, or when law enforcement agents dismantle a trafficking organization, the goal should always be the same — reducing drug use. . . . When we treat people for addiction, when we counsel young people to avoid drug use, and when trafficking organizations are dismantled, it means nothing unless drug use is reduced.[5]

Of most interest to us are claims of those types in which ONDCP used statistics to support its case. Here, our goal was to discover if ONDCP honestly and appropriately used statistics to tell it like it really is, or if ONDCP misused statistics to justify the drug war and serve its own ideology as it did with its reformatted budget. We also carefully examined claims that were accompanied by visual figures. Here, our goal was to assess the degree to which the written claims match the visual evidence and vice versa. We also critically analyze the visual evidence chosen for presentation and that which is left out.

We showed in chapter 1 some examples of how ONDCP presented statistics visually in a slide show that accompanied the 2000 National Drug Control

Strategy. We carefully examined the six years of the Strategy reports looking
for similar inappropriate presentation of statistics. Further, we identified claims
of ONDCP that are indicative of failures, including failures to reduce drug use,
failures to heal America's drug users, and failures to disrupt drug markets.
Here, we relied on ONDCP claims-making related to these three areas, but
also in the area of costs attributable to drug use and abuse and costs of the drug
war (including relationships between drug use and crime, criminal justice costs
resulting from the drug war, deaths attributed to drug use, and emergency
room mentions of drug use).

The latter claims are relevant because previous ONDCP goals, as stated in
numerous years of the Strategy reports up until 2002, included reducing health
and social costs to the public of illegal drugs use and increasing the safety of
America's citizens by reducing drug-related crime and violence. Further, measurable objectives included reducing drug-related health problems.

How We Did It

We began the study by locating and printing up the past six years (2000-2005)
of the National Drug Control Strategy. Next, we carefully read and outlined
each year's report, looking for evidence of honesty and dishonesty—accurate
use of statistics as well as misleading use.

We then listed and organized claims by topic—those about drug use,
those about healing drug users, and those about disrupting drug markets. We
could not cite and discuss every claim made by ONDCP in these areas, so we
chose those that were the most broad as opposed to specific, and also selected
as many as we could that were accompanied by a discussion of a particular statistic or figure. When figures were not accompanied by a specific claim, as
many were not, we located within the Strategy the claim that came closest to
addressing the presented figure and critically analyzed it. Usually, these claims
were on the same page of the Strategy as the presented figure.

For each claim, we either attempted to verify it by referring to original statistics—the data sources that ONDCP relies on to formulate its Strategy reports—or by locating and reading other research on the same topic. In attempts to verify claims related to efforts to reduce drug use, we relied heavily
on data contained in the official sources of data most used by ONDCP, which
we discuss next.

For those claims that simply characterized a trend shown in a figure, we assessed whether the claim actually matched the trend line depicted in the figure.
Here, the key question we tried to answer was how did ONDCP characterize the
statistics depicted in its figures. Did it characterize declining trends as declines,
increasing trends as increases, stagnant trends as unchanged, and so forth?

We also analyzed claims related to additional topics, including costs of drug use and abuse, costs of the drug war, and relationships between drugs and crime. In attempting to verify these claims, we relied heavily on Brian Bennett's "truth: the Anti-drug war" Web site,[6] a site that is highly critical of the drug war and one that is meticulously researched and thoroughly presented. This Web site challenges ONDCP in many areas, including its claims about the costs of drug use and abuse.

DATA SOURCES

When making claims about drug use trends, ONDCP primarily uses several data sources for information about drug use.[7] We relied on the same sources to verify or debunk ONDCP claims:

- The *National Household Survey on Drug Abuse (NHSDA)*, now called the *National Survey on Drug Use and Health (NSDUH)*. This is a survey of people age twelve and older conducted every year since 1976 by the Substance Abuse and Mental Health Services Administration.
- The *Monitoring the Future Survey (MTF)*, which is a survey of eighth, tenth, and twelfth graders, college students, and young adults conducted every year since 1972 by the National Institute of Drug Abuse.
- *Arrestee Drug Abuse Monitoring (ADAM)*, which consists of surveys and drug testing of arrestees in more than thirty cities conducted every year since 1997 by the National Institute of Justice.

The NHSDA was redesigned in 1999, after a switch from paper-and-pencil interviews to computer-assisted interviews. Thus, household data on drug use collected prior to 1999 cannot be compared with data collected in 1999 or after. This makes long-term evaluations of ONDCP from 1988 to 2005 impossible, including assessments of ONDCP's goals stated in chapter 2. Further, as noted in the 2003 Strategy, further "improvements" in the NHSDA in 2002 make comparisons of data collected before and after 2002 inappropriate. In fact, the name of the survey was changed to the National Survey on Drug Use and Health (NSDUH).[8] That the federal government would allow its primary source of drug use trends for adults to undergo revisions twice in the middle of an evaluation period raises an interesting question itself.

According to the National Academy of Sciences' Committee on Data and Research for Policy and Illegal Drugs:

The Office of National Drug Control Policy (ONDCP) has authority to facilitate and coordinate data collection concerning illegal drugs . . .

it was at ONDCP's suggestion that the National Household Survey
of Drug Abuse was carried out each year rather than every 3 years, and
its size markedly increased. Likewise ONDCP suggested that Monitoring the Future include 8th and 10th graders rather than just 12th
graders.[9]

We do not know if the changes in the NHSDA were requested by
ONDCP or instituted for some other reason. Yet, given that ONDCP has
much influence over the national surveys on drug use, it is possible that
ONDCP requested the changes. If so, this means ONDCP may be responsible
for the fact that researchers cannot evaluate the ability of ONDCP to achieve
its ten-year goals (from 1996 to 2007) that were stated in 1998 Strategy. Recall
from chapter 2 that in the 1998 Strategy, ONDCP stated two objectives of reducing drug use and drug availability by 50% by 2007. Given the changes in
NSHDA, evaluating the effectiveness of ONDCP in achieving these goals is
impossible. This is an important point that will be revisited later in this book
(see chapter 8).

ONDCP also relies on other sources of information when discussing healing America's drug users and disrupting drug markets. These include:

- The *Drug Abuse Warning Network (DAWN)*, which consists of mentions of drug use by patients in emergency rooms tabulated every
  year since 1972 by the Substance Abuse and Mental Health Services
  Administration.
- The *Treatment Episode Data Set (TEDS)*, which consists of data on the
  demographic and substance abuse characteristics of admissions to substance abuse treatment collected every year since 1992 by the Substance
  Abuse and Mental Health Services Administration.
- *Federal-wide Drug Seizure System*, which consists of data on drug seizures made by and with the participation of DEA, FBI, Customs Service, Border Patrol, and the Coast Guard disseminated every year
  since 1998 by the Drug Enforcement Administration.
- *System to Retrieve Information from Drug Evidence (STRIDE)*, which
  consist of records of cocaine, heroin, and other illegal drugs acquired by
  undercover agents and Drug Enforcement Administration (DEA) and
  officers with the Metropolitan Police of the District of Colombia. Data
  include type, amount, purity, and price of drugs acquired/purchased.

Many other sources are cited by ONDCP in its annual Strategy, but these
are the most frequently relied on sources and the ones we used, ironically, to
counter ONDCP claims. Each of these sources is located on the Internet and
is easily accessible to readers.

The Web sites of SAMHSA and MTF also contain numerous reports filled with claims about drug use. Our goal was not to assess these claims. Yet, when these claims either bolstered or refuted those of ONDCP, we use them to support or challenge ONDCP claims-making. The Web sites for the NHSDA/NSDUH and MTF contain literally hundreds of tables with statistics pertaining to drug use trends. Mostly, we used these sources to check the statistics presented by ONDCP.

In addition to the Strategy and the sources cited, we also relied on ONDCP's *Performance Measures of Effectiveness (PME)* system, which was "designed in 1997 to inform the drug control community about the extent to which it achieves the . . . Strategy's goals and objectives and to assist in the clarification of problem areas and the development of corrective actions." The PME system was "endorsed by Congress in the Office of National Drug Control Policy (ONDCP) Reauthorization Act of 1998 . . . as the vehicle by which to assess strategic progress."[10] It was designed to evaluate the effectiveness of the National Drug Control Strategy and was to be a tool of the federal government for assessing the nation's drug war, including the performance of federal agencies to meet the goals of ONDCP.

As it turns out, the PME system has only been used to evaluate the 1998 version of the National Drug Control Strategy. ONDCP issued three reports as part of an evaluation of the 1998 Strategy goals, the last in February 2002. We discuss the findings of the final report of the PME system for one simple reason: this report states that the PME system "should be viewed as a rough gage of the national drug control community's progress toward the desired end states" or, in other words, whether the drug war is meeting its goals. Since it appears to be the only evaluation by ONDCP of the effectiveness of the drug war, we felt it would be useful in our analysis.

We return to the findings of the PME evaluations in chapter 7. For now, it is important to keep in mind that the PME reports make clear that ONDCP expects *consistent* declines in drug use, drug availability, and health and social costs of illicit drug use. Any evaluation of ONDCP's effectiveness must judge its progress against this standard.

LIMITATIONS OF DRUG DATA

Many of the data sources used by the Office of National Drug Control Policy (ONDCP), as well as by us in this book, have notable limitations that must be understood before our findings can be presented. These were aptly documented by a National Academy of Sciences' Committee on Data and Research for Policy and Illegal Drugs report titled *Informing America's Policy on Illegal Drugs: What We Don't Know Keeps Hurting Us*.[11] In this report, the National

Academy of Sciences (NAS) concludes "that the nation possesses little information about the effectiveness of current drug policy, especially of drug law enforcement" (which constitutes a major portion of the drug war).[12] The authors add that "at present, the quality of some data is poor, often data are simply unavailable, and policies in many areas are therefore poorly informed."[13]

Specific problems identified in the report include:

- Evaluations of enforcement activities are hindered by "the absence of adequate data on drug consumption and reliable data on drug prices"[14]
- Incomplete coverage of the drug use surveys due to missing "high school dropouts, homeless people, and people in institutions [who] may exhibit substantially higher rates of drug use than the general population"[15]
- Nonresponse and inaccurate response in the drug use surveys.[16]

The price data (STRIDE) on which evaluations of interdiction efforts rely are collected by the Drug Enforcement Administration (DEA) and other policing agencies "does not provide reliable indicators of retail price movements in actual drug markets."[17] That is, the procedures employed to collect price data "are not designed to provide representative samples of price distributions in drug markets."[18] The result is that data on what consumers actually pay for drug are not available.[19]

Incomplete coverage of drug use is due to the methodology of the Monitoring the Future (MTF) study, which is conducted in the nation's schools (those that agree to participate), and the methodology of the National Survey on Drug Use and Health (NSDUH), which is conducted in the nation's households. Nonresponses and inaccurate responses are caused by people not wanting to admit to their illicit drug use.

The first problem makes it impossible to conclude whether drug interdiction efforts are increasing or decreasing drug prices. This is problematic, but we are unable to assert that it affects long-term trend data one way or the other. When we evaluate price data in chapter 5, keep in mind the limitations of the data itself.

The result of incomplete coverage and nonresponse and inaccurate response is an undercounting of drug use and abuse in the United States. This means that data presented by ONDCP about drug use are surely undercounts of the true amount of drug use in the United States. When we evaluate drug use trends in chapter 4, keep this in mind, too. Yet, the key point for our analysis of ONDCP claims and discussions of drug use trends is that nonresponses and inaccurate responses are thought to be stable over time. That is, these limitations do not affect ONDCP's ability (or ours) to assess drug use trends over time. Two drug policy experts agree, saying that despite the weaknesses of the

NSDUH and MTF data, "the surveys probably capture the general trends in occasional drug use, with some exaggeration in the speed of upturns and downturns. . . . Turning points are probably identified with reasonable accuracy."[20]

Finally, trends in drug dependency are not known, given that the NSDUH and MTF do not accurately measure abuse trends. It is thought that dependent users are underrepresented among respondents and are more likely to lie in their responses. Because of this, drug dependency data are suspect.[21] Despite such problems, policy-makers must make choices according to available data. The war on drugs should be based on empirical evidence, as we argued in chapter 1, and these are the data available to inform American drug policy.

Chapter Four

Claims of Success in Reducing Drug Use

In this chapter, we critically analyze ONDCP claims-making concerning federal efforts to reduce drug use. We examine claims about general drug use trends for adults and youth, as well as specific claims about marijuana, cocaine, heroin, Ecstasy, and other drugs. We address the claims year by year in a roughly chronological order.

In its annual Strategy reports, ONDCP generally claims success in reducing drug use. This is true when the statistics warrant it and when they do not.

General Drug Use Trends for Adults and Youth

2000 Strategy

In the 2000 Strategy, it is claimed: "Since 1996, the number of current [illicit drug] users remained steady, with statistically insignificant changes occurring each year."[1] A figure on the same page shows current drug use trends unchanged since 1988, the year ONDCP was created, yet the figure begins with a statistic from 1985 (like the figure in the PowerPoint© slide show discussed in chapter 1). Beginning with 1985 data assures that the figure is more suggestive of a decline.

There are at least two problems with the statistics presented in the figure. First, as noted in chapter 1, the use of 1985 as a starting point of trend data is misleading for an evaluation of ONDCP goals since ONDCP was not created until 1988. Second, the trend in drug use looks noticeably different when the

1988 starting point is used, as no decline is depicted with 1988 as the starting point. A counterargument is that it is fair to use any starting date to show the effectiveness of the war on drugs, since it began prior to the founding of ONDCP. Perhaps 1991 is the fairest starting point to assess annual drug use trends with Monitoring the Future (MTF) data. MTF data were not collected annually on all three grades — eighth, tenth, and twelfth — until 1991.

The 2000 Strategy also claims in a bold headline that "juvenile drug-use rates level off."[2] Citing statistics from the National Household Survey on Drug Abuse (NHSDA), ONDCP notes a meaningful decline in current drug use among the nation's youth (aged 12–17 years): "This decline was the first statistically significant drop in four years." Yet, for 18–25 year olds, "current use of any illegal drug has been rising since 1994." In other words, NHSDA data suggest a zero-sum gain. When considered against ONDCP's goal of reducing drug use, both statements can be read as admissions of failure. First, the first drop in four years in drug use by 12–17 year olds is in opposition with ONDCP's goal of *consistently* reducing drug use. Second, increasing drug use by 18–25 year olds is also in opposition to ONDCP's goal of *consistently* reducing drug use. ONDCP's Performance Measures of Effectiveness (PME) system, introduced in chapter 3, makes it clear that ONDCP expects the drug use trend to consistently decline.

Further, a figure on the same page using MTF statistics shows a general upward trend in current use of illicit drugs among eighth, tenth, and twelfth graders since 1991. Again, since the same type of figure is presented in the 2001 Strategy, we replicate it later in our discussion of those data.

2001 Strategy

In the 2001 Strategy, ONDCP claims: "Since 1992 the number of current [illicit drug] users had gradually increased, with statistically insignificant changes occurring each year."[3] The figure on the same page shows no changes in past-month drug use since 1988, yet again it begins with a statistic from 1985. Figure 4.1 depicts that figure.

Looking at the trend beginning in 1988 (when ONDCP was created) or 1991 (the first year for which MTF data were collected each year for all grades) shows a flat or unchanged trend in overall drug use in the United States. Here, ONDCP intentionally presents statistics to suggest declining drug use trends even when the statistics suggest no change in drug use since the founding of ONDCP.

Further, ONDCP's claim about growing numbers of illicit drug users is overshadowed by the figure that deals with past-month drug use. These are two different statistics. ONDCP has chosen to highlight the one in its figure that does not depict a statistically significant increase.

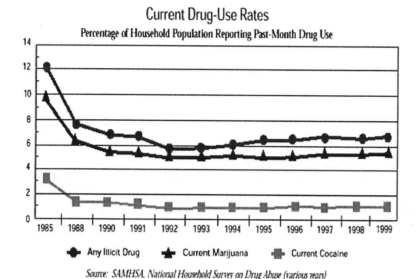

Current Drug-Use Rates
Percentage of Household Population Reporting Past-Month Drug Use

Source: SAMHSA, National Household Survey on Drug Abuse (various years)

FIGURE 4.1 ONDCP Characterizes Increasing Drug Use as Statistically Insignificant (NHSDA), 2001 Strategy

ONDCP again cites NHSDA data in the 2001 Strategy to claim some successes in reducing youth drug use. For example, it reports a 21% decline in current illicit drug use by youth aged 12–17 years from 1997 to 1999. Yet, it also notes consistent increases in current illicit drug use by 18–25 year olds during this time period, suggesting another zero-sum gain.

The accompanying figure on the same page shows MTF data from 1991 through 2000. Figure 4.2 depicts this illustration. This figure clearly shows an overall upward trend in past-month drug use among eighth, tenth, and twelfth graders. Here, ONDCP presents a figure indicating increasing drug use trends (using MTF statistics) but chooses to highlight in writing recent short-term declines is drug use trends (using NHSDA statistics for 12–17 year olds).

The 2000 and 2001 versions of the Strategy show clear failure in the area of reducing overall drug use among adults and juveniles when data are analyzed from 1988 (or 1991) to 2000. Yet, some signs in the documents offer hope for reducing drug use in the future. For example, in the 2000 Strategy, ONDCP claims that seventh through twelfth graders were more likely to disapprove of drug use between 1998 and 1999.[4] A figure showing MTF data for past-month use of marijuana by eighth graders from 1991 to 1999 suggests greater disapproval results in less overall use, whereas less disapproval is found to be associated with more overall use.[5] The same figure is shown in the 2001 Strategy,[6]

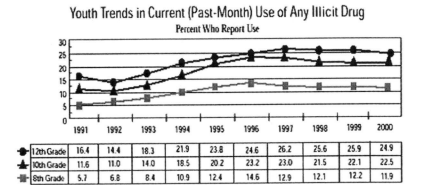

FIGURE 4.2   ONDCP Claims Reductions in Drug Use Among Students (MTF),
2001 Strategy

and more evidence is offered suggesting that teen attitudes are less favorable
toward drug use. It is possible that less use results in greater disapproval, but
this is not considered by ONDCP.

Overall the 2000 and 2001 versions of the Strategy are filled with evidence
of failure to reduce adult and juvenile drug use. ONDCP, however, does not
admit this.

2002 Strategy

In the 2002 Strategy, new goals related to reducing drug use are stated, including two-year and five-year objectives. Two-year goals include: "A 10 percent reduction in current use of illegal drugs by 8th, 10th, and 12th graders" and "A 10
percent reduction in current use of illegal drugs by adults aged 18 and older."
Five-year goals include: "A 25 percent reduction in current use of illegal drugs
by 8th, 10th, and 12th graders" and "A 25 percent reduction in current use of illegal drugs by adults aged 18 and older." The 2002 Strategy notes: "Progress toward all goals will be measured from the baseline established by the 2000 National Household Survey on Drug Abuse."[7]

It is interesting that ONDCP states new goals in 2002. While they are
clearly related to the overall goal of reducing drug use, and while they can be
understood as measurable objectives under this broader goal, ONDCP doesn't
explain why these goals are first mentioned in 2002 rather than in earlier years or

in every version of the Strategy. We can guess that it relates in part to the changes in the NHSDA (as discussed in chapter 3). We also believe ONDCP had good reason to expect some drug use declines among young people, based on projections made earlier by the Substance Abuse and Mental Health Administration (SAMHSA). For example, after discussing that when new illicit drug users (incidence) declines, so too does overall drug use (prevalence), SAMHSA writes:

> Assuming this relationship between incidence and prevalence continues to hold, the continuing high levels (between 2.5 and 3.0 million initiates per year) of marijuana incidence between 1995 and 2001 indicate that substantial declines in youth prevalence may not occur in the near future. However, the [National Survey on Drug Use and Health] NSDUH incidence estimates for youths under age 18 indicate a decline from 2000 to 2001 (from 2.1 million to 1.7 million), which suggests that youth prevalence may decline. The NSDUH youth lifetime prevalence and MTF past month prevalence estimates do show decreases from 2001 to 2002.[8]

If researchers at ONDCP read SAMSHA's yearly NSDUH reports, they could reasonably expect youth drug use to decline in the near future—even over the next couple of years. A short-term goal to reduce youth drug use rates over a two-year period would be a safe goal to put forth based on this statistical projection by SAMSHA. Following this logic, ONDCP should not expect declines in adult drug use because adult incidence has increased.

The 2002 Strategy begins with more bad news, including MTF data in which "most indicators were flat." It says:

> what *Monitoring the Future* had to say was deeply disturbing. Though drug use among our Nation's 8th, 10th, and 12th graders remains stable, it nevertheless is at levels that are close to record highs. More than 50 percent of our high school seniors experimented with illegal drugs at least once prior to graduation. And, during the month prior to the survey, 25 percent of seniors used illegal drugs, and 32 percent reported being drunk at least once.[9]

Clearly, these data are inconsistent with the goals of ONDCP. A startling admission is offered in the 2002 Strategy on the same page: "This situation is not new. Indeed, drug use among our young people has hovered at unacceptably high levels for most of the past decade. *As in the 1960s and 1970s, drug use has once again become all too accepted by our youth.*"[10]

We characterize this admission as startling because, generally speaking, ONDCP appears to downplay (or ignore entirely) statistics that depict a failure to achieve drug war goals. Here it admits unacceptably high drug use trends for "most of the past decade." And of course, there is a significant difference between the 1960s and 1970s and the current day—the existence of ONDCP with all its resources to reinforce the dominant ideology that drug use is wrong and that drugs are bad. According to the 2002 Strategy, ONDCP has failed to reduce drug use since its creation in 1988, despite all its efforts and the tens of billions of dollars it has budgeted over the past fifteen years.

Another admission of failure is later offered: "Bureaucracies are famously self-protective, but this document will depart from standard government practice by conceding that our drug fighting institutions have not worked as effectively as they should."[11] Considering that from 1988 (the year ONDCP was created) through 2001 (the latest year for which data were available), drug use has remained either unchanged or has increased, this is a relatively mildly worded admission of failure.

We consistently see these kinds of admissions of failure in the ONDCP Strategy reports, hidden in plain view for all who are reading carefully enough. ONDCP, however, does not generally characterize its failures as failures. Instead, it uses them to justify the war on drugs. Ironically, ONDCP must admit some failure in order to heighten awareness of the problem of drugs. Yet, never does ONDCP question the American approach to fighting drugs or consider alternative approaches used elsewhere. This serves to reinforce status quo approaches to solving drug problems.

2003 Strategy

In the 2003 Strategy, the same new goals related to reducing drug use from the 2002 Strategy are stated, including the two-year and five-year goals. Yet, the 2003 Strategy notes: "Progress toward youth goals will be measured from the baseline established by the Monitoring the Future survey for the 2000–2001 school year. Progress toward adult goals will be measured from the baseline of the 2002 National Household Survey on Drug Abuse."[12] Thus, one source of data and the baseline for evaluating these goals are different from the goals stated in the 2002 Strategy, where ONDCP said it would use the *2000 NHSDA* as a baseline for adult *and* youth drug use.

An explanation for why ONDCP shifted baseline years and data sources for its two-year and five-year goals is contained in the 2003 Strategy:

> Progress toward youth goals was to have been measured entirely from the baseline of the *National Household Survey on Drug Abuse,* but recent improvements to that survey have created a discontinuity between the 2002 survey and previous years' data. Although changes

to the survey will permit more reliable estimates of drug use in future years, they prevent comparisons with use rates from the baseline year (2000). Fortunately, there is another survey that measures drug use among young people while preserving continuity over time. As a result, the Strategy will measure progress toward the two- and five-year goals as follows: drug use by young people will be measured at the 8th, 10th, and 12th grade levels using the *Monitoring the Future* survey, with the 2000-2001 school year as a baseline. . . . Given the discontinuity problem, and with no available substitute for measuring adult use (*Monitoring the Future* focuses on teen use), measuring the two- and five-year goals for adults poses a different challenge. This Strategy meets the challenge by measuring adult use from the baseline of the improved and redesigned 2002 *Household Survey*.[13]

We believe that most policy experts would agree that simply shifting years for an evaluation period during an ongoing evaluation due to a problem with data is not a sufficient solution. The claim by ONDCP that it "meets the challenge" is dubious at best.

The shift in tone from the previous three years of the Strategy (2000-2002) to the 2003 version of the Strategy is striking:

Last year's National Drug Control Strategy opened on an unsettling note. Just-released data from the 2000-2001 school year had confirmed the continuation of a trend, begun in the early 1990s, of near-record levels of drug use among young people. More than half of American high school seniors had tried illegal drugs at least once by graduation, while a quarter of seniors were regular users. . . . In this year's Strategy, by contrast, we are pleased to report that after a long upward trajectory, teen drug use is once again headed in the right direction -- down. In fact, data from the University of Michigan's most recent Monitoring the Future survey show the *first significant downturn in youth drug use in nearly a decade*, with reductions in drug use noted among 8th, 10th, and 12th graders, and levels of use for some drugs that are lower than they have been in almost three decades. Such *comprehensive declines are remarkably rare;* they carry the hopeful suggestion that America has, again, *begun to work effectively to reduce the drug problem.*[14]

We added emphasis to show that even when claims of success are made, there is clear evidence of long-term failure in the claims (and in the statistics presented to back up the claims). This is another example of an admission of failure in the ONDCP Strategy reports, stated plainly but used as a justification for the war on drugs. The admission of failure is that this is the "first significant downturn in youth drug use in nearly a decade," that "comprehensive declines are remarkably rare," and that we have just "begun" to reduce drug use. It is used to justify greater resources in hopes of continuing the decline without any explanation from ONDCP as to why it was unable to reduce trends for the previous ten years.

The 2003 Strategy points out the following positive results:

- "The percentages of 8th and 10th graders using 'any illicit drug' were at their lowest levels since 1993 and 1995, respectively."
- "Among 10th graders, marijuana use in the past year and past month decreased, as did daily use in the past month. Past-year marijuana use among 8th graders has dropped to 14.6 percent--its lowest level since 1994."
- "With a single exception (past-month, or 'current,' use by 12th graders), the use of illegal drugs other than marijuana fell for all three grades surveyed and for all three prevalence periods (lifetime, annual, and past month), although not all changes reached statistical significance."
- "Ecstasy use was down in all three grades. Ecstasy use in the past year and past month decreased significantly among 10th graders from 2001 to 2002. Past-year and lifetime rates were below those for 2000 in all three grades."
- "Lifetime and past-year LSD use decreased significantly among 8th, 10th, and 12th graders, and past-month use declined among 10th and 12th graders. Past-year and past-month LSD use by 12th graders reached its lowest point in the 28-year history of the survey."[15]

While it cannot be denied that such findings are welcome changes to the findings of the past three versions of the Strategy (2000–2002), the fact remains that these findings are atypical and not indicative of long-term drug use trends. In fact, even with these important changes, a figure shows past-month use of illicit drugs up over the period from 1991 to 2002.[16] Figure 4.3 depicts that figure.

Recall that one of the 2000 figures from the ONDCP PowerPoint© slide show we found when preparing to teach our "War on Drugs" course indicates that a stagnant trend from 1988 to 2000 is characterized as a declining trend based on a decline from 1985 to 1988 (see chapter 1). It is interesting that ONDCP, in the 2003 Strategy, does not characterize an upward trend over eleven years as an increasing trend. This is consistent with ONDCP's general approach to interpreting drug use trend statistics—celebrate declines even when they are short-term or occurred a decade ago, and downplay increases unless they are being used to create alarm.

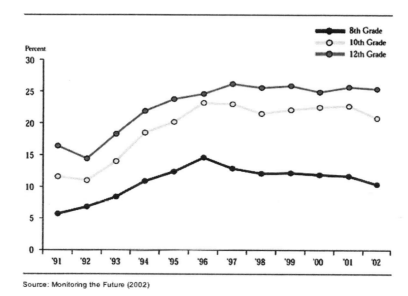

Source: Monitoring the Future (2002)

FIGURE 4.3 ONDCP Downplays Increasing Drug Use Among Students (MTF), 2003 Strategy

Furthermore, even with different forms of drug use among the nation's youth at their lowest levels since 1993, 1994, 1995, and 2000, the fact remains that they are all (with the exception of LSD) higher than in 1988 when ONDCP was created. Thus, the following are alternative conclusions to those of the ONDCP, each of which is equally true:

- Even though overall use of any illicit drug by eighth and tenth graders is at its lowest levels since 1993 and 1995, respectively, the fact remains that any illicit drug use by eighth and tenth graders is higher in 2002 than 1993 and 1995.
- Even though past-year and past-month marijuana use by tenth graders declined in 2002, it is still up significantly since ONDCP was created. Further, even though past-year marijuana use by eighth graders dropped to its lowest level since 1994, the fact remains that past-year marijuana use by eighth graders is higher in 2002 than in 1994.
- Even though lifetime, past-year, and past-month use of illegal drugs other than marijuana fell for eighth, tenth, and twelfth graders in 2002, the general trend is more use since 1988, not less.

- Even though Ecstasy use is down in 2002 for eighth, tenth, and twelfth graders, and past-month and past-year and lifetime rates were below those in 2000, the general trend is more use since 1988, not less.
- As for LSD, almost all of the declines in lifetime, past-year, and past-month use occurred over one year (from 2001 to 2002), suggesting the possibility of a one-year blip in the data. Further, past-month use of LSD for eighth graders actually remains at the same level as 1991.

We do not expect ONDCP to state such negative conclusions. Yet, ONDCP's conclusions pertaining to drug use trends are not warranted—despite being truthful—because they are based on incomplete interpretations of ONDCP's own figures and the statistics on which they are based.

Citing its findings (and ignoring such alternative conclusions), ONDCP claims in the 2003 Strategy: "We have achieved an important goal of getting drug use by our young people *moving downward*. We now must secure the equally important objective of sustaining, accelerating, and broadening that downward movement."[17]

We have three reactions to this statement. First, the primary goal of the drug war according to ONDCP is to reduce drug use, not to start it moving downward. Second, no evidence is offered that the small declines in drug use among young people in 2002 is attributable to anything ONDCP has done. Third, it is debatable that drug use is even down.

With regard to the first point, trends must obviously start moving downward before they can decline, but a single year or two of decreasing drug use does not equal success. Further, ONDCP never stated "getting drug use by our young people moving downward" as a goal. To claim it has met a goal is misleading.

With regard to the second point, if every increase and decrease in drug use is attributable to ONDCP activities, then another reasonable conclusion reached from analyzing statistics pertaining to drug use trends is that ONDCP is responsible for overall increases in drug use since 1988. ONDCP only takes credit when drug use trends decline, but takes no responsbility when drug use trends increase. The fact is that trend data fluctuate up and down due to many factors—social, demographic, moral, economic, criminal justice, and so forth—and concluding that ONDCP has achieved a goal of starting to reduce drug use among youth based on a brief fluctuation is dishonest and inconsistent with long-term drug trends.

With regard to the third point, it is debatable that drug use among youth has even declined. Table 1 of the very same 2003 Strategy shows "NHSDA data for the Estimated Number of Users of Selected Illegal Drugs, 1979-2001." The statistics reported in the table indicate that current users of any illicit drugs among adolescents increased from 2.27 million in 1999 to 2.56 million in

2001 (a rate increase from 9.8% to 10.8%). This is up from 1.9 million users in 1988 (when the rate was 8.1%), the year ONDCP was created. Current users of marijuana among adolescents increased from 1.68 million in 1999 to 1.89 million in 2001 (a rate increase from 7.2% to 8%). This is up from 1.1 million users in 1988 (when the rate was 5.4%).

While NHSDA data from 1988 to 2001 are not technically comparable due to changes in the survey methodology, the table contains the statistics from these years and so we have used them to counter ONDCP claims. Why would ONDCP ignore statistics in the table of its own Strategy report that contradict its claims?

We are confident that drug use among youth during this time did not decrease and, if anything, it increased. For example, NSDUH data from 2002 show increases in lifetime marijuana use among youth younger than eighteen years through the 1990s, increases in lifetime use for heroin, hallucinogens, and psychotherapeutics, and that lifetime cocaine use among youth younger than eighteen years reached a new peak in 2002. The data also show increases through the 1990s in new users of marijuana, cocaine, heroin, and Ecstasy.[18]

For adults, the table also reports increases. From 1999 to 2001, adult users of any illicit drug increased from 13.83 million to 15.91 million (a rate increase of 6.3% to 7.1%). This is up from 15 million users in 1988 (but down from the rate of 7.7%). The 2002 NSDUH shows 19.5 million current illicit drug users, or 8.3% of the population (which is equal to 1988).

Current marijuana users increased from 10.46 million to 12.12 million (a rate increase from 4.7% to 5.4%). This is relatively unchanged since 1988, when 12.4 million users were reported (but down from the rate of 6.2%). The 2002 NSDUH shows 14.6 million current marijuana users, or 6.2% of the population (which is equal to 1988).

Current cocaine users from 1999 to 2001 increased from 1.55 million to 1.68 million (rate remained constant at 0.7%). This is down since 1988, when 3.1 million current cocaine users were reported (when the rate was much higher at 1.6%). The 2002 National Survey on Drug Use and Health shows 2 million current cocaine users, or 0.9% of the population (which is less than 1988).

Amazingly, even MTF statistics cited in Tables 5, 6, and 7 of the 2003 Strategy show that, among eighth graders, past-month use of marijuana, hallucinogens, and cocaine is up from 1991 to 2002. Among tenth and twelfth graders, past-month use of marijuana, cocaine, and stimulants is up from 1991 to 2002.[19] In other words, although the MTF shows declines in some forms of drug use among young people, it also shows increases in other forms of drug use among the same young people.

It is possible that young people have just changed drugs—a form of substitution rather than prevention. An honest policy assessment and review of drug use statistics would discuss this possibility, or at least mention it. There is no discussion of these findings by ONDCP and no figures are offered showing these trends.

Despite its own data, ONDCP claims: "This time we intend to make the problem much smaller and build the structures that will keep [drug use] from growing larger in the future." ONDCP does not explain what it means by this other than to say it will "require a sustained focus on all aspects of drug control, as well as a balanced strategy for approaching the problem."[20] Is this an admission that prior to this year, agencies fighting the drug war have not had "sustained focus on all aspects of drug control" and that the drug war has not been "balanced"? ONDCP does not say.

Short-term thinking with regard to drug use trends seems common by ONDCP, at least as presented in the yearly editions of the Strategy. For example, in the 2003 Strategy, ONDCP writes: "Only the first year of the two-year goal period has elapsed, yet already the goal of reducing current drug use by 10 percent among 8th, 10th, and 12th graders, as measured by the Monitoring the Future survey, is well on the way to being met (with reductions of 11.1, 8.4, and 1.2 percent respectively)."[21] While this statement is an observation of fact, it is a misleading use of statistics because it suggests that ONDCP is achieving its goal of reducing drug use. Achieving short-term goals is important, but, in this case, the brief decline did not make up for longer-term increases.

Yet, ONDCP does reach back to 1979—the peak in American drug use—to show overall declines in drug use (see chapter 1 for an example). It also reaches back to 1985 in some of its figures featured in the Strategy to create the appearance of declines that have not occurred during the tenure of ONDCP, as we showed earlier. If ONDCP began its examination of drug use trends in 1971 when the war on drugs was declared by President Nixon, its figures would show increases in at least some forms of drug use, and declines in others (and, overall, little change in drug use during the entire period, despite rapidly increasing drug war expenditures and efforts).[22]

We observed that the overall tone of the 2003 Strategy is much more uplifting than the previous years. In fact, ONDCP boldly presents visual evidence that previous efforts of the drug war (prior to the creation of the ONDCP) did in fact work. For example, "the data on the prevalence of drug use shows the steep reductions in use that followed the national mobilization started in 1985 by Nancy Reagan's "Just Say No" campaign. Like smoking and other social pathologies, drug use is a problem that responds to societal pressure; when we push against this problem, it gets smaller."[23]

In fact, the figure presented as evidence shows that marijuana use had already begun to decline in 1979, six years prior to Nancy Reagan's campaign, and that cocaine use was already lower in 1985 than it was in 1979.[24] The Substance Abuse and Mental Health Services Administration (SAMHSA) reports that

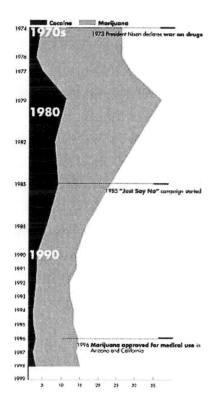

FIGURE 4.4   ONDCP Claims "Just Say No" Campaign Caused Cocaine and Marijuana Use to Decline, 2003 Strategy

overall cocaine use peaked in the early 1980s and then declined through 1991.[25] Perhaps this is why the ONDCP figure only shows trends among 18–25 year olds (rather than all users), which appear in the figure to begin to decline in 1985. Further, ONDCP does not assess the role of other factors in declining cocaine use, such as the waning of the crack cocaine epidemic. Figure 4.4 depicts this figure.

It is simply baffling as to why ONDCP would show drug use trends drawn from statistics of drug use among only 18–25 year olds. After all, it is widely accepted that Nancy Reagan's "Just Say No" campaign was aimed at children and adolescents more so than adults. We looked up two sets of statistics to check ONDCP's figure and claims regarding the "Just Say No" campaign. First we looked up NHSDA statistics for adolescents (aged 12–17 years) and for all people twelve years and older. The statistics for those twelve years and older suggest that:

- Past-month use of any illicit drug declined from 14.1% in 1979 to 12.1% in 1985 (the year "Just Say No" started), and continued to decline to 5.8% in 1992. The percentage remained relatively constant thereafter but rose to 6.4% in 1997 and 6.2% in 1998.
- Past-month use of marijuana declined from 13.2% in 1979 to 11.5% in 1985 (the year "Just Say No" started), and continued to decline to 4.6% in 1994. The percentage remained relatively constant thereafter but rose to 5.1% in 1997 and 5% in 1998.
- Past-month use of cocaine declined from 2.6% in 1979 to 2.4% in 1985 (the year "Just Say No" started), and then increased to 3% in 1988. Afterwards, past-month use declined to 0.7% in 1993 and remained at about that rate until 1998.[26]

The statistics for those aged 12–17 years (adolescents) suggest that:

- Past-month use of any illicit drug declined from 16.3% in 1979 to 13.2% in 1985 (the year "Just Say No" started), and continued to decline to 5.3% in 1992. The percentage began to rise thereafter, reaching 11.4% in 1997 and 9.9% in 1998.
- Past-month use of marijuana declined from 14.2% in 1979 to 9.9% in 1985 (the year "Just Say No" started), and then increased to 10.2% in 1988. Afterwards, past-month use declined to 3.4% in 1993 and then rose thereafter, reaching 9.4% in 1997 and 8.3% in 1998.[27]

These statistics, offered by SAMSHA, show that drug use for all people twelve years and older, as well as for those aged 12–17 years (adolescents) began to decline prior to "Just Say No" and did not universally decline from 1985 through 1988 (after "Just Say No" began). This example alone demonstrates that ONDCP selectively uses statistics to prove a point, even when an examination of all drug use statistics (and especially the most relevant) does not warrant the conclusion. We do not know why ONDCP chose to highlight the "Just Say No" campaign as an effective one, but other examples in the same Strategy report give us some hints.

For example, ONDCP highlights the "major reductions in smoking that followed the 1964 Surgeon General's report linking cigarettes with health problems, and the imposition of federal restrictions on tobacco sales in 1992."[28] A figure on the same page, using statistics for all people eighteen years and older (rather than only for 18–25 year olds), visually demonstrates that for adults, two government efforts—one educational in 1964 and the other legal in 1972—resulted in reductions in cigarette smoking. ONDCP attempts to link the "Just Say No" campaign to similar reductions in illicit drugs. Yet, for illicit drugs, it presents data only for 18–25 year olds even though the "Just Say No" program was aimed at kids. This is a selective and inappropriate use of statistics.

Even a cursory review of MTF data, which is available for twelfth graders during the 1980s, shows that the Nancy Reagan effort was not effective. For example, for twelfth graders:

- Past-month use of any illicit drug declined from a high of 38.9% in 1979 to 37.2% in 1980, 36.9% in 1981, 32.5% in 1982, 30.5% in 1983, 29.2% in 1984, 29.7% in 1985, and 27.1% in 1986. Past-month use then declined every year thereafter until 1992, when it reached 14.4%. After that, it increased every year until 1997 when it reached 26.2% and then leveled off and slightly declined until 2004 when it was 23.4%.
- Past-month use of marijuana declined from a high of 37.1% in 1978 to 36.5% in 1979, 33.7% in 1980, 31.6% in 1981, 28.5% in 1982, 27% in 1983, 25.2% in 1984, 25.7% in 1985, and 23.4% in 1986. Past-month use then declined every year thereafter until 1992, when it reached 11.9%. After that, it increased every year until 1997 when it reached 23.7% and then leveled off and slightly declined until 2004 when it was 19.9%.
- Past-month use of cocaine declined from a high of 5.8% in 1981 to 5% in 1982, and 4.9% in 1983. After that past-month use rose again between 1983 and 1985, when it reached 6.7%, a new high. After 1985, past-month use declined every year until 1993, when it reached 1.3%. After that, it increased every year until 1999 when it reached 2.6% and then leveled off and slightly declined until 2004 when it was 2.3%.[29]

Of all these trends, the only one that is consistent with the claim by ONDCP that "Just Say No" was effective is the declines in past-month use of cocaine among twelfth graders, which began to decline between 1985 and 1986 and consistently declined thereafter for more than a decade. MTF statistics for eighth and tenth graders were not available until 1991, but "Just Say No" did not cause declines among twelfth graders. Nor is there evidence it did so for adolescents, according to NHSDA statistics from the time period. ONDCP's claims regarding the effectiveness of the "Just Say No" campaign simply fly in the face of statistics.

Interestingly, ONDCP also presents a figure concerning total alcohol consumption through the twentieth century. In the figure, the years 1919–1933 are identified as the years of prohibition. During these years, total alcohol consumption is depicted as rapidly increasing. Not surprisingly, despite making claims about both tobacco use and illicit drug use, ONDCP makes no claim about alcohol use. The careful Strategy reader would wonder why ONDCP makes no claims about the significance for the drug war of rising alcohol consumption during alcohol prohibition, given the clear parallels between alcohol prohibition and drug prohibition.[30]

A statement in the 2002 Strategy provides a similar example of how ONDCP claims sometimes appear unwarranted: "During the late 1980s and early 1990s, an engaged government and citizenry took on the drug issue and forced down drug use, with declines observed among 12th graders in every year between 1985 and 1992."[31] While the statement about declining drug use among twelfth graders is true, 1985 marks roughly the midpoint of the falling drug use trends shown in MTF data rather than the beginning.[32] In other words, Nancy Reagan did not cause drug use to go down—it was already declining.[33]

In the 2002 Strategy, the ONDCP acknowledges that it has lost ground since and writes: "To make up the ground we have lost, we need only to recover the lessons of the recent past. We *know* that when we push against the drug problem it recedes."[34] Other than the faulty Nancy Reagan "Just Say No" claim, the Strategy does not contain any evidence—no statistics—backing up this confident claim. We wondered, after reading this claim, when during the drug war were federal agencies pushing against the drug problem? And when were they slacking? It is hard to tell when, given the consistent increases in the drug war budget throughout the 1980s and 1990s.

The 2003 Strategy showed that 93% of Americans do not use drugs regularly, as measured in past-month use. Thus, a significant possibility is that drug use is really not a problem in the United States. ONDCP could state that its goal is to make sure that more Americans do not use drugs—to keep drug use in a free society at a stable and perhaps reasonable rate such as 7%—yet it does not. It is possible, even probable, that drug use would be higher in this country if illicit drugs were legalized and marketed by private corporations in our free capitalistic society.[35] It might be more difficult for ONDCP to justify its consistent budget increases since 1988 in order to maintain a constant level of illicit drug use, however.

2004 Strategy

The 2004 Strategy is much like the 2003 Strategy in that the ONDCP is not only much more optimistic about its chance of winning the drug war, but also because it more boldly claims it is winning the drug war. It paints a dire picture of drug use in the United States, admits that it has not been successful in the past, but restates its new goals and puts a positive spin on its ability to achieve them. For example, right at the beginning of the Strategy, the ONDCP reports:

> Two years ago, the President's first National Drug Control Strategy reported the unsettling news that *for the sixth straight year, more than 50 percent of 12th graders had used an illegal drug at least once by graduation*. In his 2002 State of the Union address, the President

set a national goal of reducing youth drug use by 10 percent within two years. It was an ambitious goal, and to many it seemed improbable in light of the string of serial increases that preceded it. Yet that goal has been met.[36]

We again added emphasis to show that even when claims of success are made (such as "that goal has been met"), some questions remain unanswered. First, what percentage of twelfth graders now admit having tried an illicit drug at least once since graduation? The implication of the above claim is that it has fallen to less than 50%. No data are offered to indicate this is the case.

We examined MTF statistics from 2003 and found that 51% of twelfth graders reported illicit drug use at least once by graduation. This represents the eighth consecutive year that more than 50% of high school seniors admit to using an illicit drug at some point in their lives.[37] ONDCP implied it had stopped this streak, when in fact it had not.

Second, even if less than 50% of high school seniors had reported using an illicit drug, does this mean that lifetime drug use is less common among twelfth graders since 1988 when ONDCP was created? No statistics are offered to indicate this is the case.

ONDCP reports in the 2004 Strategy that the most recent MTF data show an "11 percent drop in the past-month use of illicit drugs between 2001 and 2003. . . . Monitoring the Future, which measured behavior at the 8th, 10th, and 12th grades found significant reductions among all three levels."[38] While it is good news that MTF data show that illicit drug use by youth has declined, ONDCP does not indicate where the declines occurred and how much of the declines were attributable to each grade level. Instead, a figure on the same page illustrates a single trend line, created by combining statistics on past-month drug use by all grade levels. Figure 4.5 shows that figure.

We have several reactions to the figure and the accompanying claim. First, we question the wisdom of presenting combined drug use trends because it is possible that the combination masks important trends specific to each grade. Recall that in the 2002 and 2003 Strategy reports, ONDCP stated a goal of reducing by 10% the "current use of illegal drugs by 8th, 10th, *and* 12th graders." MTF data show two-year declines in past-month drug use among eighth graders (20.6%), tenth graders (16.4%), and twelfth graders (6.6%).[39] In other words, when broken down by grade level, we see ONDCP has not achieved its two-year goal of reducing drug use by 10% for twelfth graders. Given the large reductions in the other grades, we do not understand the unwillingness to let the statistics speak for themselves by showing true reductions in each grade level. ONDCP combines the data to arrive at a single statistical trend for all grades in order to claim it has met its goals, which it has not. We know this is inappropriate because in the 2003 Strategy,

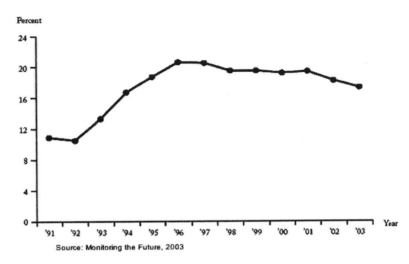

FIGURE 4.5   ONDCP Combines Drug Use Statistics on Current Drug Use into One
Trend to Meet a Two-Year Goal (MTF), 2004 Strategy

ONDCP did report statistics separately for each grade level. Recall that
ONDCP reported declines of 11.1%, 8.4%, and 1.2% for eighth, tenth, and
twelfth graders, respectively.

Second, the statistics show clearly that the overall trend since 1991 is still an
upward one. That is, use is significantly higher in 2003 than in 1991. Here, as before, ONDCP focuses on a short-term decline and a two-year goal, rather than
on long-term increases and its long-term goals ever since ONDCP was created.

Third, while the above figure does show that current drug use among students overall has declined slightly since 1996, the overall levels are still relatively unchanged since 1994. ONDCP does not discuss why drug use trends are
stagnant despite consistent budget increases since 1994.

Fourth, while the nature of the MTF means that the ONDCP cannot
present statistics prior to 1991 for all grades, we wonder why it does not show
trends among twelfth graders since the first year data were collected. The
MTF data for twelfth graders were first available in 1975. We suspect it is because MTF data for past-month drug use by twelfth graders show that it is actually higher than it was in 1988 when ONDCP was created. In fact, MTF data
show past-month drug use among twelfth graders was 21.3% in 1988 but 24.1%
in 2003.[40] Thus, after more than three decades of the drug war and about a
decade and a half of leadership by ONDCP, the level of current drug use by
twelfth graders is unchanged. This is true despite greater spending, increased
use of punishment, and expanded criminal justice and public relations efforts
aimed at reducing drug use.

One ONDCP description of the successes it has outlined sounds more like an admission of failure—ONDCP notes that recent MTF declines "represent the first decline in drug use across all three grades in more than a decade. Moreover, it is a decline in its second year."[41] While this statement is technically true, a quick glance at the figure showing student drug use trends illustrates that another two-year decline occurred from 1996 to 1998. After this two-year decline, drug use stagnated until 2001. It is highly likely that ONDCP will not reach the ten-year goal it stated in the 2000 Strategy of reducing drug use (and drug availability) 50% by 2007.

A final reaction to the figure that combines drug use trends for all MTF grades is that the data on which ONDCP claims it has met the president's goal of reducing youth drug use by 10% within two years are not the correct data on which to base this conclusion. Recall that this was a goal stated by President George W. Bush in the 2002 State of the Union address, made January 29, 2002. The 10% decline referred to in the ONDCP claim occurred between 2001 (before the 2002 State of the Union speech) and 2003.

At the time of the publication of the 2004 Strategy, the 2004 MTF data were not available. Therefore, ONDCP simply went back to one year prior to the president's speech to obtain and use statistics to show it met a goal that had not yet even been stated! This is clearly an inappropriate use of statistics.

When the 2004 MTF data were released, we looked up drug use rates from 2002 to 2004, the two-year period which actually followed the president's statement of the goal. It showed that past month use of any illicit drug fell:

- For eighth graders from 10.4% in 2002 to 8.4% in 2004.
- For tenth graders from 20.8% in 2002 to 18.3% in 2004.
- For twelfth graders from 25.4% in 2002 to 23.4% in 2004.[42]

Thus, for eighth graders, current drug use fell 24% from 2002 to 2004 in line with the president's goal. For tenth graders, current drug use fell 14% in line with the president's goal. For twelfth graders, current drug use fell 8.5%, which is short of the two-year goal of 10% stated by the president. We could not combine the data for eighth, tenth, and twelfth graders to see if drug use among all grades declined from 2002 to 2004 by 10%, but we are confident it did.

Is it possible that when ONDCP wrote: "in his 2002 State of the Union address, the President set a national goal of reducing youth drug use by 10 percent within two years" that it meant something else? Could it have been referring to the 2001 Strategy instead, where it set the goal of "[a] 10 percent reduction in current use of illegal drugs by 8th, 10th, and 12th graders"? If so, then evaluating the goal from 2001 to 2003 would be appropriate. We located and read the president's 2002 State of the Union address. Strangely, the word *drug* only appears two times in the speech, and not once does he state a goal of reducing drug use by 10% over two years.[43] We are unsure why ONDCP attributed the goal to the 2002 State of the Union address.

Among the successes touted in the 2004 Strategy, ONDCP notes:

- "These remarkable survey results apply to nearly all of the most commonly used substances, but particularly to marijuana and dangerous hallucinogens. Use of the 'rave drug MDMA (Ecstasy) has been cut in half, while LSD use has dropped by nearly two-thirds, to the lowest level in nearly three decades."[44]
- "Use of any illicit drug in the past 30 days ('current use') among students declined 11 percent, from 19.4 to 17.3 percent. Similar trends were seen for past-year use (down 11 percent) and lifetime use (down 9 percent)."[45]
- "Use of marijuana . . . also declined significantly. Past-year and current use both declined 11 percent; lifetime use declined 8.2 percent."[46]
- "The use of the hallucinogens LSD and Ecstasy among youth has plummeted. Lifetime use of LSD fell 43 percent, to 3.7 percent, and past-year and current use both dropped early two-thirds. Past-year and current use of Ecstasy were both cut in half."[47]
- "Lifetime and past-year use of inhalants declined 12 and 11 percent, respectively."[48]
- "Use of amphetamines, including methamphetamine, dropped 17 percent for both past-year and current use."[49]

Given the positive results over the last two years (using MTF data), ONDCP claims: "These findings confirm the wisdom of a balanced strategy, with appropriate emphasis on treatment, prevention, and enforcement."[50] Recall from chapter 2 that, of 2005 FY funding requests, 55% were for supply reduction and 45% were for demand reduction (which consists of treatment and prevention). More specifically, 29.4% was for treatment (with research), 25.3% was for domestic law enforcement, 20.6% was for interdiction, 15.6% was for prevention (with research), and 9.1% was for international spending. The majority of this requested funding is reactive in nature, suggesting an imbalanced Strategy.

ONDCP specifically notes two successes for which it is responsible. First, it claims that LSD use is down because of "a law enforcement-led disruption of U.S. supply." Second, it claims that Ecstasy use is down as a "result of successful prevention efforts."[51]

Our reactions to these claims are many. First, we contend that the drug war is not balanced, as discussed in chapter 2, but instead focuses far more on reactive measures such as law enforcement and punishment than proactive measures such as prevention and (especially) treatment. ONDCP admits in the 2004 Strategy that most (55%) of the federal drug control budget is spent on "law enforcement budgets, international programs, drug-related intelligence spending, and interdiction activities."[52] This is true even with the other reactive costs (such as spending on policing, courts, and corrections) are not included in the budget.

Second, ONDCP offers no statistics or other evidence to back up its claims that the drug declines are attributable to its law enforcement or prevention efforts. Yet, the claim is made yet again that: "When we push drug use down" it goes down.[53]

Finally, what about adult drug use trends? Literally, *no* data are offered in the 2004 Strategy to assess the president's goal of reducing adult drug use by 10% within two years. This is because at the time the report was issued, 2003 National Survey on Drug Use and Health (NSDUH) data were not yet available. When the 2003 NSDUH were released, we examined drug use trends from 2001 to 2003 to see if the goal of "[a] 10 percent reduction in current use of illegal drugs by adults age 18 and older" had been met. The statistics show that past month use of any illicit drug:

- Remained steady for 18 to 25 year olds, from 20.2% in 2001 to 20.3% in 2003.[54]
- Increased slightly for 26 to 34 year olds, from 10.5% in 2001 to 10.7% in 2003.[55]
- Declined slightly for those aged 35 and older, from 4.6% in 2001 to 4.4% in 2003.[56]

Thus, for adults aged 18–25 years, current drug use increased 0.5% from 2001 to 2003, in opposition to the president's goal. For adults aged 26–24 years, current drug use rose 2%, in opposition to the president's goal. For adults aged 35 and older, current drug use fell 4.5%, which is short of the two-year goal of 10% stated by the president. We could not combine the data for all adult age groups to see if drug use among all grades declined from 2001 to 2003 by 10%, but it is clear that it did not.

It is strange that ONDCP claims to have met its goals of reducing drug use by 10% when it only assessed one of the two populations using only one of the two data sets it has set out to evaluate and, even then, using the incorrect time period. Adult drug use trends are literally ignored in the 2004 Strategy report. This is a selective and inappropriate use of statistics.

2005 Strategy

The 2005 Strategy is the most optimistic of the six years reviewed here. Overall, it claims success in reducing drug use and focuses on accountability. For example, it begins:

Three years ago this month, President Bush released the Administration's first National Drug Control Strategy. Consistent with his view of government, it was a document that clearly laid out a plan for accountable results in achieving a single goal--reducing drug use. . . . The President's decision to hold his Administration accountable for helping drive down drug use followed a decade during which the use of drugs by young people had doubled. It came at a time when fully half of 12th graders had used an illegal drug at least once by graduation. It was seen, and rightly, as an audacious challenge to the skeptics, who invariably counsel despair when it comes to illegal drugs.[57]

ONDCP claims that not only has the goal of reducing youth drug use by 10% over two years been met, it has been exceeded: "Youth drug use has dropped by 11 percent over two years, and now a third year of data puts the program ahead of schedule for the five-year goal, with a three-year drop of 17 percent."[58] To illustrate success, ONDCP presents a figure depicting past-month use of any illicit drug by eighth,tenth, and twelfth graders combined as in the 2004 Strategy. Figure 4.6 shows that figure.

Examination of the figure shows that youth drug use, according to Monitoring the Future (MTF), is down for three straight years (2001-2004). It also shows that youth drug use has generally declined since 1996. All of this is good news and is consistent with ONDCP's goal of reducing drug use. Yet, youth drug use is still higher in 2004 than in 1991 and is generally up since MTF began measuring drug use by youths in all three grade levels. ONDCP does not acknowledge this or discuss its meaning.

Further, the 17% decline cited by ONDCP is for all three grade levels combined. ONDCP again does not disaggregate drug use trends for each grade level. This is misleading since ONDCP stated its goal of reducing by 10% the "current use of illegal drugs by 8th, 10th, *and* 12th graders" in the 2002 and 2003 Strategy reports.

Additionally, the "half of 12th graders had used an illegal drug at least once by graduation" claim is made again. Here, as in the 2004 Strategy, ONDCP implies that now less than half of twelfth graders have tried an illegal drug at least once by graduation. In fact, the 2004 MTF shows that 51.1% of twelfth graders admit to using some illicit drug in their lives.[59] In other words, President Bush's accountability pledge came at a time when more than half of twelfth graders had used an illegal drug by graduation. Three years later, more than half of twelfth graders still have used an illegal drug by graduation.

Finally, ONDCP again presents no statistics or figures pertaining to adult drug use. Instead, it explains: "Figures for adult drug use will become available with the publication, this summer, of the 2004 National Survey on Drug Use

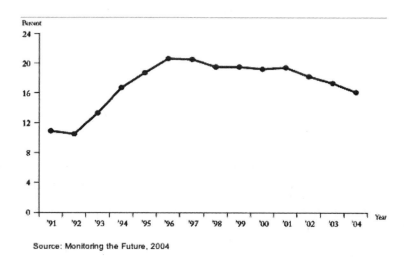

Source: Monitoring the Future, 2004

FIGURE 4.6   ONDCP Again Combines Drug Use Statistics on Current Drug Use into One Trend to Meet a Two-Year Goal (MTF), 2005 Strategy

and Health [NSDUH]."[60] ONDCP could examine adult drug use trends through the 2003 NSDUH, but it chose not to. Perhaps this is because an examination of trends for adult use would show that ONDCP is not meeting its goal of reducing adult drug use by 10%, as we indicated earlier. This is another selective misuse of statistics.

ONDCP highlights some positive findings with regard to drug use in the 2005 Strategy. Referring to combined statistics from MTF for 8th, 10th, and 12th graders since 2001, ONDCP notes that:

- Use of any illicit drug in the past 30 days (so-called current use) declined 17 percent, from 19.4 percent to 16.1 percent. Similar declines were seen for past-year use (down 13 percent) and lifetime use (down 11 percent).
- Marijuana, the most commonly used illicit drug among youth, also declined significantly. Current use declined 18 percent, while past-year use declined 14 percent.
- Use of the hallucinogens LSD and MDMA (Ecstasy) plummeted, with past-year and current use of LSD down by nearly two-thirds and lifetime use down by 55 percent. Past year and current use of Ecstasy were each cut by more than half, while lifetime use was down 41 percent.

- Use of amphetamines, traditionally the second most commonly used illicit drug among youth, also dropped over the past three years. Lifetime use declined 20 percent, while past-year use fell 21 percent and current use fell 24 percent. Past year and current use of methamphetamine among youth declined 25 percent each.[61]

It is important to note that, here, ONDCP is highlighting youth drug use trends from 2001 to 2004. That is, all the declines noted are short-term declines and not indicative of long-term trends. The statistics cited also only come from MTF, whereas NSDUH data for youth are not presented or discussed.

Marijuana

2000 Strategy

The 2000 Strategy illustrates that first-time use of marijuana increased from 1991 to 1994 and has "not changed significantly since 1994."[62] This suggests no declines from 1991 to 1999. Yet, ONDCP claims that "past-month marijuana use among eighth graders was stable during the past year but decreased 14 percent since 1996." On the same page, figures based on NHSDA statistics show the current number of past-month users of marijuana has remained steady since 1990, that the number of first-time users is up since 1987, and that the average age of marijuana use has declined slightly since 1987. Each of these figures suggests outcomes counter to the drug war goals, yet ONDCP does not discuss the implications of these statistical trends for the drug war.

2001 Strategy

The 2001 Strategy shows a zero-sum gain in marijuana use among young people: "There has been an increasing trend toward marijuana use since 1997 among young adults, age 18–25 years . . . and a decreasing trend since 1997 for youths age 12–17 years."[63] Yet, the number of new users of marijuana is reported to have increased from 1990 to 1996, remained stable in 1997, and then dropped in 1998. A figure on the same page shows new marijuana users significantly up since 1989, and ONDCP admits that "the rates of marijuana initiation for youth during 1995 through 1998 are at their highest levels since the peak levels in the late 1970s." This is clearly counter to its goal of reducing marijuana use, as is the fact that the age of first marijuana use has remained stable since 1989.

2002–2005 Strategy

Aside from the brief quotes noted earlier about marijuana put forth in the 2003 and 2004 versions of the Strategy, the 2002–2005 versions of the Strategy make no specific claims related to marijuana use and show no figures referring to marijuana use trends. Instead, tables are included at the end of the Strategy reports whereby trend data can be examined. This is possibly because the data from 1988 to present are not consistent with ONDCP's drug war goals. Indeed, it appears ONDCP ignores statistics that point to outcomes counter to the drug war.

COCAINE

2000 Strategy

The 2000 Strategy reports that cocaine use is said to have "stabilized in the United States between 1992 and 1998." Using 1985 as a starting point, ONDCP notes that past-month cocaine use declined until 1992, but "did not change significantly through 1998."[64] The number of hard-core cocaine users was also unchanged, although "the number of first-time users of any form of cocaine rose between 1996 and 1997." The Strategy notes that this is still lower than in the early 1980s when new initiates were higher (and when there was no ONDCP). Figures using NHSDA statistics on the same page show no changes in the number of past-month users of cocaine since 1990, no changes in new users since 1988, and a slight decline in average age of first use since 1988. Again, these figures suggest failure to meet the goal of reducing drug use, yet ONDCP also does not discuss the implications of these statistical trends for the drug war.

2001 Strategy

In the 2001 Strategy, the picture is much the same, with "stabilized" cocaine use in the United States between 1992 and 1999. ONDCP is quick to point out that: "Past-month cocaine use declined from 3 percent of the population in 1985 to 0.7 percent in 1992 and did not change significantly through 1999, in which 0.8 percent of the population reported past-month use."[65] The problems with using a statistic from 1985 as a starting point for trend analysis were noted earlier.

Statistics presented in figures on the same page (using NHSDA data) begin in 1990 and show no change in past-month cocaine use since 1990, but show an increase in first-time users since 1994 and a slight decline in average

age of first cocaine use.[66] Additionally, it is noted that MTF data show an over-all increase in youth cocaine use initiation: it increased from 1992 to 1996 and has remained stable since then. Thus, the 2001 Strategy shows that cocaine use is not being reduced in line with ONDCP goals.

2002–2005 Strategy

The 2002–2005 versions of the Strategy make no specific claims related to co-caine use and show no figures referring to cocaine use trends. Instead, tables are included at the end of the Strategy reports whereby trend data can be examined. This is also possibly because the data from 1988 to present are not consistent with ONDCP's drug war goals. As with marijuana, ONDCP ignores statistics that point to outcomes counter to the drug war.

HEROIN

2000 Strategy

In the 2000 Strategy, ONDCP claims that heroin use "appears to be declining after an upward trend between 1992 and 1997.[67] Yet, figures on the same page using NHSDA statistics show a general upward trend in past-month use from 1988 through 1998, an increase in new users since 1987, and a consistent decline in the average age of first-time users. ONDCP notes that the changes in use are not "statistically significant" increases, but conveniently ignores that nei-ther are they declines. Data for youth offered on the same page show "consis-tent" increases in heroin use since 1991. None of these outcomes is consistent with the ONDCP goal of reducing drug use, and ONDCP again fails to dis-cuss the implications of these statistics trends for the drug war.

2001 Strategy

The 2001 Strategy claims: "Heroin use in the United States has stabilized since 1992."[68] This is a different conclusion from the 2000 Strategy. Figures on the same page illustrate a general upward trend in past-month use of heroin from 1990 to 1999 and an overall increase in heroin initiation rates since 1990. While ONDCP reports that MTF data show declines in past-year use by eighth graders from 1996 to 2000, it reports stable levels in past-year use by tenth graders between 1997 and 2000 and a huge increase in past-year use among twelfth graders from 1991 to 2000. Average age of first-use of heroin is down since 1990. Thus, the 2001 Strategy illustrates that heroin use has not been reduced in line with the drug war's goals. ONDCP does not acknowledge this.

2002–2005 Strategy

The 2002–2005 versions of the Strategy make no specific claims related to heroin use and show no figures referring to heroin use trends. Instead, tables are included at the end of the Strategy reports whereby trend data can be examined. Again, this is possibly because the data from 1988 to present are not consistent with ONDCP's drug war goals. As with marijuana and cocaine, ONDCP ignores statistics that point to outcomes counter to the drug war.

ECSTASY

2000 Strategy

The 2000 Strategy notes that past-year use of Ecstasy increased from 1998 to 1999 among students (MTF data). Ecstasy trends are depicted in a figure from 1996 through 1999, and MTF statistics show an increase over the time period. ONDCP also reports an increase in the number of emergency room mentions of Ecstasy use from 1993 to 1997.[69]

2001 Strategy

In the 2001 Strategy, ONDCP expresses concern about continued increases of Ecstasy use by eighth, tenth, and twelfth graders (MTF data), under the headline "Emerging drug-use trends among youth." Here, ONDCP also honestly points out that lifetime use, past-year use, and past-month use of Ecstasy increased significantly from 1999 to 2000.

The 2001 Strategy begins its section on Ecstasy with the following fact: "Emergency room mentions [of Ecstasy] increased from sixty-eight in 1993 to 2,200 in 2000."[70] The Strategy characterizes youth use as "widespread" and claims that: "Trial use of Ecstasy has increased from five percent in 1995 to seven percent last year [1999] to ten percent this year [2000]."[71] A figure on the same page illustrates a clear upward trend in past-year use in Ecstasy since 1998 for tenth and twelfth graders and an increase from 1999 for eighth graders. These increases are noted as very significant one- and two-year increases, ranging from 44% to 82%.

Clearly, through the 2001 Strategy, Ecstasy use trends are a major concern for ONDCP. Given the dramatic increases, it is understandable why. With regard to Ecstasy, ONDCP makes no effort to hide or manipulate statistics, at least not through 2001. Instead, it uses them to generate alarm about the drug.

2002–2005 Strategy

The 2003 and 2004 versions each show only one figure referring to Ecstasy use trends.[72] These figures illustrate Ecstasy trends among eighth, tenth, and twelfth graders from 1997 to 2003, with declines from 2000 to 2003. Figure 4.7 depicts MTF Ecstasy trends from the 2004 Strategy. The trends shown in the figure illustrate that use first increased and then decreased, suggesting no real change in Ecstasy use overall. ONDCP does not characterize the trend as unchanged. Instead, it celebrates the recent declines, as noted earlier.

This is simply an inappropriate interpretation of statistics. If a trend increases and then decreases by roughly the same amount, the correct interpretation of the trend is that it is unchanged.

As in the 2004 Strategy, ONDCP presents in the 2005 Strategy a figure depicting past-month use of Ecstasy for eighth, tenth, and twelfth graders. Note that here it shows three trend lines, one for each grade level, as opposed to its combined trend date user earlier by ONDCP to prove it was meetings its two-year goal of reducing youth drug use by 10%. We replicate it here as Figure 4.8.

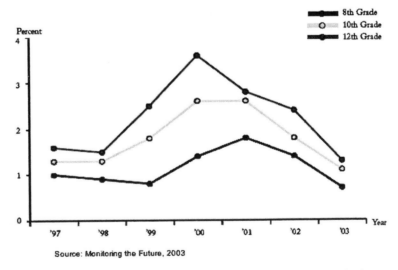

FIGURE 4.7   ONDCP Characterizes an Unchanged Trend in Ecstasy Use by Students as a Declining Trend (MTF), 2004 Strategy

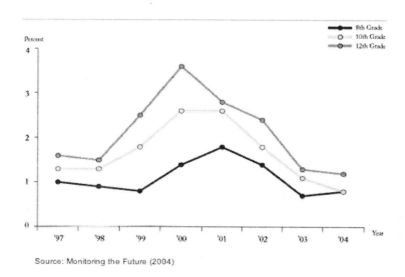

Source: Monitoring the Future (2004)

FIGURE 4.8   ONDCP Again Characterizes an Unchanged Trend in Ecstasy Use by Students as a Declining Trend (MTF), 2005 Strategy

The figure illustrates that Ecstasy use among youth rapidly declined since 2000 and 2001. Yet, the figure also shows that, since 1997, Ecstasy use is generally unchanged. That is, an analysis of a long-term trend shows that Ecstasy use increased, then decreased, and overall remained unchanged since 1997. ONDCP only focuses on the recent declines.

OTHER DRUGS

Steroids, Methamphetamine, and Inhalants

The 2000 and 2001 versions of the Strategy show an increase in steroid use in the late 1990s through 2000. In the 2000 and 2001 versions of the Strategy, increases of new meth users are also reported in the 1990s, as are increases in the rate of first-use of meth for young adults aged 18–25 years. As noted in the 2001 Strategy: "The rate of first-use among youths age 12–17 rose significantly from 1990 to 1998." and there were "slight declines" (but not statistically significant) among eighth, tenth, and twelfth graders in annual use of meth between 1998 and 2000.[73] No figure is offered by ONDCP, which would show overall increases in meth use in the United States.

Instead, in the 2000 Strategy, ONDCP claims some success in reducing meth use—use of the drug by twelfth graders declined from 1998 to 1999 and lifetime use by 12–17 year olds declined from 1997 to 1998.[74] The Strategy also shows very small declines from 1996 to 1999 in inhalant use by eighth, tenth, and twelfth graders. Here, ONDCP highlights statistics that show a short-term decline in some drugs.

The 2001 Strategy shows a continued decline in past-month inhalant use among youth aged 12–17 years from 1996 through 2000, although the "rate of first use among youths age 12–17 rose significantly from 1990 to 1998."[75]

Hallucinogens/LSD

The 2001 Strategy also reports stable past-month use of all hallucinogens between 1995 and 1999 among people ages twelve and older (NHSDA data). Yet, it also notes a "statistically significant increase" in overall hallucinogen use since 1994.[76] Again, no figure is offered by ONDCP, which would show overall increases in hallucinogen use in the United States.

Aside from the quotes noted earlier about LSD put forth in the 2003 and 2004 versions of the Strategy, the 2002–2005 versions of the Strategy make no specific claims related to LSD and few to other drugs. They also show no figures referring to trends in LSD use or use of other drugs. Instead, tables are included at the end of the Strategy reports whereby trend data can be examined. For some reason, beginning with the 2002 Strategy, ONDCP provides less useful information about even drug use trends for policy-makers and the public. This is inconsistent with ONDCP's claim of increased accountability in the drug war.

Psychotherapeutics

The 2004 Strategy does contain a telling admission about a form of drug use that has been relatively ignored in the nation's drug war—prescription drug abuse:

> Surveys confirm that the nonmedical use of prescription drugs has emerged in the last decade as a major problem. The illegal diversion, theft, and medical mismanagement of prescription drugs (particularly opioid pain medications) have increased and, in some areas, present a larger public health and law enforcement challenge than cocaine or heroin.[77]

In fact, ONDCP admits that the misuse of pain relievers, tranquilizers, stimulants, and sedatives "was the second leading category of illicit drug use in 2002, following marijuana. An estimated 6.2 million Americans . . . have used a pscyhotherapeutic drug for nonmedical reasons in the month prior to the survey."[78] Most of the abuse is of pain relievers. According to ONDCP, MTF statistics show a similar pattern of use among young people: "The abuse by high-school seniors of the brand-name narcotic Vicodin is more than double their use of cocaine, Ecstasy, or methamphetamine. This drug has become a deadly youth fad, with one out of every ten high-school seniors reporting nonmedical use."[79]

Is it possible that high school students have just switched drugs over the past few years—from LSD, Ecstasy, and other club drugs—to prescription drugs? If so, ONDCP's claims of success in reducing this kind of drug use must be tempered by the realization that other forms of drug use have simultaneously increased. What appears to have occurred is not a reduction in drug use but rather a form of substitution, where law enforcement and prevention efforts have simply shifted users from one drug to another. More evidence of this is offered later in the 2004 Strategy where it is noted that

> nonmedical use of narcotic analgesics as a reason for an emergency room visit rose 163 percent between 1995 and 2002. More alarming, trend data from DAWN for the years 1995–2002 shows [sic] a dramatic rise in emergency room mentions of single-entity oxycodone (formulations of the narcotic without other drug combinations), from 100 mentions in 1999 to nearly 15,000 mentions in 2002.[80]

ONDCP does not consider substitution, nor does it offer a figure showing the huge increases in new users of psychotherapeutics. Such a figure might cause the reader to question ONDCP's claims.

Interestingly, ONDCP explains that psychotherapeutics cannot be banned because it "would undermine the legitimate medical purposes that they serve and would increase the suffering of many." Instead, ONDCP promotes greater monitoring of drug retailers and a network of state-level prescription monitoring programs (PMPs) that "are designed to facilitate the collection, analysis, and reporting of information on the prescribing, dispensing, and use of pharmaceuticals."[81] ONDCP claims the effectiveness of PMPs "can be seen in a simple statistic: In 2000, the five states with the lowest number of Oxy-Contin prescriptions per capita all had PMPs" while "the five states with the highest number of prescriptions per capita all lacked them."[82]

ONDCP thus acknowledges that some drug problems cannot be solved through a drug war. Yet, it fails to see the legitimate medical uses of some illicit drugs, including marijuana.[83]

The use of the previous "simple statistic" is also interesting, because it does not prove the effectiveness of PMPs. What it suggests is some kind of relationship, but not a causal relationship.[84] In fact, the statistic does not prove that a lack of PMPs is even related to more *illegal or inappropriate* Oxy-Contin prescriptions.

We actually believe PMPs will be effective at reducing prescription drug abuse. Yet, if PMPs are successful, their success might indicate the potential effectiveness of regulation as opposed to prohibition.[85] ONDCP, as the lead agency in the nation's drug war, does not consider this.

In the 2005 Strategy, ONDCP again cites evidence of increases in use of psychotherapeutics: "Monitoring the Future began collecting data on the non-medical use of OxyContin in 2002. In 2004, there was a 24 percent increase in past year use of OxyContin for all three grades combined compared to 2002, from 2.7 percent to 3.3 percent."[86] Yet, ONDCP does not depict this increase in a figure, consistent with past versions of the Strategy. Later in the Strategy, ONDCP admits increases in the use of psychotherapeutics:

> Surveys show that the non-medical use of prescription drugs, particularly narcotic painkillers, continues to rise in several populations. The number of people who had used pain relievers non-medically at least once during their lifetime increased 5 percent, to 31.2 million Americans, from 2002 to 2003. Among young adults, the non-medical use of any psychotherapeutics in the past month ("current" use) increased from 5.4 to 6.0 percent. Also among young adults, current non-medical use of pain relievers increased by 15 percent, from 4.1 to 4.7 percent.[87]

Here, again, ONDCP presents no figure depicting the rapid increase in use of psychotherapeutics. It also urges a nonprohibition approach to solving the problem, as in the 2004 Strategy:

> Although this is an emerging drug abuse problem, the challenge it presents is of a different order from the traditional drug threats. Existing as they do in every pharmacy in every city and town in America, prescription drugs are both more ubiquitous and more susceptible to regulatory control, with the mechanisms to reduce the threat of prescription drug misuse substantially within the scope of state and Federal regulatory authority. What is needed is continued improvement in the surveillance of practices like "doctor shopping" coupled with more careful and responsible medical oversight, preserving legitimate access to needed medicines while deterring unlawful conduct.[88]

ONDCP again notes the success of Prescription Monitoring Programs (PMPs) and implies they are responsible for "a 54 percent decline in current use of illicit drugs in just one year" in rural America, "driven in large measure by a 78 percent drop in the non-medical use of pain relievers."[89] Here, ONDCP asserts that PMPs are partly responsible for declining drug use trends in rural areas, including drugs over which PMPs have no control.

ONDCP Emphasizes Prevention (But Does Not Fund It)

Despite the lack of actual strategies aimed at prevention pursued by ONDCP in the drug war, ONDCP begins to emphasize prevention in the 2002 Strategy: "Prevention is . . . the most cost-effective approach to the drug problem, sparing society the burden of treatment, rehabilitation, lost productivity, and other social pathologies. . . . We know that prevention works. We know that, if we prevent young people from using drugs through age 18, the chance of their using drugs as adults is very small."[90] Interestingly, no explanation is given as to why prevention does not then receive the majority of the ONDCP budget, or at least a more sizable portion. As shown in chapter 2, in FY 2005, prevention receives 15.6% of the drug war budget. In FY 2006, requests for prevention fell to 12.6%.

According to many scholars, crime prevention is less popular with politicians because it is inconsistent with the get tough on crime and drugs perspective. Yet, it offers much more promise than reactive measures of criminal justice.[91] What is interesting is that ONDCP is not putting its money where its mouth is when it comes to prevention. That is, its claims don't match its budget.

Additionally, in the 2003 Strategy ONDCP characterizes drug prevention programs as "invaluable" to "educating young people about the dangers of drug use and reinforcing a climate of social disapproval of drug use." Yet, it notes that "drug prevention makes for a difficult public policy discussion because prevention activities are not, for the most part, discrete, government-funded programs. In fact, they can best be understood as the sum of the efforts parents and communities make in bringing up young people."[92] This seems like an admission by ONDCP that the drug war does not emphasize prevention, is not willing to commit resources to concrete prevention programs, and assumes that prevention is something that must occur outside of the formal agencies of the government.

In the 2004 Strategy, ONDCP claims for the first time that one of its prevention programs—the *Media Campaign*—works to reduce approval of drugs: "Youth in all three grades surveyed (eighth, tenth, and twelfth) say that such ads have made their attitudes less favorable toward drugs to a 'great extent' or 'very great extent,' and made them less likely to use drugs in the future."[93]

ONDCP does not say how many youth in all three grades reported this, but instead it claims such findings are proof that they are "saving more lives." Yet, no data on drug-related deaths are offered to prove this. Additionally, drug-induced deaths have increased rapidly since 1988, when ONDCP was created (see chapter 6). This is true when drug use went up and when it went down.

Importantly, MTF data are inconsistent with the overall claim on the part of the government that youth disapproval of drug use has increased. In fact, for most forms of illicit drug use for most grade levels, disapproval of drug use and perceived harmfulness of drug use have gone down or remain unchanged.[94] Further, consider the most recent statistics on drug use at the time of this writing. In 2004, 51% of high school seniors, 40% of tenth graders, and 22% of eighth graders reported using an illegal drug at least once in their lives.[95] For all persons 12 years or older in 2003, 46% had used an illegal drug at least once in their lives.[96]

According to the National Institute of Drug Abuse's research in to the effectiveness of ONDCP ads, about 80% of young people and 70% of parents recall being exposed to anti-drug ads every week. Most important, the research on these ads show that most will not work to reduce drug use by youth. Many may even increase drug use in the long run for reasons that are not well understood.[97] There is little evidence that advertisements are effective, especially when it comes to reducing youth drug use. This is discussed further in chapter 8. For ONDCP to claim otherwise is dishonest and inconsistent with the evidence.

Yet, in the 2005 Strategy, ONDCP again tries to sell the effectiveness of its Media Campaign in the 2005 Strategy. It notes: "Exposure to anti-drug advertising (of which the federally funded media campaign is the major contributor) has had an impact on improving youth anti-drug attitudes and intentions. Among all three grades, such ads have made youth to a 'great extent' or 'very great extent' less favorable toward drugs and less likely to use them in the future."[98]

Later, ONDCP cites research on the importance of and effectiveness of parental involvement and monitoring on youth behavior. It notes that "surveys show that two-thirds of youth ages 13 to 17 say losing their parents' respect is one of the main reasons they do not smoke marijuana or use other drugs."[99] ONDCP uses this as a justification for requesting $120 million to fund its National Youth Anti-Drug Media Campaign. While we do not doubt that parental involvement and monitoring are crucial to reducing the risk of all antisocial behaviors,[100] we question the logic of using proven science to justify spending on a disproven program.

Chapter Five

Claims of Success in Healing America's Drug Users and Disrupting Drug Markets

In this chapter, we critically analyze ONDCP claims-making concerning federal efforts to heal drug users and disrupt drug markets. We address the claims year by year in a roughly chronological order.

In its annual Strategy, ONDCP generally does not claim success in healing America's drugs users. Simply stated, relevant statistics do not warrant such claims.

CLAIMS OF SUCCESS IN HEALING AMERICA'S DRUG USERS

The 2000 Strategy notes that the objectives related to healing America's drug users include not only providing treatment to drug abusers, but also reducing drug-related health problems including infectious disease (which we presume includes reducing the number of drug-related deaths and emergency room mentions of drugs).

Since ONDCP, beginning in the 2002 Strategy, focuses on drug treatment exclusively when discussing efforts to heal drug users, we examine ONDCP claims regarding treatment in this chapter. Claims regarding deaths and emergency room mentions of drugs are examined in chapter 6 when we discuss claims regarding costs of the drug war.

Extent of Need for Treatment

2000–2001 Strategy

It should be noted that there are actually very few comments of any kind with regard to treatment in the 2000 and 2001 versions of the Strategy. The only discussions of treatment relate to the extent of need for treatment by dependent drug users and drug abusers in the United States. In the 2000 strategy, for example, ONDCP claims that there are "approximately five million drug abusers who need immediate treatment."[1] This same number is reported in the 2001 Strategy,[2] although later it reports that "3.6 million people met diagnostic criteria for dependence on illegal drugs in 1999."[3]

2002 Strategy

The 2002 Strategy cites National Household Survey on Drug Abuse (NHSDA) data showing that "2.8 million Americans are 'dependent' on illegal drugs, while an additional 1.5 million fall in the less severe 'abuser' category."[4] Thus, 4.3 million Americans presumably have an illicit drug problem.

Later in the Strategy, ONDCP explains: "Our understanding of treatment need advanced significantly with the release . . . of new data from the *National Household Survey on Drug Abuse.* By incorporating into the survey questions distilled from the *Diagnostic and Statistical Manual of Mental Disorders* (DSM-IV), we are now for the first time able to estimate" the number of dependent drug users and drug abusers, where

> drug dependence—characterized by significant health problems, emotional problems, difficulty in cutting down on use, drug tolerance, withdrawal, and other symptoms—is more severe than drug abuse. Abuse is characterized by problems at work, home, and school; problems with family or friends; voluntary exposure to physical danger; and trouble with law enforcement.[5]

By its own admission, ONDCP notes in the 2002 Strategy that "the treatment system is not able to help all those deemed to be in need of drug treatment; according to conservative estimates, only an estimated 800,000 individuals had received drug treatment in the year prior to the survey."[6] That is, only 800,000 of 2.8 million dependent users and 1.5 million abusers received treatment. Stated differently, only 18.6% of people who need treatment actually got it.

2003 Strategy

In the 2003 Strategy, ONDCP notes that only about 1 million Americans enter drug treatment each year and that 101,000 who seek treatment are not able to receive it.[7] In other words, most of those who need drug treatment do not seek it and many of those who do seek it still do not get it.

As with claims dealing with reducing drug use, here again we consistently see these kinds of admissions of failures in the ONDCP Strategy reports, hidden in plain view for all who are reading carefully enough. Yet, ONDCP does not admit failure readily. Instead, it uses its own failures to call for stepped up efforts in the drug war.

In the 2003 Strategy, ONDCP revises its estimate for the extent of treatment need by drug users: "Despite substantial drug prevention efforts, some 16 million Americans still use drugs on a monthly basis, and roughly six million meet the clinical criteria for needing drug treatment."[8] Later in the same document, ONDCP claims that there are "5.6 million Americans who meet the diagnostic criteria for needing drug treatment (criteria developed by the American Psychiatric Association, not police departments or prosecutors)."[9] It is not clear if these 5.6 million are the same "roughly 6 million" referred to earlier.

Two things are clear from this statement. First, only one million of six million users who need treatment actually receives it. Second, only roughly 6 million of the 16 million past-month users of illicit drugs are in need of treatment. The former suggests ONDCP is failing to achieve its goal of healing drug users through treatment. Now, according to ONDCP, only one in six, or 16.6% of people who need treatment actually got it. The latter shows there is a difference between drug use and drug abuse. Yet, ONDCP does not differentiate between the two.

Instead, the 2003 Strategy contains more rhetoric related to the dangers of drug use than previous years, blurring the clear lines between use and abuse. It claims: "Medical research has established a clear fact about drug use: once started, it can develop into a devastating disease of the brain, with consequences that are anything but enticing."[10] ONDCP characterizes drug use as a disease and says:

> It spreads because the vectors of contagion are not addicts in the streets but users who do not yet show the consequences of their drug habit. Last year, some 16 million Americans used an illegal drug on at least a monthly basis, while 6.1 million Americans were in need of treatment. The rest, still in the "honeymoon" phase of their drug-using careers, are "carriers" who transmit the disease to others who see only the surface of the fraud.[11]

Not only has treatment need now grown to "6.1 million Americans" instead of 5.6 million or "roughly six million," this quote reads as if we can expect the number to grow even larger in the future because of the spread of the contagious disease to new users. Since ONDCP is supposed to be leading the effort to prevent the need for drug treatment (by preventing illicit drug use), this can be read as an admission of failure.

The 2003 Strategy predicts that treatment need will grow because drug use is a lie that is contagious: "Drug use promises one thing but delivers something else—something sad and debilitating for users, their families, and their communities. The deception can be masked for some time, and it is during this time that the habit is 'carried' by users to other vulnerable young people."[12]

We examined the two most recently published books on the effectiveness of the war on drugs to see if they agreed with ONDCP's assessment of the contagious nature of drug use. One set of authors asserted: "Because drug use is spread mainly through social contacts and because most users sooner or later desist from use, patterns of drug use over time can have some of the characteristics of a contagious epidemic."[13] The other authors also agreed. They wrote that because most first-time drug use occurs due to being offered a drug by a friend, it is logical to characterize drug use as contagious: "Drug use thus spreads much like a communicable disease; users are 'contagious,' and some of those with whom they come into contact become 'infected.'"[14]

There are exceptions to the "contagion" rule, however. First, "with heroin, cocaine, and crack, long-term addicts are not particularly contagious. They are more socially isolated than new users, and knowing the pitfalls of prolonged use, may not want to expose others. Moreover, they usually present an unappealing picture of the consequences of addiction."[15] Second, there have been only three drug use epidemics in the United States—heroin use in the 1960s, powder cocaine use in the 1970s and early 1980s, and crack cocaine use in the 1980s.[16] This is not particularly alarming given the number of outbreaks of physical disease in the history of the United States.

Finally, most of those who have tried illicit drugs, know others who have, or have read any bit of research about illicit drug use, would challenge ONDCP's claim that drug use is contagious, despite the agreement by drug policy experts. Drug use can lead to devastating consequences—yes—and it is important that (especially) young people know this. Yet, typically drug use does *not* lead to such outcomes. Unlike being exposed to a deadly disease, which is likely to sicken or kill you, being exposed to drug use does not significantly increase the likelihood of becoming a regular or permanent user of drugs.

The typical drug user—an older teenager or young person in his or her early twenties—uses drugs only a few times, quits within five years, and does not suffer or cause any significant damage.[17] Most people who try drugs do not continue. Drug policy experts suggest: "If there is a typical continuing user, it is an occasional marijuana smoker who will cease to use drugs at some point during his twenties."[18] Most of the costs of drug use are thus not attributable to users but to drug abusers. Because of this, goals of the drug war—such as limiting supply of drugs through demand reduction strategies of interdiction and eradication instead of reducing demand among the worst of the drug users (drug abusers) — are illogical.

Finally, illicit drug use often leads to various pleasurable and even beneficial outcomes for users. ONDCP's characterizations of illicit drug use are incomplete and thus, inaccurate. One writer notes that "responsible drug use, unlike responsible alcohol use, is considered an oxymoron. To *use* a prohibited substance is defined as *abuse,* whether or not the user is addicted."[19] Perhaps it is the illicit nature of use that explains why ONDCP considers all drug use abuse, or at least characterizes all use as a significant problem. This is true even though "studies show that most drug users are not addicts, yet all users of illegal drugs are subject to the same severe penalties and are frequently forced into treatment, if not prison."[20]

An admission by ONDCP of the difference between drug use and abuse is offered in its 2003 Strategy: "The nearly 12 million current drug users whose use has not progressed to dependence face an uncertain future. Their likelihood of eventually crossing over into addiction ranges from one in three to roughly one in ten, depending on the drug."[21]

A couple of important factors should be pointed out about these statistics. First, other research puts the risk of abuse lower than 10–33%.[22] For example, according to notable drug policy experts: "Some fraction of people who begin using any drug move on to heavy use of that drug, with all the ill consequences specific to that drug that heavy use entails. . . . It has been estimated that 23 percent of those who try heroin, 17 percent of those who try cocaine, and 9 percent of those who try marijuana become clinically dependent on the drug (the rates for tobacco and alcohol are 32 percent and 15 percent, respectively)."[23] Even assuming that ONDCP's statistics are accurate, another way of looking at it is one's risk of *not* becoming a drug abuser range from two in three (66%) to nine in ten (90%).

Second, it is well established that some people have higher risks of becoming drug abusers based on their genetic makeup, their early familial experiences, the prevalence of drug use and abuse in their homes, the amount of stress they are under, and so forth. Not every individual has the same odds of becoming a drug abuser simply determined by the type of drug she consumes.[24]

Drug experts with the National Academy of Sciences' Committee on Data and Research for Policy and Illegal Drugs assert that "the addiction process involves multiple factors that vary across drugs, individuals and the environment."[25] That is, it is not just the morality of potential users and prices and availability of drugs (things ONDCP attempts to manipulate) that matter. Other factors relevant for whether people use and abuse drugs include "individual, family, peer, neighborhood, and social risk factors" (things ONDCP cannot manipulate).[26]

2004 Strategy

The 2004 Strategy contains many of the same types of questionable claims about drug use as previous years. For example, ONDCP says that "many people use drugs because they know someone who is using and not suffering any apparent consequences. The disease of drug dependence spreads because the vectors of contagion are 'asymptomatic' users who do not yet show the consequences of their drug habit, and who do not have the slightest awareness of their need to seek help."[27]

The need for drug treatment is stated in the 2004 Strategy as 7 million users (out of 19.5 million users). Of these, just over 1 million receive treatment. Now, only 14.3% of people who need treatment actually got it. Again, ONDCP admits that about 100,000 people who are aware that they need drug treatment each year do not get it, while the other six million who need treatment do not know they need it because they are in denial.[28]

In the 2004 Strategy, ONDCP writes that we must close the "denial gap" by confronting "drug use honestly and directly, offering the compassionate coercion of family, friends, and the community, including colleagues in the workplace, to motivate the change that brings recovery."[29] This strikes us as an ironic statement given the blurring by ONDCP of drug use and drug abuse and drug dependence. ONDCP does not differentiate between normal, recreational, and even some forms of adaptive drug use and the type of use that is problematic and leads to various forms of dysfunction. An honest and direct discussion of drug use must acknowledge the difference.

For example, historical research suggests that "the human use of psychoactive drugs is both primordial and nearly universal. In almost every human culture in every age of history, the use of one or more psychoactive drugs was featured prominently in the contexts of religion, ritual, health care, divination, celebration (including the arts, music, and theater), recreation, and cuisine."[30] This does not mean that society must tolerate rampant drug use or problematic drug abuse. It simply appears that ONDCP cannot (or does not) differentiate between what is normal and what is not when it comes to drug use.

2005 Strategy

In the 2005 Strategy, ONDCP again blurs the lines between drug use and drug abuse:

> As risky behaviors go, drug use ranks among the worst. While it is difficult to draw precise inferences from the data available, the likelihood that an adult who uses drugs on at least a monthly basis (a so-called "current" user) will go on to need drug treatment is approximately one in four—high enough to constitute a substantial risk but low enough that many individuals are able to deny the obvious risks or convince themselves that they can "manage" their drug-using behavior. One

drug treatment practitioner compares the problem to that of people who do not wear seatbelts. Although such people are risking self-destruction at every turn, every trip that ends safely actually reinforces the erroneous belief that seatbelts do not matter.[31]

Note that the risk of drug abuse (one in four) has been modified from just the previous year's estimate when ONDCP said it was somewhere between one in ten and one in three.

In the 2005 Strategy, ONDCP goes on to again blame users for falling into abuse:

There is a word for this problem—"denial." Addicts deny the nature and severity of their problem even in the face of mounting evidence to the contrary. Denial explains why such a small percentage of the more than four million Americans who meet the clinical definition of dependence and are therefore in need of drug treatment actually seek it in a given year. . . . Not only does denial keep people from seeking help, it also maintains the destructive behavior long enough to allow the disease of addiction to gain an even firmer hold and be transmitted to peer groups and friends. The power and tenacity of denial are thus real and must be met with a force of equal and opposite magnitude.[32]

Note that the need for treatment is now "more than four million" rather than "5 million" stated earlier in the same document.[33] ONDCP does not explain how the need for treatment fell from 7 million in the 2004 Strategy to 5 million in the 2005 Strategy, especially given the fact that most people who need drug treatment do not get it.

ONDCP's statistics on the ability to provide treatment to those who need it suggest that as the years go by, the drug war is less and less able to provide treatment. In the 2002 Strategy, ONDCP reported that 18.6% of drug users who needed treatment got it, while in the 2003 Strategy, the number fell to 16.6%. In the 2004 Strategy, only 14.3% of drug users who needed treatment got it. This is clearly not consistent with ONDCP's goal of healing drug users through treatment. ONDCP makes no mention of how many received treatment in the 2005 Strategy.

Drug Courts

2004 Strategy
Beginning in the 2004 Strategy, ONDCP begins to tout the effectiveness of drug courts as a way to coerce people involved in the criminal justice system to enroll in treatment. It writes: "Drug courts use the authority of a judge to

require abstinence and altered behavior through a combination of clear expectations, graduated sanctions, mandatory drug testing, case management, supervised treatment, and aftercare programs — a remarkable example of a public health approach linked to a public safety strategy."[34] A figure shows the rapid growth of drug courts in the United States through the 1990s, and it is stated that nearly 1,200 drug courts operate in the country, in all 50 states.[35] Indeed, research shows that drug courts are highly effective.[36]

2005 Strategy
The 2005 Strategy continues to sell drug courts, and a figure presented by ONDCP shows a continued increase in drug courts nationwide.[37] ONDCP explains:

> Drug court programs have a real effect on criminal recidivism. A National Institute of Justice study compared rearrest rates for drug court graduates with those of individuals who were imprisoned for drug offenses and found significant differences. The likelihood that a drug court graduate would be rearrested and charged for a serious offense in the first year after graduation was 16.4 percent, compared to 43.5 percent for non-drug court graduates. By the two-year mark, the recidivism rate had grown to 27.5 percent, compared to 58.6 percent for non-graduates.[38]

We believe that such claims are accurate and consistent with the research.

Drug Testing

2004 Strategy
More controversial claims are made in the 2004 Strategy regarding drug testing in schools. After acknowledging that drug use initiation among youth under the age of eighteen years is a serious problem (suggesting that efforts to stop drug use among youth are not working), ONDCP begins to sell student drug testing. It claims: "Following up with brief interventions for young people who do try illegal drugs (or alcohol) is critical. This Strategy highlights the importance of student drug testing, a prevention approach that accomplishes . . . deterring drug use while guiding users to needed treatment or counseling."[39] It then calls student drug testing a "remarkable grassroots tool" and requests $25 million for student drug testing programs. The rationale for student drug testing is stated as:

> Student drug testing programs advance the Strategy's goal of intervening early in the young person's drug career, using research-based

prevention approaches to guide users into counseling or drug treatment, and deterring others from starting in the first place. The purpose of random testing is not to catch, punish, or expose students who use drugs but to prevent drug dependence and to help drug-dependent students become drug-free in a confidential manner.[40]

The claim that "Student drug testing programs work" is supported by three studies mentioned by ONDCP, including one at a single high school in Oregon and another at a high school in New Jersey.[41] Compare this to the conclusion of the National Academy of Sciences's Committee on Data and Research for Policy and Illegal Drugs that states we simply do not have quality enough data whether drug testing is effective, including about whether it deters use, how much it costs, and whether it is cost-effective.[42]

Yet, the front page of the Web site for the Monitoring the Future (MTF) survey contains a link announcing new information.[43] Ironically, at the time of this writing, on this page is the announcement of a recent, comprehensive study announcing: "Student drug testing not effective in reducing drug use." The conclusion that "drug testing of students in schools does not deter drug use" is based on "a large, multi-year national sample of the nation's high schools and middle schools."[44]

The study's conclusion that schools with drug testing and those without it have virtually identical drug use rates runs directly counter to the ONDCP claim about the effectiveness of student drug testing: ONDCP claims that "student drug testing programs work" while the national study concludes "drug testing of students in schools does not deter drug use." Is ONDCP unaware of the most comprehensive study available on student drug testing programs, whose results are broadcast on the official Web site of MTF, now the most widely cited drug use study by ONDCP?

That the study analyzed four years of data (1998–2001) and 722 schools (including 497 high schools and 255 middle schools) lends credence to the validity of its findings. Additional data from 2002 (and 169 more schools) found no differences in student drug use among schools with random drug testing programs ($n = 7$) and those without random drug testing programs ($n = 162$). We find it hard to imagine that ONDCP is unaware of a study posted on the Monitoring the Future website. Therefore, it is probable that ONDCP is actively promoting a policy that it knows does not work. If this is true, it is clearly inappropriate.

It should be noted that the ONDCP begins its discussion of drug testing in schools in the 2004 Strategy with some alarming statistics concerning drug use by young people. A figure shows that 1,741,000 young people began using marijuana in 2001, followed by 1,124,000 new users of pain relievers, 757,000 new users of hallucinogens, 590,000 new users of Ecstasy, and

353,000 new users of cocaine. On the same page, ONDCP claims that "every day approximately 4,800 American youth under age 18 try marijuana for the first time—a number roughly equal to the enrollment of six average-size high schools."[45] Here again, ONDCP presents statistics that suggest it is not meeting its primary goal of reducing drug use. Instead of even considering that these statistics point to failure, ONDCP uses them to cause alarm and advocate for a policy—drug testing—that the evidence suggests does not even work.

2005 Strategy
The 2005 Strategy notes $25.4 million in spending on drug testing programs for FY 2006.[46] To justify the expense, ONCDP does not present statistical evidence that drug testing works, nor does it cite the national study noted earlier showing that student drug testing programs are ineffective. Instead, it presents anecdotal evidence from a Catholic High School in Chicago, Illinois, and a school system in Polk County, Florida.[47]

The Polk County, Florida case is particularly interesting because in the case study presented, ONDCP writes:

> While shopping at a grocery store near her home in central Florida, Audrey Kelley-Fritz found all the proof she needed that her county's student drug testing program was working. "I had a kid taking my groceries out to the car at the Publix," says Kelley-Fritz, who runs a student drug testing program for Polk County high school students. "He said he didn't have anything to worry about with the school's new drug testing policy, but he was after two of his friends, saying, 'I keep telling them they have to give it up before school starts, because they [school officials] are going to find out.'" "Now that is what I like to hear," says Kelley-Fritz. "Not only are we making it easier for the one kid to say no in a party situation—this kid is exerting positive peer pressure on his teammates."[48]

This is amazing that ONDCP claims success based on the statement of one woman who had one interaction with a bagger at a grocery store.

Later, ONDCP continues:

> Polk County had ample reason to believe that a student drug testing program would help drive down drug use. One of the county's high schools had started a testing program for student athletes in 1997 and saw marijuana use drop by 30 percent virtually overnight. The program was cancelled after four years because of a budget crunch, and drug use quickly returned to pre-testing levels.[49]

Here, ONDCP generalizes from a single school to all schools. And yet, ONDCP's claim that "marijuana use drop[ped] by 30 percent virtually overnight" is impossible. Marijuana stays in the body for up to one month.[50] Thus, detection of a 30% reduction in marijuana use could not occur "virtually overnight."

ONDCP asserts that "Drug testing is powerful, safe, and effective, and it is available to any school, public or private, that understands the devastation of drug use and is determined to confront it. Many schools urgently need effective ways to reinforce their anti-drug efforts. Drug testing can help them."[51] Beyond this, ONDCP claims that drug testing makes other methods more effective, too:

> By giving students who do not want to use drugs an "out," testing reduces the impact of peer pressure. By giving students who are tempted by drugs a concrete reason not to use them, testing amplifies the force of prevention messages. And by identifying students who are using illegal drugs, testing supports parental monitoring and enables treatment specialists to direct early intervention techniques where they are needed.[52]

Here, ONDCP explains the logic of drug testing, but provides no summary of studies of drug testing (which show that it does not work).

Based on our review of ONDCP's annual Strategy, it is safe to conclude at least five things about ONDCP's claims regarding healing America's drug users. First, deaths attributable to illicit drugs and emergency room mentions of illicit drug use are on the rise, inconsistent with ONDCP's goal of healing America's drug users (see chapter 6). Second, ONDCP does not have a solid grasp on the actual need for treatment. Third, the drug war fails to provide treatment for most dependent drug users and abusers who need it. Fourth, one's chance of progressing to dependence is fairly small. Fifth, some of the claims in ONDCP's Strategy are inconsistent with research and common sense.

We discuss the first point in more depth in chapter 6, which deals with costs of the drug war. With regard to the second point, if there are 19.5 million users and only 7 million who need treatment (as noted in the 2004 Strategy), then 12.5 million users have *not* progressed to dependence. If there are 16 million past-month drug users and 12 million of them have not progressed to dependence (as noted in the 2003 Strategy), then only 4 million have progressed to dependence. Compare this to the "5.6 million," "roughly 6 million," and "6.1 million" figures offered earlier. We presume the other 2 million or so who "need treatment" are drug abusers, but this is not specified by ONDCP. In the most recent document—the 2005 Strategy—ONDCP claims both that 5 million and 4 million people need treatment.

With regard to the third point, only between 14.3% and 18.6% of people who need drug treatment receive it.[53] This can also be seen as a failure rate of between 81.4% and 85.7%. ONDCP blames dependent drug users for failing to recognize the need for treatment and characterizes them as being in a state of denial. Here ONDCP seems to contradict itself by calling drug dependence an illness while simultaneously refusing to fully understand the significance of drug dependence as an illness. Further, ONDCP says little about what it has done to make sure that treatment is available to drug users since 1988 when it was created.

With regard to the fourth point, if one's chance of progressing to dependence ranges from "one in three to roughly one in ten" (as claimed in the 2003 Strategy), the odds of not becoming dependent would be roughly 66% to 90%, as noted earlier. When compared to tobacco, a legal drug, dependency rates for illicit drugs appear to be quite low. Research suggests that rates of drug dependence are higher for nicotine than for marijuana, cocaine, or alcohol.[54]

Still, ONDCP predicts doom for "the relatively asymptomatic casual drug user whose use is not obvious and may go for months or years before a triggering event such as an automobile accident, an overdose, or an arrest."[55] Yet, in the 2005 Strategy, ONDCP implies that illicit drugs are more problematic in terms of causing dependence than the legal drugs alcohol and tobacco. It presents a figure illustrating the number of dependent users by substance. Figure 5.1 shows this figure.

Here, ONDCP questions alternatives to prohibition by questioning whether we should "treat drugs like alcohol and cigarettes?"[56] That there are more dependent users of tobacco and alcohol than illicit drugs is true, yet this is attributable to the fact that alcohol and tobacco are more habit-forming to users. Additionally, alcohol and tobacco are legally available and widely marketed to consumers. Comparing legal drugs to illegal drugs, in this case, is comparing apples to oranges. ONDCP does not admit that some illicit drugs cause few dependency problems.

With regard to the fifth point—that some ONDCP claims are inconsistent with research and common sense—both research and logic actually appear to contradict claims in the areas of the inevitability of drug abuse, the deadly nature of drug use, and the effectiveness of drug testing. ONDCP itself admits that most users are not abusers and that most will not become abusers. The most deadly drugs are legal, whereas most illicit drug use does not produce death.[57] And drug testing is ineffective.[58]

CLAIMS OF SUCCESS IN DISRUPTING DRUG MARKETS

In its annual Strategy, ONDCP generally does not claim success in disrupting drug markets. The relevant statistics also do not warrant such claims. Yet,

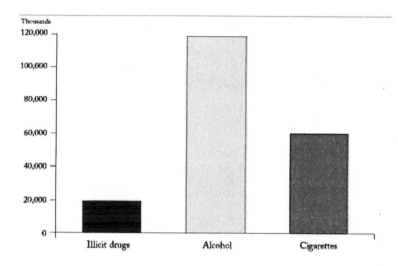

FIGURE 5.1   ONDCP Implies Greater Tobacco and Alcohol Dependency (Total Number of Users) Is Due to Legal Status, 2005 Strategy

ONDCP again makes optimistic claims and stresses the importance of disrupting drug markets.

2000 Strategy

One measure of supposed success in disrupting markets is the reported ease with which young people can obtain drugs. In the 2000 Strategy, it is reported that Monitoring the Future (MTF) data show: "Eighth graders who reported that marijuana was 'fairly easy to get' dropped from 50.6 to 48.4 percent" from 1998 to 1999.[59] That half of eighth graders say they can easily obtain marijuana after decades of the drug war takes a back seat to a very small decline over a one-year period. Here, ONDCP selectively uses statistics to highlight a short-term change in a trend that is favorable to its case.

On the same page, ONDCP admits: "Marijuana is the most readily available illegal drug in the United States" and later a figure shows that the average price per gram of marijuana has declined during the 1990s. ONDCP characterizes the declines from the figure as "relatively stable over the past decade."[60] Figure 5.2 shows these so-called stable trends. We see a decline in the average price of marijuana at the retail level.

Here, ONDCP mischaracterizes a trend showing statistics on marijuana prices.

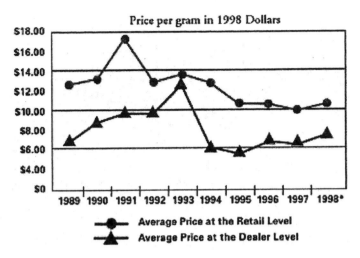

FIGURE 5.2   ONDCP Characterizes Marijuana Prices as Stable, 2000 Strategy

Another figure on the same page shows that federal seizures of marijuana during the same period skyrocketed, obviously not affecting prices. Nor did seizures apparently affect THC content, as the 2000 Strategy reports an increase in THC levels in marijuana from 1985 to 1998.[61] These outcomes are inconsistent with ONDCP goals, yet ONDCP does not acknowledge it.

The 2000 Strategy also notes that: "Cocaine continues to be readily available in nearly all major metropolitan areas." Figures on the same page show that the average price for a pure gram of cocaine has fallen since 1990, although the Strategy claims that "the retail price of pure cocaine has remained relatively stable since 1994."[62] Here again, ONDCP mischaracterizes a trend showing statistics on cocaine prices. Figure 5.3 shows the supposedly stable price of cocaine, which appears to us to actually be declining at both the retail and dealer levels.

Other figures on the page show that purity has remained unchanged since 1990, and that federal seizures of cocaine have remained unchanged since 1990. Again, this is inconsistent with ONDCP goals.

The 2000 Strategy presents the average price of heroin in figures, and it is down since 1991. Heroin purity is shown to be up since 1989 (but steady since 1992) and seizures are variable (up and down) since 1990. ONDCP claims: "Heroin purity is a reflection of the drug's availability. Unprecedented retail purity and low prices in the United States indicate that heroin is readily accessible."[63] These data suggest that the drug war goal of disrupting heroin markets is not being achieved, yet ONDCP does not acknowledge that.

In the 2000 Strategy, ONDCP illustrates that seizures of meth increased rapidly since 1996, as did meth lab seizures, yet the average price for a pure

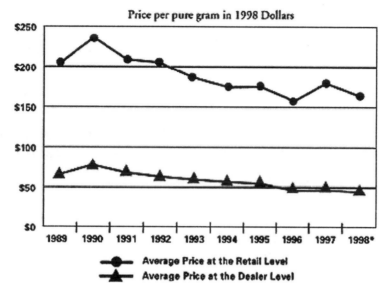

Average Price For Cocaine

Price per pure gram in 1998 Dollars

*Based on annualized data through June 1998
Source: 1999 ONDCP-Adjusted from DEA STRIDE Data*

FIGURE 5.3   ONDCP Characterizes Cocaine Prices as Stable, 2000 Strategy

gram of meth dropped during the 1990s. The drug is widely available according to the Strategy. ONDCP notes an increase in the availability of meth between 1997 and 1998 and states: "Methamphetamine is the most prevalent drug clandestinely manufactured in the United States."[64]

The information about Ecstasy is similar. The 2000 Strategy explains: "Numerous data reflect the increasing availability of [Ecstasy] in the United States."[65] Figures on the same page show Ecstasy seizures up tremendously from 1998 to 1999, but no statistics are presented about fluctuations in prices of the drug. A few pages later ONDCP claims that "designer drugs in most parts of the country are easily obtainable and used primarily by adolescents and young adults at clubs, raves, and concerts."[66]

2001 Strategy
In the 2001 Strategy, the picture is much the same as it was in 2000: "Marijuana is the most readily available illegal drug in the United States. Further, an upswing in the number of investigations, arrests, and seizures in and around high schools, is indicative of the ease with which youth can access this dangerous

drug."[67] When a drug is easy to obtain, logically the drug war is not effectively meeting its goal of disrupting drug markets. Yet, ONDCP does not acknowledge this. Additionally, note how ONDCP characterizes marijuana as a dangerous drug. Many experts disagree.[68]

The 2001 Strategy also indicates that federal seizures of marijuana have again increased and that price is still down since the late 1980s. The 2001 Strategy also notes increased levels of Tetrahydrocannibinol (THC) content.[69] None of these results in consistent with the drug war goal of disrupting drug markets. Successful drug market disruption would raise drug prices, reduce drug purity, and reduce drug availability. Yet, again, ONDCP does not acknowledge it.

In the 2001 Strategy, the ONDCP notes that cocaine arriving in the United States in the first six-months of 2000 increased nearly 40% over the first six months of 1999.[70] No changes in price are noted and ONDCP admits that "improvements in the criminal distribution and production of cocaine and crack have increased their availability in suburban and rural communities."[71] Again, none of these results is consistent with the drug war goal of disrupting drug markets. Yet, again, ONDCP does not acknowledge that. Other measure of successful drug market disruption would include reductions in the amount of drugs entering the country, increased seizures of drugs, and, ultimately, reductions in drug use.

As in the 2000 Strategy, the 2001 Strategy presents the average price of heroin in figures, which has declined since 1991. Heroin purity is shown to be up since 1989 (but steady since 1992) and seizures are variable (up and down) since 1990. ONDCP claims: "Heroin purity is a reflection of the drug's availability. Unprecedented retail purity and low prices in the United States indicate that heroin is readily accessible."[72] Using the exact same words from the 2000 Strategy, the ONDCP states that heroin is readily accessible in the United States. Yet, the fact that these statistics indicate a failure to disrupt heroin markets is lacking.[73]

The 2001 Strategy notes that seizures of meth labs by law enforcement increased significantly between 1998 and 1999, but that they then declined through October 2000.[74] It also states: "U.S. methamphetamine availability at the retail level increased from 11.9 metric tons in 1997 to 15.9 metric tons in 1998. For 1999 and 2000, methamphetamine availability is estimated at 15.5 metric tons." In other words, there was more meth available in 2000 than in 1997, inconsistent with ONDCP's goal of reducing availability. Yet, ONDCP does not acknowledge its failure.

A figure on the same page shows the average retail price per pure gram of meth falling since 1992 and a general downward trend in the average price at the dealer level. These data suggest that the drug war goal of disrupting meth is not being achieved. Yet, ONDCP characterizes the trend as remaining

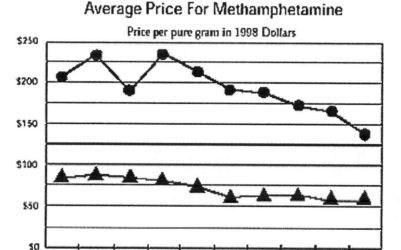

FIGURE 5.4   ONDCP Characterizes Methamphetamine Prices as Constant, 2001 Strategy

"constant." In characterizing drug use trends, ONDCP is clearly distorting the meaning of the statistics. Figure 5.4 shows the "constant" price of meth.

The 2001 Strategy reports an increase in the perceived availability of Ecstasy among twelfth graders—in fact, it is "the largest one-year percentage point increase in the availability measure among 12th graders for any drug class in the 26-year history of the MTF study."[75] Not surprisingly, on the same page, ONDCP notes "increasing availability of [Ecstasy] in the United States—in metropolitan centers and suburban communities alike." Thus, the 2001 Strategy illustrates that Ecstasy use has not been reduced in line with the drug war's goals.

The 2001 Strategy reports increased Ecstasy seizures in the United States between 1998 and 2000 and explains that "criminal groups that have proven capable of producing and smuggling significant quantities of [Ecstasy] into the United States are expanding distribution networks from coast to coast."[76] Further, the Strategy notes that Ecstasy "has spread into branches of the military," meaning that internal investigations concerning Ecstasy in the military have increased. All of these data suggest that the drug war goal of disrupting Ecstasy is not being achieved. Yet, ONDCP does not explicitly acknowledge this.

2002 Strategy

Interestingly, no statistics on availability, price, or purity of illicit drugs are visually presented and discussed in the 2002, 2003, 2004, and 2005 versions of the Strategy. We suspect the data are not consistent with their goals, for the previous versions (which contained figures and discussions) showed outcomes counter to ONDCP objectives.[77]

ONDCP does provide data on prices, purity, deaths, emergency room mentions, drug arrests, costs to society, drug seizures, asset forfeiture, and so forth. The are contained in ONDCP's fact sheet titled *Drug Data Summary*. Yet, this fact sheet is located in a very difficult to find location — at the very bottom of one of ONDCP's Web sites titled, "Federal Drug Data Sources."[78] Removing these data from the Strategy makes the Strategy a less useful tool for policy analysis and evaluating the drug war.

Again, when statistics counter the drug war's goals, ONDCP simply ignores them in terms of its Strategy. We cannot imagine how removing these data make the Strategy a better document, one that is accountable to the American people and a more useful tool for policy-makers. An honest policy evaluation would examine the trends rather than hide them. Honest policy evaluations require the assessments of the failures of the policy, not just the successes.[79]

ONDCP claims, in its 2002 Strategy, that: "Few areas of public policy boast linkages as clear as those that exist between the availability and use of illegal drugs. Simply put, the demand for drugs tends to vary with their price and availability. Disrupting this market relationship provides policymakers with a clear lever to reduce use."[80] This, apparently, does not take into account the power of addiction. Even if addiction were not an unconsidered problem, we know that since ONDCP existed, drug availability has generally not declined and prices have not increased. That ONDCP does not acknowledge these facts is evidence of dishonest claims-making.

2003 Strategy

The 2003 Strategy says marijuana is "so widespread in today's schools that nearly half of all high school seniors report having tried it by graduation."[81] Perhaps this is why use is not down because federal efforts to disrupt markets have failed.

Here again, we consistently see admissions of failures in the ONDCP Strategy reports, hidden in plain view for all who are reading carefully enough. As noted earlier, the irony is that ONDCP must admit some failure in order to heighten awareness of the problem of drugs.

The 2003 Strategy, as in previous years, also admits:

In 1974, according to data compiled by the Drug Enforcement Administration (DEA), the average THC content of marijuana was less than 1 percent. Twenty-five years later, potency was averaging around 7 percent, with some samples in the 30 percent range. Recent research published in the *British Journal of Psychiatry* suggests a 15-fold increase in THC content and concludes that "the modern cannabis smoker may be exposed to doses of THC many times greater than his or her counterpart in the 1960s and 1970s." The Journal concludes that this "single fact has made obsolete much of what we once knew about the risks and consequences of marijuana use."[82]

This is simply an amazing claim. Like many of its claims about the need for drug treatment, ONDCP's claims about THC content in marijuana vary widely across the years and even across different documents. As for the Strategy reports, there is little discussion of the issue over the years, yet on the ONDCP Web site, there is much contradictory information about this issue. Ideally, ONDCP would simply present the statistics along with their sources and allow the reader to verify the validity of the numbers.

Two marijuana experts refute ONDCP's claim that THC content is significantly higher today:

> When today's youth use marijuana, they are using the same drug used by youth in the 1960s and 1970s. A small number of low-THC sample sized by the Drug Enforcement Administration are used to calculate a dramatic increase in potency. However, these samples were not representative of the marijuana generally available to users during this era. Potency data from the early 1980s to the present are more reliable, and they show no increase in the average THC content of marijuana. Even if marijuana potency were to increase, it would not necessarily make the drug more dangerous. Marijuana that varies quite substantially in potency produces similar psychoactive effects.[83]

Yet, ONDCP Director John Walters claims that "Parents are often unaware that today's marijuana is different from that of a generation ago, with potency levels 10 to 20 times stronger than the marijuana with which they were familiar."[84]

A reaction by one researcher clarifies the clear discrepancies in these claims:

- Marijuana and sinsemilla *are* on average getting stronger, but certainly not 10 or 20 times stronger. In any event, high potency cannabis products have *always* been available.

• Most seized marijuana (and presumably most of the marijuana available for sale) is actually not very potent.[85]

After a careful analysis of statistics pertaining to THC content in various forms of marijuana—obtained from the University of Mississippi's Marijuana Potency Monitoring Project, sponsored by the National Institute on Drug Abuse (NIDA)—independent researcher Brian Bennett explains that:

> If we narrow our focus to just "marijuana," the lowest recorded average potency was measured in 1973 at 0.83 percent THC. By contrast, the highest recorded average potency for "marijuana" was measured in 2001 at 4.72 percent THC. These numbers indicate that today's "marijuana" weighs in at less than 6 times as potent as that from the last generation.[86]

Even if we assume that ONDCP's statistics on THC content are accurate, what does this say about the drug war? Does it result in higher potency of drugs—e.g., better marijuana and other drugs—reaching the market? If so, is this consistent with ONDCP's drug war goals? ONDCP does not address this issue. Price and availability suggest that minimal market disruption is occurring. Despite the apparent ineffectiveness of interdiction, the importance of interdiction is highlighted even in the 2003 Strategy:

> An effective, balanced drug policy requires an aggressive interdiction program to make drugs scarce, expensive, and of unreliable quality. Yet it is an article of faith among many self-styled drug policy "experts" that drug interdiction is futile, for at least two reasons: with millions of square miles of ocean (or "thousands of miles of border," or "millions of cargo containers"), interdictors must be everywhere to be effective. Not being everywhere, it follows that transit zone interdictors from the departments of Defense and Homeland Security are consigned to seizing a small and irrelevant portion of the flow of cocaine, to pick the drug that currently is generating the most emergency room admissions.[87]

Here, ONDCP assails experts opposed to the drug war for basing their arguments that interdiction is futile on "faith" yet simultaneously seems to be arguing in favor of interdiction based on faith (without evidence). In other words, even when the evidence shows that interdiction does not affect price, quality, or availability of drugs (in the direction desired by ONDCP), ONDCP still assures success. Even when the relevant statistics point clearly to failure, ONDCP still claims:

In 2001, U.S. Government and partner nations seized or otherwise interdicted more than 21 percent of the cocaine shipped to the United States, according to an interagency assessment. When added to the additional 7 percent that is seized at our borders or elsewhere in the United States, current interdiction rates are *within reach of the 35 to 50 percent seizure rate* that is estimated would prompt a collapse of profitability for smugglers unless they substantially raise their prices or expand their sales to non-U.S. markets.[88]

If we read this statement correctly, it tells us that—even after fighting the drug war for decades—government agencies have not been able to seize enough drugs to make a real difference. Further, ONDCP claims it is "within reach" of 35-50% success, yet its own statistics suggest it seizes only about 28% of cocaine entering the United States. Let's say the government must actually seize 50% of cocaine (the ONDCP upper range) to make it unprofitable, then we are still 44% away from our goal.[89] Here, ONDCP presents statistics to show that it is close to making a difference. Strangely, the statistics show the opposite, that we are not close to making a difference.

What really would matter, it would seem, is how much more drugs have law enforcement agencies been able to seize over the years and has that changed use patterns? Seizures of virtually all illicit drugs are up since 1988, but prices have not risen and overall use of illicit drugs is not down. This suggests drug seizures have not had their intended effects. This outcome is inconsistent with ONDCP goals.

Next, ONDCP admits that we probably should not be surprised that our interdiction efforts have not been successful. In the 2003 Strategy, it claims that its focus on disruption if the market has not been consistent:

> As a government, faced with the obvious and urgent challenges of punishing the guilty and taking drugs off the street, our focus on targeting the drug trade as a business—with a view to increasing its costs—has been episodic. We need to do a more consistent job of ratcheting up trafficker costs at a tempo that does not allow the drug trade to reestablish itself or adapt.[90]

ONDCP also notes a "lack of collaboration" between law enforcement agencies and a failure to agree on "a set of trafficker targets." ONDCP admits in the 2003 Strategy that a "consolidated list of top trafficker targets" has *finally* been created.[91] Thus, it appears that although ONDCP has made more and more efforts to disrupt drug markets since 1988, has seized more drugs over this period, and has spent more and more taxpayer dollars, its efforts were never aimed at clear targets or coordinated. This is inconsistent with a carefully planned drug control policy.

Further, ONDCP admits that its High Intensity Drug Trafficking Areas (HIDTA) program, "created in 1990 to focus law enforcement efforts on the Nation's most serious drug trafficking threats . . . had not demonstrated adequate results and that over time the initial focus of the program has been diluted."[92] In other words, a program in effect since 1990 has not worked. ONDCP admits the failure, but does not consider the possibility that such findings prove interdiction may be futile. Nor does ONDCP suggest that the HIDTA should be ended because it is ineffective. Each of these is a significant admission of failure. Yet, in the 2003 Strategy, these claims are buried among many others, most of which attempt to sell the drug war by focusing on positive outcomes related to drug use based on faulty statistics.

2004 Strategy

In the 2004 Strategy, ONDCP again explains the importance of disrupting drug markets: "The main reason supply reduction matters to drug policy is that it makes drugs more expensive, less potent, and less available."[93] On the same page, ONDCP claims: "We are now attacking the drug trade in all of its component parts, and we have made progress on all fronts."

Simply stated, we find this to be an outlandish claim, and no statistics are offered with regard to this specific claim. Ironically, a review of data through 2003 shows that ONDCP has not made drugs more expensive, less potent, or less available.

Given the available evidence, ONDCP's pride in its interdiction efforts is surprising. The National Academy of Sciences's Committee on Data and Research for Policy and Illegal Drugs concludes that we simply do not have enough quality data to conclude whether interdiction is effective, including about whether drug offenders are deterred by the law and police, how drug offenders are replaced when they are removed from the market, and how drug offenders adapt to challenges posed by interdiction efforts.[94] Interestingly, the Committee presents a figure using ONDCP data on cocaine and heroin prices and spending on law enforcement, international enforcement, and interdiction. The figure shows that, from 1981 to 1998, as spending on enforcement increased, the price of cocaine and heroin fell.[95] This is directly contrary to what ONDCP wishes to achieve. Still, the Committee concludes that "little is known about the effectiveness of law enforcement operations against retail drug markets . . . the consequences of increasing or decreasing current levels of enforcement are not known."[96] We feel this conclusion is far too cautious.

In the 2004 Strategy, ONDCP makes claims such as this to prove the effectiveness of interdiction efforts: "The U.S. Government's master list of targeted trafficking organizations is shorter this year, thanks to the elimination of eight major trafficking organizations during the past fiscal year. . . . Another seven organizations were weakened enough to be classified as 'significantly disrupted'."[97] We have no way of verifying such claims or analyzing the data on which they are based because ONDCP does not offer any evidence.

ONDCP also claims success in some countries in terms of reducing overall drug production, such as cocaine production in Colombia. It also claims that the critics' claim of a "balloon" market or "push-down-pop-up" market is *no longer* true. ONDCP admits:

> It is true that criminal enterprises invariably attempt to reestablish themselves in an environment with the most permissive rule of law. It is also true that traffickers have more than once been driven out of a country by drug control efforts only to reconstitute their business in a neighboring country—as in the mid-1990s, when plummeting coca cultivation in Peru was offset by rapid planting in neighboring Colombia.[98]

ONDCP boldly claims: "But *not this time*. Crucially, progress in Colombia has not been offset in traditional growing areas in Peru. Nor have regular increases in cultivation in Bolivia come close to offsetting the drop in Colombia."[99]

It is indeed possible that ONDCP is correct that *finally* something has changed with regard to cocaine production in South America. Yet, it should be noted that before the 2004 Strategy, the balloon or push-down-pop-up market was the rule in South America. In fact, figures on the ONDCP Web site serve as evidence of it. Figure 5.5—not included in any of the versions on the Strategy we reviewed—illustrates that in the 1990s until 2000, while cocaine production fell in Peru and Bolivia, it surged in Colombia.[100] ONDCP even refers to this as "spillover." Our main reaction to this new success in preventing spillover is curiosity—what has changed with regard to the war on drugs in South America that has led to this new finding? This is not explained by ONDCP.

Here, ONDCP has missed providing critical information on what about its drug war abroad has changed and made it more successful. Another possibility is that ONDCP has claimed success as a result of statistical anomaly. Perhaps Colombia had an off-year in cocaine production and will in the future return to its previously higher levels of production. Only time will tell if this is true. What is clear is that ONDCP is using a one-year decline in cocaine production as proof of an effective drug war, even among a long history of failures to achieve similar results.

In contrast to the situation with coca, the statistics about poppy cultivation are quite unambiguous. As noted earlier, heroin production is on the rise. The demise of the Taliban in Afghanistan and the new political dynamics within the country have led to a substantial increase in poppy cultivation. According

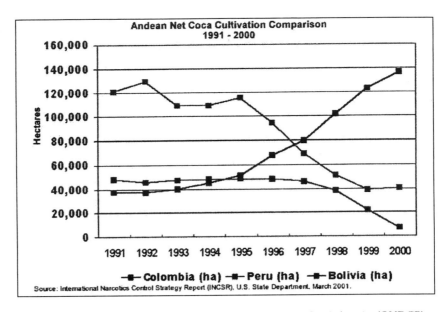

FIGURE 5.5   Spillover or Displacement in Cocaine Production, South America (ONDCP)

to ONDCP itself (though not in the Strategy), poppy cultivation in Afghanistan for 2004 was estimated at 206,700 hectares, compared with 61,000 in 2003, and 30,750 in 2002.[101] Market disruption in Afghanistan has not been successful.

Finally, what is the net effect of these attempts at market disruption through eradication and interdiction? Are drugs actually less available in the United States because of it? Has use gone down because of it? MTF data show slight declines in use and perceived availability of powder cocaine between 2002 and 2003 (the latest data available at the time of the publication of the 2004 Strategy), although between 20% and 40% of eighth, tenth, and twelfth graders still say it is "fairly easy" or "very easy" to obtain cocaine.[102] This is after decades of the drug war.

Recently, a researcher with the Congressional Research Service wrote:

Efforts to significantly reduce the flow of illicit drugs from abroad into the United States have so far not succeeded. Moreover, over the past decade, worldwide production of illicit drugs has risen dramatically: opium and marijuana production has roughly doubled and coca production tripled. Street prices of cocaine and heroin have fallen significantly in the past 20 years, reflecting increased availability.[103]

A more recent policy evaluation of the war on drugs found that crop eradication has negligible effects and that success is extremely rare,[104] and that
interdiction has only a small effect and possibly meaningless effect on drug
prices.[105] In fact, that drug prices have declined may suggest larger worldwide
availability of drugs. Domestic enforcement does raise prices within the United
States and, without it, drug prices would be cheaper.[106] Yet, if use went up in
the absence of domestic enforcement, it would likely be due to heavy users
using more drugs rather than more users overall. Finally, it should be pointed
out that critical analyses of drug enforcement spending increases from the
1980s to 2000 were accompanied by sizable declines in drug prices, suggesting
that increase funding for domestic enforcement did not achieve the desired
outcome.[107] In fact, as arrests per million dollars in cocaine sales increased
from 1981 to 2000, the retail price of cocaine per gram declined.[108] ONDCP is
not unaware of these facts or does not feel they are relevant to its case.

2005 Strategy

In the 2005 Strategy, ONDCP reasserts its commitment to disrupting drug
markets. It writes: "The strategy of the U.S. Government is to disrupt the market for illegal drugs—and to do so in a way that both reduces the profitability
of the drug trade and increases the costs of drugs to consumers. In other words,
we seek to inflict on this business what every legal business fears—escalating
costs, diminishing profits, and unreliable suppliers."[109]
    One expects ONDCP to finally provide evidence that its efforts to disrupt
drug markets work. Instead, ONDCP again tries to convince the reader that
its efforts simply make sense:

> Like every other business, the supply of and demand for illegal drugs
> exist in equilibrium; there is a price beyond which customers, particu-
> larly young people, will not pay for drugs. It follows that, when sup-
> plies are disrupted, prices go up, or drug supplies become erratic.
> Prices rising too much can precipitate a crisis for the individual user,
> encouraging an attempt at drug treatment. Use, in turn, goes
> down.[110]

While this is certainly logical enough, ONDCP makes no mention of
what is actually happening to drug prices. In fact, drug prices are not up but instead are generally down. It may trouble some that ONDCP continues to sell
market disruption as a means to increase prices and reduce use despite the statistical evidence that shows prices falling rather than increasing.

We were able to locate relevant statistics to address availability, price, and purity. These data suggest ONDCP itself knows drugs are available, that prices are unchanged or falling, and that drug purity has not fallen. First, we accessed ONDCP's *Pulse Check* reports.[111] These reports present " findings on drug use patterns and drug markets as reported by ethnographers, epidemiologists, treatment providers, and law enforcement officials in sites throughout the Nation."[112] The latest report, at the time of this writing, suggests that ONDCP is not achieving its goals when it comes to market disruption.[113]

Second, we accessed a report on ONDCP's Web site, *The Price and Purity of Illicit Drugs*. This report claims:

> In summary, prices for powder cocaine, crack, and heroin declined sharply in the 1980s and have declined more gradually since then, with periodic interruptions by modest price spikes that have usually persisted for a year or less. . . . Marijuana prices have followed a very different pattern, increasing from 1981 to 1991, then declining through 2000 and increasing over the past three years. . . . The average purities of these drugs of these drugs have varied substantially by drug, occasionally with divergent trends.[114]

ONDCP concludes:

> Perhaps the most striking observation about illicit drug prices is simply that they are extraordinarily high price per unit weight, even though prices have declined over the past 20 years. . . . The overall trend for powder cocaine, crack, and heroin showed a steep decline during the 1980s, a spike in prices in 1989–1990, then relatively stability, with a modest decline during the 1990s and early 2000s. . . . Marijuana prices rose from 1981 to 1991, fell through 2000, and have since rebounded somewhat . . . Cocaine purity is typically fairly high at all quantity levels . . . and heroin today is much more pure than it was in the early 1980s.[115]

That these two sources are on ONDCP's Web site prove that ONDCP cannot claim it is unaware of the data. ONDCP statistics presented on its own Web site simply contradict what ONDCP claims in its own Strategy. It is outrageous that ONDCP sells a policy that evidence suggests is a failure, given that its own data show ONDCP should know the policy is ineffective. Third, a report from the Drug Enforcement Administration (DEA) titled *Illegal Drug Price and Purity Report* also shows that drugs are still widely available, cheap, and pure. Among its findings, which focus on the years 1998–2001:

- Cocaine prices nationwide have remained relatively stable over the time period, particularly for ounce and gram quantities, suggesting that cocaine was readily available to the user. "Crack" cocaine prices also remained stable, indicating it too was readily available nationwide.
- Cocaine purity levels decreased at the kilogram level from 82 percent in 1998 to 69 percent in 2001. Ounce and gram levels have also decreased from 69 percent in 1998 to 53 percent in 2001 and from 69 percent to 56 percent, respectively.
- Heroin is readily available in many U.S. cities as evidenced by the unprecedented level of average retail, or street-level, purity.
- Overall heroin purity at the kilogram level increased slightly, but remained below 70 percent in 2001. However, gram- and ounce-purity levels declined slightly, but remained over 50 percent.
- Prices for commercial-grade marijuana have remained relatively stable over the past decade . . . the average commercial-grade potency THC levels have increased from 4.19 percent in 1999 to 4.72 percent in 2001. Average sinsemilla potency THC levels have decreased from 13.38 percent to 9.03 percent over the same time period.
- National methamphetamine prices at the pound level decreased significantly from 1998 to 1999, but increased in 2000 and remained stable in 2001. Nationally, methamphetamine prices at the ounce level increased slightly at the upper end of the price range and prices at the gram level remained stable.
- The national purity level for methamphetamine dropped dramatically; however, as methamphetamine makers found alternative chemicals, the purity has begun to increase.[116]

Fourth, the National Drug Intelligence Center's *National Drug Threat Assessment* shows that drugs are still widely available. Among its specific findings:

- Marijuana is widely available throughout the United States, and this availability is relatively stable overall.
- Powder cocaine is readily available throughout the United States, and overall availability appears to be stable.
- Crack cocaine is available throughout the country, particularly in urban areas, and availability appears to be stable overall.
- Heroin is readily available throughout most major metropolitan areas in the United States and is becoming more available in many suburban and rural areas, particularly in the Northeast/Mid-Atlantic region of the country.
- Methamphetamine is widely available throughout the Pacific, Southwest, and West Central regions, and availability has risen to high or

moderate levels in most areas of the Great Lakes and Southeast regions. Methamphetamine availability in the Northeast/Mid-Atlantic region remains low; however, several law enforcement agencies in the region have reported increased availability of the drug over the past year.

- MDMA is available in all regions of the country. Law enforcement reporting indicates increasing MDMA availability while most other data (seizure, case initiation, indictment, and arrest) indicate stable to slightly decreasing availability.
- The production, distribution, and abuse of other dangerous drugs (ODDs), including the club drugs GHB, ketamine, and Rohypnol as well as the hallucinogens LSD, PCP, and psilocybin, pose only a moderate overall threat to the country. The availability and use of these drugs are moderate and relatively stable.
- The diversion and abuse of pharmaceuticals, including narcotics, depressants, and stimulants, pose an increasing threat to the country. . . . Pharmaceutical narcotics such as (Vicodin), oxycodone (OxyContin), hydromorphone (Dilaudid), and codeine are available and abused throughout the country. The demand, availability, and abuse of these drugs are high and appear to be increasing. . . . The availability of depressants (including barbiturates and benzodiazepines) varies regionally. . . . Stimulants . . . are widely available in most areas.[117]

Most of these outcomes are inconsistent with ONDCP's goal of disrupting drug markets. Yet, ONDCP never admits failure in any area related to market disruption.

In the 2005 Strategy, ONDCP does note one success in its effort to disrupt drug markets—cocaine production in the Andes. It claims it has, "for the third straight year, decrease[d]."[118] A figure on the same page shows declining cocaine cultivation from 2001 to 2003. Figure 5.6 reproduces that figure.

The figure actually indicates a decline over two years (2001–2002 and 2002–2003) rather than three. Further, the amount of cocaine cultivated in Colombia in 2003 is only slightly lower than in 2000. As in the 2004 Strategy, ONDCP in the 2005 Strategy claims no evidence of displacement from Colombia to other countries in the region: "Crucially, progress in Colombia has not been offset by increases in Peru or Bolivia. There was a net decrease in the total area cultivated in those countries in 2003, including a remarkable 15 percent drop in Peru. Only trace amounts of coca are cultivated in neighboring Venezuela, Ecuador, Panama, and Brazil."[119]

New data suggest that displacement and eradication failure are occurring. Increased production is developing in Peru. Coca producers (cocaleros) are gaining greater political power in Bolivia. And a U.S. government report recently

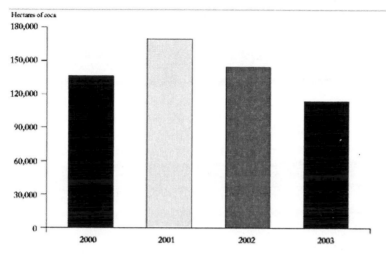

Source: U.S. Government

FIGURE 5.6   ONDCP Claims a Three-Year Decline in Cocaine Cultivation, Colombia, 2005 Strategy

acknowledged that coca eradication is not flourishing in Colombia: "The report by the White House Office of National Drug Control Policy said that despite a record-setting aerial eradication offensive, 281,694 acres of coca remained in Colombia at the end of 2004 — an increase from the 281,323 acres left over after spraying the year earlier."[120]

Instead of acknowledging such facts, ONDCP attempts to make the case that eradication of drugs works: "Large-scale eradication is an effective means of targeting trafficker networks because most growers are affected, reducing the production available to all traffickers. With Colombia producing one-third less cocaine than it was just two years earlier, there simply is less to go around."[121]

One thus expects young people to indicate that cocaine is less available and cocaine use to fall. Yet, ONDCP does not show evidence that this is true. Instead, in the 2005 Strategy, ONDCP asserts that "making drugs harder to find means fewer teens using drugs" and it shows figures depicting trends on availability and use of Ecstasy[122] and LSD.[123] In fact, the figures illustrate that availability barely declined from 2001–2004, whereas use of these drugs declined much more significantly. ONDCP does not consider other factors that could have led to declines in use, or the possibility that youth have simply changed drugs (substitution). Further, another interpretation of the statistical trends is possible. It is possible that as youth use declines, so does perceived availability. That is, as youth are looking less for particular drugs, they are probably more likely to indicate that the drugs are less available.

As shown in ONDCP's figures, that perceived availability of Ecstasy and LSD have declined does not imply that these drugs are hard to obtain. ONDCP's figures show that 50% still say Ecstasy is available ("fairly easy" or "very easy" to get) and that 35% of youth say LSD is available ("fairly easy" or "very easy" to get). Finally, ONDCP presents no such figures on drugs that are more widely used by youth (and available to them). This suggests that ONDCP has purposely selected two drugs of use by youth—both of which show declining trends—in order to prove that declines in availability led to declines in use.

In the 2005 Strategy, ONDCP claims it has now been able to seize or destroy half of the world's cocaine in a given year:

> In 2003, the United States and our allies seized or forced the jettisoning of 210 metric tons of cocaine headed through the transit zone before it could reach U.S. consumers. Adding in seizures in South America, Mexico, and elsewhere, the United States and our allies removed 401 metric tons of cocaine—about half of the world's potential production—from distribution channels. In 2004, those figures rose to 248 and 430 metric tons, respectively—against a backdrop of declining production in Latin America.[124]

Recall that in the 2004 Strategy, ONDCP claimed:

> In 2001, U.S. Government and partner nations seized or otherwise interdicted more than 21 percent of the cocaine shipped to the United States, according to an interagency assessment. When added to the additional 7 percent that is seized at our borders or elsewhere in the United States, current interdiction rates are *within reach of the 35 to 50 percent seizure rate* that is estimated would prompt a collapse of profitability for smugglers unless they substantially raise their prices or expand their sales to non-U.S. markets.

Although we may be comparing apples and oranges here, ONDCP first says it seized 28% of cocaine shipped to the United States. The next year it claims it seized about half of the world's potential production of cocaine. We assume that if ONDCP's logic about causing a collapse of profitability for cocaine smugglers is true, eliminating 50% of the cocaine from the market would do it. Yet, ONDCP does not make such a claim in the 2005 Strategy.

Instead, ONDCP presents figures showing worldwide seizures are up from 1999 to 2004[125] and seizures of US bound cocaine are up from 1999 to

2004.[126] ONDCP makes no case that this has led to declines in use, however. ONDCP also stresses the importance of asset forfeiture, and notes that "DEA's asset seizures are up from $383 million during fiscal year 2003 to $523 million in 2004, and the number of seizures valued at more than $1 million rose by more than half."[127] ONDCP makes no efforts to document the significance of such seizures for its drug war goals.

ONDCP then revisits the issue of its top illegal drug organization targets:

> Over the past two years, the U.S. Government has identified 58 major trafficking organizations, 12 of which have links to terrorist organizations, and added them to the Consolidated Priority Organization Target (CPOT) list. In two years, we have dismantled 14 organizations while severely disrupting an additional eight. The heads of 17 CPOT organizations—nearly 30 percent of the total CPOT targets—have been arrested. Organizations dismantled during fiscal year 2004 were responsible for shipping an estimated 44 metric tons per year of cocaine—and 500 kilograms per year of heroin—to the United States.[128]

While this is consistent with ONDCP's goal to disrupt the organizations responsible for growing, manufacturing, shipping, and distributing drugs into this country, ONDCP fails to discuss the issue of replacement. What happens when these top figures are arrested? Does the ability to provide drugs actually go down? Does demand for the drugs go down? Or do some other top figures simply step in and take their places? If this occurs—replacement—then efforts to disrupt CPOT are doomed to fail.

ONDCP also discusses the issue of opium and poppy production in Afghanistan in a section titled "Securing the Future of a Free and Democratic Afghanistan."[129] It explains:

> In 2004, Afghanistan produced some 207,000 hectares of opium poppy. Current cultivation levels equate to a potential production of 4,950 metric tons of opium. This represents a 239 percent increase in the poppy crop and a 73 percent increase in potential opium production over 2003 estimates. . . . If all of Afghanistan's opium were converted to heroin, the result would be 582 metric tons of heroin. By comparison, Colombia and Mexico combined produced roughly 22 metric tons of pure heroin in 2003, more than enough to satisfy U.S. consumption. The level of opium and heroin production in 2004 does pose an immense threat to Europe, Southeast Asia, Iran, Pakistan, and Russia—all major consumers of Afghan heroin.[130]

ONDCP presents figures showing increasing opium production in Afghanistan[131] and an explosion of poppy cultivation in Afghanistan.[132] ONDCP makes no mention of why we are seeing the large increases in opium and heroin production in Afghanistan. It likely has everything to do with the overthrow of the Taliban government in Afghanistan by U.S. military forces, so it is strange that ONDCP does not acknowledge this or at least explain why overthrowing the Taliban—a worthwhile goal in the nation's war on terror— might lead to this outcome. Instead, ONDCP links this increase in opium and heroin production to terrorism and other bad outcomes:

> According to United Nations estimates, illicit poppy cultivation and heroin production in Afghanistan and the region generate nearly $3 billion, equivalent to about 60 percent of Afghanistan's gross domestic product. This level of illicit income fosters instability and supports criminals, terrorists, and militias. Further, the large incomes from the opium crop and heroin trafficking inhibit the normal development of the Afghan economy by sidetracking the labor pool and diminishing the attractiveness of legal farming and economic activities.[133]

ONDCP explains that it will assist the Afghan government by beginning "a public affairs campaign designed to discourage poppy cultivation and dissuade participation in any aspect of the drug trade."[134] Second, ONDCP will help the Afghan government increase law enforcement:

"We will help the Afghans build a special narcotics prosecution task force and aid construction of judicial and detention facilities expressly for counternarcotics cases."[135] Third, ONDCP "will create new opportunities for growing legitimate and high-value crops. . . . Micro-credit programs, improved irrigation, and access to improved seeds and better roads will make turning away from poppy cultivation a viable alternative."[136] Fourth, ONDCP will assist with Afghan government with an "aggressive eradication program."[137] Finally, according to ONDCP:

> The fifth pillar is interdiction. Our goal is to help the Government increase the size and mobility of its counternarcotics police while accelerating the pace of their efforts. More police forces will be trained, high-impact targets arrested, drug-related intelligence sharing improved, and the pressure points of the drug trade identified and suppressed. We will help with the construction of border checkpoints that will assist in narcotics interdiction. Because interdiction occurs on both sides of the border, we will also work with Afghanistan's neighbors to formulate a regional strategy, and help them build their capacity to protect their own borders.[138]

Interestingly, here ONDCP links drugs to all kinds of bad outcomes: "A vibrant drug trade fosters corruption, undermines the rule of law, can finance terror, and will destabilize the region. It threatens all that the courageous Afghan people have achieved. In a troubled region's newest democracy, there is simply no place for the drug trade."[139] ONDCP does even not consider the possibility that none of this would be possible without prohibition and our war on drugs.

Finally, in the 2005 Strategy, ONDCP discusses its efforts to target synthetic drugs. Beginning with methamphetamine, ONDCP notes that "production appears to be increasing in that the amount of methamphetamine seized within Mexico rose during 2003, as did seizures along the U.S.-Mexico border in 2003 and 2004."[140] That meth production is rising is inconsistent with ONDCP's goal of disrupting drug markets, yet ONDCP does not acknowledge this. ONDCP does demonstrate rising meth seizures on the southwest border and successful efforts in Canada that have led to "a 92 percent reduction in methamphetamine precursor seizure events inbound from Canada . . . and a 96 percent drop is such seizures by weight. . . . Traffickers appear to have largely abandoned their once-plentiful Canadian precursor source."[141]

Yet, a figure presented by ONDCP shows declining seizures of meth "super-labs." ONDCP explains: "A recent trend toward declining seizures of so-called "super labs" (laboratories capable of producing at least ten pounds of methamphetamine in a day) suggests that production of methamphetamine is moving out of the country, possibly in response to reduced availability of precursor chemicals like bulk pseudoephedrine."[142] If ONDCP is right here, it means it is not disrupting meth labs but rather is moving them, which is a form of displacement that is inconsistent with market disruption.

As for Ecstasy, ONDCP claims that "since the success of major enforcement efforts in the United States, Canada, and Europe, Ecstasy use continues to decline in the United States."[143] This is an interesting claim since a figure presented earlier in the 2005 Strategy actually shows Ecstasy use leveling off to levels previously seen in the late 1990s rather than continuing to decline. But, even assuming Ecstasy use is still declining, use of other drugs like psychotherapeutics is increasing. Displacement from one drug to another is inconsistent with ONDCP's goals.

Chapter Six

Costs of the Drug War

In this chapter, we critically analyze ONDCP claims-making concerning the costs of drug use and abuse, as well as costs of the drug war. This includes economic costs, deaths, emergency room mentions of illicit drugs, and crime. We address the claims by type of costs in a roughly chronological order.

Our review of the annual Strategy suggests that ONDCP states goals and objectives of its drug war, consistently asserts proof of its benefits, and often claims successes even when not warranted. Yet, as noted in chapter 1, a fair assessment of any policy—including the drug war—must also consider the costs associated with the policy. Any policy in which harms outweigh benefits can be considered a failing policy.[1] As the findings of this chapter suggest, ONDCP does not evaluate the drug war this way, for it attributes all costs of the drug war to drug users and abusers.

Economic Costs

2000 Strategy

In the 2000 Strategy, figures show growing economic costs of alcohol and drug abuse from 1985 through 1995, including growing health care costs and increased criminal justice costs.[2] Figure 6.1 illustrates these increases.

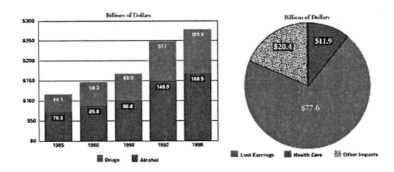

FIGURE 6.1   ONDCP Admits Growing Costs of Drug Abuse, 2000 Strategy

The costs depicted in the figure include criminal justice costs (i.e., the costs to apprehend, convict, and punish drug offenders). The 2000 Strategy notes that drug offenders accounted for 19% of the total growth in state prison populations between 1990 and 1998 and that drug inmates made up 60% of all federal inmates in 1997. This means the drug war is responsible for about one-fifth of the costs of state prisons in the 1990s and 60% of federal prison costs in at least one year in the 1990s.

The Strategy also notes increased costs associated with incarceration and greater national spending on incarceration than on education. Evidence is also presented showing clear evidence of racial disparities in incarceration.[3] Each of these could be considered a cost of the drug war, yet ONDCP does not treat them that way.

ONDCP attempts to minimize such statistics by stating in the 2000 Strategy that "drug offenders account for *only* 19% of state prison population growth while large numbers of violent offenders are responsible for 51% of the growth."[4] At the same time, it is noted that "the number of parole violators who are returned to prison for drug offenses has doubled since 1990. Drug offenders also account for more than half (52 percent) of the total rise in the number of parolees who have their parole revoked and returned to State prison."[5] In other words, drug offenders are a significant source of incarceration; this costs society billions of dollars a year. ONDCP never discusses whether these costs are worth it—that is, whether the benefits justify such costs.

2001 Strategy

In the 2001 Strategy, ONDCP puts forth some alarming statistics about the costs of drug use and abuse:

Illegal drugs exact a staggering cost on American society. In 1995, they accounted for an estimated $110 billion in expenses and lost revenue. This public-health burden is shared by all of society, directly or indirectly. Tax dollars pay for increased law enforcement, incarceration, and treatment to stem the flow of illegal drugs and counter associated negative social repercussions. NIDA [the National Institute on Drug Abuse] estimated that health-care expenditures due to drug abuse cost America $9.9 billion in 1992 and nearly twelve billion dollars in 1995.[6]

Note that ONDCP counts components of the drug war—law enforcement, incarceration, and treatment—as part of the costs of drug use and abuse. Many would argue that these are costs of the drug war and do not directly or necessarily flow from drug use. Instead, they reflect policy choices by the government among a variety of policy options, some of which do not involve significant criminal justice operations.

2002 Strategy

The 2002 Strategy notes in a box titled "Consequences of Drug Use" that "the total economic cost to society of illegal drug use in 2000 was an estimated $160 billion, *a 57 percent increase from 1992*".[7] This includes $110.5 billion in productivity losses, $35.2 billion for costs such as goods and services lost to crime, criminal justice responses and social welfare, and $14.9 billion for health care costs. Again, many of these costs are actually not attributable to drug use and abuse but instead to the drug war. We return to this issue later in the chapter.

For now, it is important to note that the above claim is another subtle admission of failure. ONDCP states the economic costs to society of drug use and abuse grew 57% from 1992 to 2000. Since one of ONDCP's goals through the 2002 Strategy included reducing health and social costs to the public of illegal drug use, rising economic costs are a sign of failure, not success. ONDCP does not consider this statistic as indicative of failure.

2002–2005 Strategy

As noted in chapter 1, beginning in 2003, these kinds of costs are no longer included in the annual Strategy reports. Instead, they have been removed and are separately included in its report, *The Economic Costs of Drug Abuse in the United States 1992–1998*.[8] This is inconsistent with careful policy analysis that requires consideration of both the benefits and the costs of the policy. The 2000 and

2001 versions of the Strategy contained many useful figures, tables, and statements related to such costs of the drug war. Policy-makers could thus at least
try to weigh the costs versus the benefits of the drug war. The 2002 Strategy
contained only the one box dealing with the costs. The 2003 and 2004 versions
of the Strategy simply removed such costs from the equation. The 2005 Strategy discusses costs again, but only briefly and in a very limited way.

In its report, *The Economic Costs of Drug Abuse in the United States
1992–1998,* ONDCP writes:

> The societal cost of drug abuse in the United States was $143.4 billion
> in 1998. The majority of these costs are productivity losses, particu-
> larly those related to incarceration, crime careers, drug abuse related
> illness, and premature death. . . . The overall cost of drug abuse rose
> 5.9 percent annually between 1992 and 1998 increasing from $102.2 to
> $143.4 billion. This increase is greater than the combined increase in
> the adult population and consumer prices of 3.5 percent annual
> growth during that period. The primary sources of this increase are
> increases in productivity losses related to incarceration and drug abuse
> related illness.[9]

Here, ONDCP admits that the costs of drug abuse are rising, inconsistent
with its goal of reducing health and social costs to the public. It also admits
that most of the costs are due to prohibition, which is what leads to incarceration and is probably increasingly responsible for drug abuse related illness, as
we will show later in this chapter.

In the 2005 Strategy, ONDCP returns to characterizing drug abuse as
highly costly. It writes that "new estimates of the amount of money Americans
spend on illegal drugs reveal something remarkable about the extent to which
the concentration of drug users in our cities hurts those cities economically."[10]
In support of this claim, ONDCP presents two figures, one showing the
amount of money users spend on illegal drugs in some American cities[11] and
the other showing the estimated costs of drug abuse in the same cities.[12]
ONDCP notes that:

> In seven American cities, estimated annual expenditures by drug users
> total $1 billion or more—money that is drained out of the legitimate
> economy. Not surprisingly, three of the same cities have to spend $1
> billion or more in costs directly attributable to their residents' drug
> use, with health care costs the single biggest expense. (An additional
> 18 cities broke the barrier of $1 billion in costs when indirect costs such
> as drug-related illnesses and opportunity costs are included.) . . . Such
> costs represent an unacceptable drain on the economies of America's

cities—an underreported problem that exports vast amounts of individual and government capital that could be put to work in the service of everything from job creation to education reform.[13]

Here, ONDCP presents statistics from unpublished sources that cannot be verified. Further, ONDCP asserts that drug use only takes money out of the economy. In fact, every dollar made in illegal drug markets eventually comes back into the legal economy in the form of purchases of goods and services. ONDCP does not consider this.

ONDCP also does not explain why health care costs are so high for drug users. Presumably, it is because drug use is simply bad for people. Yet, another possibility is that drug use in a prohibition regime is more dangerous—that is, drug prohibition might make drug use more dangerous. ONDCP does not discuss this issue.

ONDCP makes a startling claim that the costs of drug use would be higher if not for the drug war:

> The enormous social consequences of drug use would be far worse were the price and availability of illegal drugs not so successfully circumscribed by the activities of interdiction and law enforcement. The drug trade is a market phenomenon. As we interrupt the supply of drugs we make them more scarce and more expensive, diminishing drug use and leading some to seek treatment.[14]

ONDCP offers literally no evidence here to show that it has "successfully circumscribed" the "availability of illegal drugs" through its "interdiction and law enforcement" activities. As we showed in chapter 5, no statistical evidence warrants ONDCP's claims about successful interdiction and law enforcement efforts.

As previously noted, neither the 2003 Strategy nor the 2004 Strategy contain statistics related to economic costs associated with the drug war.[15] Yet, in the 2003 Strategy, ONDCP claims that "drug arrests account for a small fraction of total arrests . . . and U.S. prevention and treatment programs are the most developed and best funded in the world."[16]

Further, ONDCP claims that "U.S. medical research on treatment and prevention, led by NIDA, is unsurpassed and heavily outweighs the amounts spent on enforcement- and interdiction-related *research*."[17] This is true, and a figure on the same page proves it. Yet, the reader might ask why statistics are not presented here about actual dollars spent overall on all aspects of the drug war rather than just research dollars.

Comparing dollars spent on treatment and prevention research relative to law enforcement research is misleading, since law enforcement reactions to drugs are not based on research but rather stem from common sense and historically practiced policing strategies that developed in response to other forms of criminal activity and then were simply utilized for the drug war. According to the National Academy of Sciences's Committee on Data and Research for Policy and Illegal Drugs: "Funding for research on enforcement policy is minimal, particularly when compared with the amount spent on carrying out enforcement policy." In fact, the amount spent on actual law enforcement operations as part of the war on drugs is at least one hundred times greater than the amount spent on enforcement research.[18]

It is an undeniable fact that the majority of money spent on the drug war is for law enforcement and punishment. Here, ONDCP is misleading the public through use of statistics by reporting only on research dollars spent on the war on drugs rather than on all dollars spent on the war on drugs. This is consistent with ONDCP's attempt to convince readers of the Strategy that its drug war is both balanced and nonpunitive.

NONPUNITIVE DRUG WAR?

In the 2003 Strategy, ONDCP suggests that those who claim the U.S. drug war is too punitive are off-base. It notes that "drug arrests account for a small fraction of total arrests" and that:

> U.S. prevention and treatment programs are the most developed and best funded in the world (President Bush has pledged to increase the drug treatment budget by $1.6 billion over five years). U.S. medical research on treatment and prevention, led by [the National Institute on Drug Abuse] NIDA, is unsurpassed and heavily outweighs the amounts spent on enforcement- and interdiction-related research.[19]

While these statements are technically true, so, too, are the following statements. First, the drug war is highly punitive and leads to massive increases in incarceration. For example, according to the National Academy of Sciences' Committee on Data and Research for Policy and Illegal Drugs:

> Between 1981 and 1999 the nation's expenditures on enforcement increased more than tenfold. The escalation in domestic enforcement is manifest in an inventory of criminal justice processing facts: in 1998, 1.6 million people were arrested for drug offenses, 3 times as many as in 1980, and 289,000 drug offenders were incarcerated in state prisons, 12 times as many as in 1980 (23,900).[20]

Second, the percentage of drug arrests of all arrests has increased slowly but consistently since the creation of ONDCP. We discuss the incarceration increases and arrest increases in chapter 7, which offers our own assessment of the benefits and costs of America's drug war.

Third, most money spent because of the drug war—including costs reflected in the 2003 Strategy budget and those that are not (such as indirect costs of the drug war)—is for reacting to drug use through punishment rather than preventing drug use and treating those who need help. If ONDCP simply presented statistics related to drug war costs (as we do in chapter 7) American citizens could see for themselves that most drug war spending is for punitive measures. Further, money invested in prevention and treatment research does not necessarily translate into treatment and prevention programs and thus perhaps should not be included in ONDCP's drug war costs.

As with previous versions of the Strategy, ONDCP characterizes its drug war as balanced in the 2005 Strategy. This year, ONDCP explains why balance is so important:

> "Balance" is a word that is not often used in the field of drug control. As previous iterations of the Strategy have noted, effective prevention programs are helped when adults and individuals in positions of responsibility are clear and unambiguous in their opposition to drug use. When prevention works, the load on the treatment system is eased. Drug treatment programs are more effective when the market for illegal drugs is disrupted and drugs are not pure, inexpensive, and readily available. Interdiction programs take drugs off the market in tandem with the success of treatment and prevention efforts, preventing what could otherwise be a glut in availability that could draw in new users.[21]

Here, ONDCP explains the logic of a balanced approach, noting why it should work. Yet, ONDCP does not provide statistical evidence to show that prevention works, drug treatment programs are effective, drug markets have been disrupted (so that drugs are not pure, inexpensive, and readily available), or that interdiction programs are effective. Yet, ONDCP explains that its balanced drug war is

> evident in the way the drug budget is constructed . . . the President's drug control budget request for fiscal year 2006 proposes to spend 38.7 percent of the drug control budget on drug treatment and prevention. . . . The budget allocates the remaining 61.3 percent among law enforcement budgets, international programs, drug-related

intelligence spending, and interdiction activities—program areas that have expanded in recent years principally because of the growth of programs combating heroin production in Afghanistan.[22]

As noted in chapter 2, the FY 2006 drug control budget is stated as 61% for law enforcement, international programs, and drug-related intelligence spending (most of which is reactive and crime control or military-oriented spending). Only 39% of the budget is for treatment and prevention, and much of this is for research rather than real services. To ONDCP, this is balanced.

We are not surprised that ONDCP sells the drug war as balanced and nonpunitive since one of its purposes is to justify America's war on drugs. Yet, it is still dishonest of ONDCP to mislead the American people in order to continue a policy that should exist only if it is intelligently permissible to them.

BLURRING COSTS OF DRUGS AND COSTS OF THE DRUG WAR

One thing that really stands out in ONDCP discussions of costs of drug use and abuse is that it blurs costs of the drug war with costs of drug use and abuse. Independent researcher Brian Bennett culls out costs of the drug war from ONDCP figures and, not surprisingly, reaches a totally different conclusion from ONDCP. He shows that most of the costs related to drug use and abuse in the United States actually are attributable to America's response through the drug war.[23]

As noted earlier, ONDCP estimates costs of the drug war in its report, *The Economic Costs of Drug Abuse in the United States 1992–1998*.[24] Note first that the title suggests that it only deals with drug abuse (not drug use). Yet, in the report, there is no differentiation between drug use (the majority of drug use) and drug abuse (the smallest amount of drug use).

ONDCP statistics on the costs of drugs are misleading because they suggest that it is drug use and abuse per se that is costly. ONDCP calculates health care costs (including community-based specialty treatment, federal-based specialty costs, support that includes prevention, training, and prevention and treatment research, and medical consequences), productivity losses (premature death, drug abuse related illness, institutionalization/hospitalization, victims of crime, incarceration, and crime careers), and costs of other effects (goods and services lost to crime and social welfare).

Bennett's analysis of ONDCP's costs figures shows that, from 1992 to 2000, only 25% of the $1.3 trillion total should be attributed to drug use and abuse. The other 75%, or just over $1 trillion, is better characterized as spending on the war on drugs. Bennett attributes costs for health care, premature death, institutionalization/hospitalization, victim productivity, crime victim property damage, and social welfare to drug use and abuse. He characterizes the following as drug war costs: lost wages due to incarceration; police services; legal system costs; state and federal corrections costs; local corrections costs; federal drug budget costs; private legal costs; drug abuse related illness costs; and crime careers costs.

If Bennett is correct, costs of the drug war are 4.3 times greater than the costs of drug use and abuse. In chapter 1, we explained that when actual dollar costs of a policy outweigh dollar costs of the problem the policy is aimed at curing, the policy can be considered a failing policy. Of course, it is possible that drug use and abuse costs would be higher if not for the costly drug war, but we have no way of knowing this.

In discussing the drug use costs, Bennett notes the following:

- The largest share of health care costs are for community-based treatment programs and treating HIV/AIDS patients that are drug-related.
- The premature death statistic is "bogus . . . as it's based on *all* deaths called drug-related (even those caused by pharmaceuticals), but mostly because it is an estimate of *lifetime* earnings lost by those who died." Bennett explains: "Most drug-induced deaths are caused by using drugs of unknown quality in unknown dosages. Were the drugs legal, it is likely that overdoes death rates would be much lower."[25]
- The institutionalization/hospitalization costs are for lost earnings while people are in drug treatment programs.
- The victim's productivity costs are lost wages by victims of drug-related crime.
- The crime's victim's property damage are costs for damage done to victims of drug-related crime.

We would assert that those costs related to drug-related crime are mostly attributable to the drug war. There is little question that the illicit nature of drugs leads many to commit crimes, either to defend their lucrative drug careers (e.g., dealers, manufacturers, distributors) or to acquire money to buy drugs they cannot currently afford (e.g., users and abusers). Most drug crimes are attributable to the drug war, as we will show later in this chapter.

In discussing drug war costs, Bennett notes the following:

- Some of the support costs, including treatment and training, include dollars spent related to alcohol treatment and training.
- The vast majority of people arrested, convicted, and punished for drug crimes would not be involved in the criminal justice system if not for prohibition (e.g., lost wages due to incarceration would not occur for

most of the people incarcerated for drug crimes if not for prohibition, since most are incarcerated for possession).

- The vast majority of police service costs related to drugs would be eliminated if not for prohibition (e.g., 80% of people arrested for drug crimes are arrested for possession of drugs, an offense that by itself causes no harm).
- The vast majority of legal service costs related to drugs would be eliminated if not for prohibition.
- The vast majority of local, state, and federal corrections costs related to drugs would be eliminated if not for prohibition.
- The statistic for drug abuse related illnesses is "a totally invented cost" (and it is, based on an assumption about how many people who use drugs for more than 100 days in their lives would get sick; ONDCP then multiplies that number by the cost of living index from the Bureau of Labor Statistics).[26]
- The crime careers statistic is also "entirely invented." Bennett explains: "This category is supposed to represent the costs of drug dealers and addicts not having regular jobs. If all drugs . . . were regulated the same way, these people would either get regular jobs or continue to commit crimes to maintain their lifestyles."[27]

We agree that those costs related to drug abuse related illnesses are mostly attributable to the drug war, as are the costs associated with the crime careers numbers. Sickness and death are largely due to the illicit nature of drug use and lost wages due to profitable drug crimes are largely the result of the illicit nature of drugs. Bennett concludes that, no matter how you look at it, "it is costing a lot more to fight [the] drug war than drug is supposedly costing us."[28]

What is most important about how ONDCP treats statistics here is that it simply invents a dollar figure for financial costs due to premature deaths, illnesses, and crime careers. Coupled with treating drug war costs as costs of drug use and abuse, ONDCP is able to use statistics to generate alarm about the harmful nature of drugs.

It is interesting to examine the list of drug-related harms created by the National Academy of Sciences's Committee on Data and Research for Policy and Illegal Drugs. They include:

- Physical/mental illnesses
- Diseases transmitted to others
- Accident victimization
- Health care costs (drug treatment)
- Health care costs (drug-related illnesses, injuries)
- Reduced performance in school

- Reduced performance at the workplace
- Poor parenting, child abuse
- Psychopharmacological crime and violence
- Economically motivated crime and violence
- Fear and disorder caused by users and dealers
- Criminal justice costs
- Corruption of legal authorities
- Strain on source-country relations
- Infringements on liberty and privacy
- Violation of the law as an intrinsic harm.[29]

Many of these harms could also better be considered drug war costs. The authors of the committee's report concur: "No responsible analysis of the harmful consequences of drug use can ignore the possibility that many of the harms of drug use are either caused or augmented by the legal prohibition against these drugs and its enforcement." Among those discussed by the committee include government intrusion into the lives of citizens, an increased likelihood of drug overdose, an increased likelihood of illness an death due to sharing illegal syringes, and crime and violence due to the high price of illegal drugs.[30]

Thus, in prohibition, increased dangers of illicit drugs could lead to increased physical illness and increased propensity for diseases transmitted to others. This would account for additional health care costs due to drug-related illnesses, as well. Economically motivated crime and violence is surely increased by higher prices in a prohibitory scheme, as fear and disorder attributed to an illegal drug market are in neighborhoods. This would account for higher criminal justice costs. Corruption of legal authorities also thrives on the drug war, as it did during alcohol prohibition. Finally, legal rulings empowering law enforcement to fight the war on drugs infringes on civil liberties and personal privacy.

Deaths

2000–2001 Strategy

In the 2000 and 2001 versions of the Strategy, ONDCP presents statistics related to drug deaths and emergency room mentions of drug use as proof of the dangers of illicit drugs (but not as evidence of a failure to meet its goal of healing drugs users or to reduce costs of drug use and abuse).

Figures in the 2000 Strategy show increased drug-induced deaths every year from 1990 through 1997.[31] The 2001 Strategy also shows continued increases in drug-induced deaths through 1998. ONDCP writes:

Illegal drug use is responsible for the deaths of thousands of Americans annually. In 1997, the latest year for which death certificate data are published, there were 15,973 drug-induced deaths in America. Drug-induced deaths result directly from drug consumption, primarily overdose. In addition, other causes of death, such as HIV/AIDS, are partially due to drug abuse. Using a methodology that incorporates deaths from other drug-related causes, ONDCP estimates that in 1995 there were 52,624 drug-related deaths. This figure includes 14,218 drug-induced deaths for that year, plus mortalities from drug-related causes. SAMHSAs Drug Abuse Warning Network (DAWN) collects data on drug-related deaths from medical examiners in forty-one major metropolitan areas. DAWN found that drug-related deaths have steadily climbed throughout the 1990s.[32]

A steady climbing of drug-related deaths in the United States in the 1990s is inconsistent with ONDCP's goal of reducing health and social costs to the public of illegal drug use and its objective of reducing drug-related health problems. Yet, ONDCP does not admit or even address this. In footnotes, ONDCP attempts to expand the number of deaths due to illegal drugs by explaining the various ways in which drugs can kill people:

> Overdose deaths, including accidental and intentional drug poisoning, accounted for 90 percent of drug-induced mortalities in 1995. Other drug-induced causes of death involved drug psychoses, drug dependence, and nondependent use of drugs. . . . Based on a review of the scientific literature, 32 percent of HIV/AIDS deaths were drug-related and included in the estimate of drug-related deaths. The following were also counted: 4.5 percent of deaths from tuberculosis, 30 percent of deaths from hepatitis B; 20 percent of deaths from hepatitis non-A/non-B; 14 percent of deaths from endocarditis; and 10 percent of deaths from motor vehicle accidents, suicide (other than by drug poisoning), homicide, and other deaths caused by injuries.[33]

2002 Strategy

The 2002 Strategy also shows increases in drug-induced deaths — "19,102 people died in 1999 (or 52 such deaths per day) . . . as the direct result of drug-induced causes . . . there was a steady increase in drug-induced deaths between 1990 and 1998 — from 9,463 to 16,926."[34] In fact, most of these deaths are not actually *caused* by illicit drugs.

Independent researcher Brian Bennett examines Centers for Disease Control Mortality Data and claims:

> In summary, over the 20 year period 1979-1998, slightly more than one-tenth of one percent of *all* deaths in the US were due to the use of illegal drugs. During that time, a total of 214,575 deaths were called *drug-induced*--but only 21 percent of these were due to the use of 'illegal' drugs [or 2,236 deaths per year]. Of the 44,727 deaths attributed to illegal drug use, 22,735 were caused by accidental heroin overdose . . . while another 15,551 died from accidental cocaine overdose. . . . That is a total of 38,286 (or 86 percent) of all deaths due to illegal drugs. One has to wonder how greatly this number of *accidental* deaths could be reduced if the people using the drugs had products of known quality and dosage to work with.[35]

2003-2005 Strategy

Beginning with the 2003 Strategy, ONDCP simply does not discuss drug-induced deaths in its Strategy reports. They thus have been removed by ONDCP from its policy evaluations. Because of this, we examined statistics on deaths attributable to illicit drugs and found that they are increasing. We created Figure 6.2 to show the rising number of deaths directly attributable to illicit drugs. Deaths attributable to illicit drugs have generally and consistently risen since the creation of ONDCP in 1988.[36]

That more people are dying from illicit drugs every year suggests either that more people are using illegal drugs or that illicit drugs are becoming more dangerous to users. Remember, one policy goal of ONDCP is to create "inconsistent quality" of drugs. Thus, the illicit nature of drugs guarantees that the contents of illicit drugs will remain unknown and unpredictable, and seems to assure that more people will die as a result of drug use. This runs counter to the drug war goal of healing America's drug users and serves to increase the costs of the drug war.

Many scholars claim that there would be less death and sickness related to illicit drug use if drugs were legally available and regulated for safety.[37] If true, these outcomes can be understood as costs of the prohibitionist war on drugs policy. Out of curiosity, we decided to try to determine if drugs were more dangerous in 2000 than in 1979. Although the number of deaths attributable to illicit drugs has increased since 1979, this could be either due to a larger population in the United States or a larger drug-using population. We chose 1979 because it was the peak in illicit drug use and 2000 because this was the last year for which data were available on deaths attributable to illicit drugs at the time of this writing.

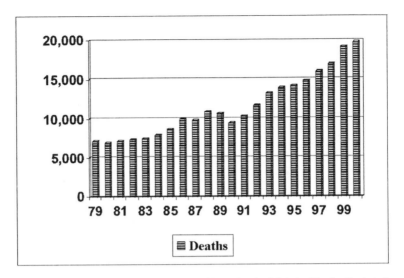

FIGURE 6.2   Deaths Attributable to Drugs (Sourcebook of Criminal Justice Statistics)

The U.S. population in 1979 was 225,055,487 people and in 2000 was 281,421,906 people.[38] The U.S. population thus grew 25% between 1979 and 2000.

There were 7,101 drug-induced deaths in 1979 and 19,698 drug-induced deaths in 2000. The number of drug-induced deaths was thus 177% larger in 2000 than in 1979. This means that the increase in drug-induced deaths (177%) is not attributable to population growth (25%) in the United States. In fact, when controlling for population size, the rate of drug-induced death in 2000 (7.0 deaths per 100,000 people) was 122% larger than in 1979 (3.16 deaths per 100,000 people).

Ironically, there were many more drug-induced deaths in 2000 than in 1979, even though there were far fewer current drug users in 2000 (14 million) than 1979 (25.4 million). Therefore, we calculated the drug-induced death rate per user in 1979 (27.96 deaths per 100,000 users) and compared it with the drug-induced rate per current user in 2000 (140.7 deaths per 100,000 users) and found that drug-induced deaths per current drug user were 403% more common in 2000 than in 1979. This suggests that current drug users were four times more likely in 2000 to die from a drug-induced death than current drug users in 1979. This is inconsistent with ONDCP's goal of making drug users healthy. To provide some context for what this means, consider this: Had the death rate per drug user remained constant from 1979 until 2000, only one-quarter of the 19,698 drug use deaths would have occurred in 2000 — meaning 4,924 drug-induced deaths instead of 19,698. The increased deadly nature of drugs under prohibition led to 15,000 more deaths in 2000 than would have occurred had prohibition not made drugs more dangerous, assuming every-thing else remained constant.

Using ONDCP's statistics shows that the drug war appears to be making drug use more deadly, thereby increasing the costs of drug use and abuse. Two drug policy experts concur, saying, "the data suggest that the general health status of cocaine and heroin addicts is worsening, even if their numbers are not rising."[39]

Emergency Room Mentions

2000–2002 Strategy

The 2000 Strategy shows increased emergency room mentions of drug use since 1988.[40] In the 2001 Strategy, ONDCP asserts:

> The number of emergency department drug episodes has been in-creasing over the 1990s. In 1999, there were an estimated 554,932 drug-related ED episodes in the United States, compared to 371,208 in 1990, a 49 percent increase. Alcohol in combination with drugs con-tinued to be the most frequently mentioned (196,277) in ED reports. Cocaine continued to be the most frequently mentioned illicit drug, comprising 30 percent of episodes (168,763 mentions) in 1999. Co-caine was followed in frequency by marijuana/hashish (16 percent, 87,150 mentions) and heroin/morphine (15 percent, 84,409). In 1999, marijuana/hashish mentions exceeded heroin/morphine mentions, changing a rank ordering of illicit drug mentions that had been con-stant since 1990.[41]

The 2001 Strategy also shows that emergency room mentions of mari-juana, heroin, and cocaine are again up through 1999.[42] The 2002 Strategy mentions the following statistics with regard to emergency room mentions of illicit drug use: "The roughly 470 emergency rooms participating in the Drug Abuse Warning Network [DAWN] give a sense of the scope of the problem — roughly 175,000 emergency room incidents related to cocaine each year, while heroin and marijuana are each implicated in roughly 97,000 incidents."[43]

2003–2005 Strategy

The 2003 Strategy presents a single statistic about emergency room mentions. It shows a figure that depicts a "steep increase in emergency department men-tions of marijuana" from 1990 to 2001.[44] The 2004 and 2005 Strategy reports

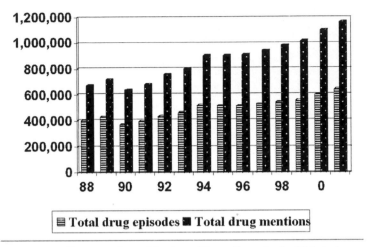

FIGURE 6.3   Emergency Room Mentions of Drugs (Sourcebook of Criminal Justice Statistics)

fail to discuss any statistics related to emergency room mentions. They, too, have been dropped from consideration by ONDCP from its policy evaluations.

Because of this, we examined statistics on emergency room mentions of illicit drugs and found that they are increasing. We created Figure 6.3 to depict the rising number of emergency room mentions associated with use of various drugs. The figure clearly shows rapid increases in emergency room mentions of drugs since the creation of ONDCP.[45] These data indicate the total number of people seen for various drug-related reasons, including overdoses, unexplained reactions, seeking detoxification, chronic effects of drugs, withdrawal, accident or injury, unknown, and other. Note that both total drug mentions and total drug episodes increased.

Recall that ONDCP's goals through the 2002 Strategy included reducing health and social costs to the public of illegal drug use, and that one measurable objective was to reduce drug-related health problems. Statistical trends on deaths and emergency room mentions of drugs are thus moving in the wrong direction. Assuming that illness and death are not healthy outcomes for drug users, these outcomes run counter to the drug war goal of healing drug users. ONDCP has chosen to simply ignore these statistics.

DRUGS AND CRIME

As for crime, in the 2000 Strategy, ONDCP claims: "A large percentage of the twelve million property crimes committed each year in America are drug-related, as are a significant proportion of nearly two million violent crimes."[46] Later, ONDCP writes that many crimes are actually "committed under the influence of drugs and alcohol or may be motivated by a need to obtain money for drugs. Substance abuse is frequently a contributing factor in family violence, sexual assaults, and child abuse."[47] In fact, the largest share of drug arrests for any year is for alcohol.[48]

A figure is offered that claims "Drug Use Correlates With Crime." The figure simply depicts Arrestee Drug Abuse Monitoring (ADAM) data showing the majority of arrestees in cities across the country test positive for some drug, most often marijuana. ONDCP does not explain that this does not mean that drug use caused the criminality, or that a person can test positive for marijuana for a significant period of time after use.[49] A similar figure offered in the 2001 Strategy[50] is shown in Figure 6.4.

Two other figures in the 2000 Strategy show increases in drug abuse arrests from 1990 and declines in drug-related murders since 1990.[51] The implication may be that increased arrests have successfully reduced drug-related murders. Yet, ONDCP does not explain whether there is a meaningful relationship between drug arrests and drug murders. Since typically most arrests are for mere possession (usually around 80%), and since a large share of murders are drug dealers killing one another for the right to sell drugs, it is unlikely that there is a meaningful relationship between these statistics. For example, drug policy experts assert that about two-thirds of drug-related homicides are market-related and thus created by competition in an illegal marketplace where legal mechanisms for solving disputes are not available.[52] Similar figures are offered in the 2001 Strategy.[53] Figure 6.5 illustrates the implied relationship between drug arrests and drug murders.

It should be noted that in the 2004 Strategy, ONDCP denies that most incarcerations are for possession. It claims that the vast majority of prisoners

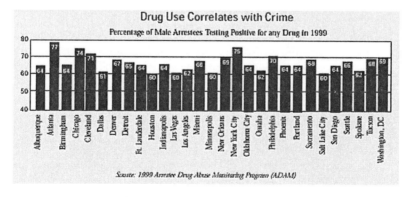

FIGURE 6.4 ONDCP Links Drug Use with Crime, 2001 Strategy

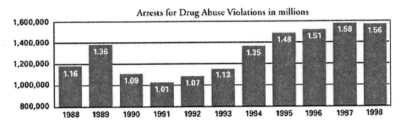

Drug-Related Arrests

Arrests for Drug Abuse Violations in millions

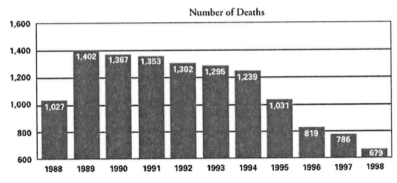

Drug-Related Murders

Number of Deaths

FIGURE 6.5   ONDCP Implies Drug Arrests Lead to Reduced Murders, 2000 Strategy

committed substantial trafficking offenses, not mere possession. It then offers statistics from the U.S. Sentencing Commission to prove its claim, reporting average quantities of drugs involved in *federal* drug trafficking cases.

It also writes: "The additional claim that law enforcement agencies are focused on locking up individuals for possession of, as opposed to trafficking in, illegal drugs is likewise inaccurate."[54] In support, ONDCP offers up statistics regarding *federal* drug cases. What is interesting about this is that the vast majority of drug cases are handled by local police (e.g., city police and county sheriffs), the majority of drug cases are handled by state courts, and the majority of drug incarcerations are at the state level. No local or state level statistics are offered by ONDCP.[55] This fits with ONDCP's basic use of statistics—if they are contradictory to the drug war and the claims ONDCP wants to promote, then leave them out or de-emphasize them.

Statistics from other sources seem to contradict ONDCP claims. According to the Bureau of Justice Statistics, data from 2001 show that 81% of all drug arrests in the United States were for possession, and 40% of all drug arrests were for possession of marijuana.[56] Further, consider the following information:

- Three-quarters of state prison inmates were convicted of drug and/or nonviolent crimes.
- More than one-third (35%) of drug inmates have criminal histories that are limited to drug offenses and 21% are first-time offenders.
- Most people sentenced to time in federal prisons for drug offenses are low-level (55%) or mid-level dealers (34%).
- Most sentenced drug offenders in state and federal prisons (58%) have no history of violence or high level drug activity.
- Nearly half (43%) of drug offenders in state prison were convicted of drug possession (27% for simple possession and 16% for possession with intent to distribute).[57]

We cannot know why ONDCP has chosen to ignore these statistics, but we suspect it is because they run counter to ONDCP's claims of a nonpunitive drug war.

The 2000 Strategy implies that drug use causes crime: "Two-thirds of sexual offenders in state prison were under the influence of alcohol or other drugs at the time of the crime."[58] In fact, the majority were under the influence of alcohol, a legal drug, so we do not understand why it is included in this statistic. ONDCP admits as much, saying: "Alcohol is implicated in more incidents of sexual violence, including rape and child molestation, than any other drug."[59] ONDCP likely includes alcohol in its figures in order to grow the statistic to "two-thirds."

The 2001 Strategy also implies that drug use causes crime. ONDCP claims a 1998 study found that "33 percent of state and 22 percent of federal prisoners said they committed their current offense while under the influence of drugs, and about one in six of both state and federal inmates said they committed their offense to get money for drugs."[60]

The 2001 Strategy notes that 16% of jail inmates in 1998 committed their offenses in order to obtain money to buy drugs.[61] There is no mention by ONDCP of the possibility that the illicit nature of drugs increases prices over what they would cost if legally available, thereby producing greater likelihood that people will commit crimes to obtain money for drugs.[62]

Further, it is claimed that: "Over 80 percent of all jail and state prison inmates said they had previously used drugs, and over 60 percent reported having regularly used drugs, i.e., and at least once a week for at least a month."[63] ONDCP cites a 1998 study that claimed "more than half of both jail (55 percent) and state prison (57 percent) inmates reported they had used drugs in the month before the offense."[64]

It is not surprising that ONDCP links drugs and crime. There is good statistical evidence that the two are related. For example, a large portion of arrestees in large cities test positive for illicit drugs, and many inmates in the nation's prisons and jails report having long histories with illicit drug use. These statistics "offer strong empirical evidence of a strong between drug use and the commission of violent crime. Correlation, however, does not imply causation."[65] According to the National Academy of Sciences Committee on Data and Research for Policy on Illegal Drugs: "Sources of data on drug use consequences are not well suited for supporting *causal* inferences. Indeed, the phrase, drug use consequences, is potentially misleading, as many apparent consequences may actually be spurious correlations."[66]

What is problematic is that ONDCP implies drugs cause crime. The evidence suggests this is simply not true. The relationship between illicit drugs and crime is far more complex than the "drugs cause crime" claim of ONDCP. Yet, illicit drugs have been linked to homicide, robbery, school violence, juvenile delinquency, and several property crimes.[67] The question is: Why? The major hypotheses of the drugs–crime relationship include:

1. Drug use causes crime.
2. Crime causes drug use.
3. Drug use and crime are caused by a third variable.
4. There is a reciprocal relationship between drugs and crime.[68]

There is no clear answer as to which of these hypotheses is most true. Evidence indicates that some drugs create a psychopharmacological effect that could logically lead to violent and/or criminal behaviors. There is also evidence that many drugs users committed crimes before they used drugs. There is also much evidence that many factors (from genetics, brain function and dysfunction, diet and nutrition, personality, intelligence levels, learning, parenting, peer influences, community characteristics, punishment, strain and stress, and many others) explain why people use drugs and commit crimes.[69] One possibility is that people who plan on being aggressive or violent may use drugs as either an excuse or a justification to embolden themselves to make the behavior possible.[70] If this is true, then it is not drugs that cause the behaviors but rather whatever caused the desire or need for violent or aggressive behaviors. Finally, it is also logical that many circumstances exist whereby drug use and criminal behavior feed off of each other and make the other more likely.

According to scholars, three main types of drug crimes include:

1. *Economic compulsive crime*—committing "economically-oriented violent crime, e.g., robbery, in order to support costly drug use."[71]

2. *Systemic crime*—"the traditionally aggressive patterns of interaction within the system of drug distribution and use" including "disputes over territory between rival drug dealers . . . assaults and homicides committed within dealing hierarchies as a means of enforcing normative codes . . . robberies of drug dealers and the usually violent retaliation by the dealer . . . elimination of informers . . . punishment for selling adulterated or phony drugs . . . punishment for failing to pay one's debts."[72]

3. *Psychopharmacological crime*—criminal behavior "as a result of short- or long-term ingestion of specific substances" that leads to a user becoming "excitable, irrational" and violent.[73]

Of these types, the smallest portion of drug crimes is psychopharmacological. The drug that most stands out for producing psychopharmacological violence is alcohol. Among other things, alcohol "lowers inhibitions, impairs judgment and motor coordination, and heightens aggression in certain situations." It has been linked to homicide, assault (including spousal assault/domestic violence), and child abuse.[74] Those under the influence of alcohol "assault family members, commit sex-related crimes, and perpetuate homicides or other violent acts." Additionally, "the drug selected most frequently by American males to ratchet up and excuse their aggressivity is alcohol."[75]

We do not see such psychopharmacological relationships with violent outcomes and many illicit drugs—most notably marijuana. For example, the National Commission on Marijuana and Drug Abuse, created in 1970, "gathered and analyzed massive quantities of data" over three years and published findings in six volumes. The results of one particular study of the effects of marijuana use on the behavior of more than 500 males between the ages of fifteen and thirty-four years "directly contradicted the assumptions and preconceived biases of the Congress and the Commission." Users rarely felt angry while on the drug or felt the urge to hurt someone, and use of marijuana typically made users "feel more peaceful and passive than before use."[76] The same study found that marijuana users committed more nonviolent offenses, but not that the marijuana use caused the criminal behaviors.

ONDCP's greatest efforts to reduce drug use have probably been focused on marijuana. This is likely due to its belief in the so-called gateway hypothesis. This is really an assumption by some, including ONDCP, that young people begin drug use with marijuana, and then eventually move on to harder drugs such as cocaine and heroin, which then could lead to criminal careers to support drug habits. ONDCP has in the past claimed that marijuana is a gateway drug, and they cite as evidence the statistic that most users of cocaine and heroin have used marijuana in the past. However, this does not support the gateway hypothesis. What would support the hypothesis is if most users of marijuana moved on to other (harder) drugs, which does not occur. Most users of marijuana never try another (harder) drug.

According to the experts, it is not typical for marijuana users to go on to harder, more dangerous, and more expensive drugs. For those who do, it is difficult to establish a causal relationship.[77] There are, in fact, at least seven interpretations of the data, including that the relationship between marijuana use and other drug use is mostly spurious, explained by other factors such as individual propensities and environmental opportunities.[78]

Some illicit drugs, including cocaine, heroin, PCP, and inhalants, may be more prone to violent or other aggressive behaviors due to effects of the drugs on the brain.[79] Others may include stimulants and barbiturates.[80]

Yet, most drug crimes are not caused by the effects of the drugs themselves but instead by their illicit nature. One scholar explains: "Because of the costliness of heroin and cocaine, it is assumed that users must resort to robbery, burglary, car theft, shoplifting, or selling drugs to pay for their habit."[81] Typically, drug crimes are *secondary crimes* committed to obtain money to buy drugs: "Many researchers have concluded that the prevalence and diversity of criminal involvement by narcotics addicts are high, and that this involvement is primarily for the purpose of supporting the use of drugs."[82] Further, the war on drugs, if successful at increasing price but not reducing demand, "will have little effect on consumption but will increase the drug sellers' earning . . . [and] may also increase property crimes by consumers who need more money to buy higher-priced drugs."[83] Of course, people also get arrested for possessing, manufacturing, and selling drugs. Each of these crimes exists only because of the criminal law.

ONDCP discusses crime and drugs in depth in its fact sheet titled *Drug-Related Crime*. The fact sheet is located on ONDCP's Web site.[84] In this fact sheet, ONDCP suggests caution in interpreting drugs-crime relationships, which seems to run counter to what ONDCP does in its Strategy reports (through 2002 when crime is discussed). It also lays out types of relationships between drugs and crime, including:

- *Drug-defined offenses*—Violations of laws prohibiting or regulating the possession, use, distribution, or manufacture of illegal drugs (examples: drug possession or use; marijuana cultivation; methamphetamine production; cocaine, heroin, or marijuana sales).
- *Drug-related offenses*—Offenses to which a drug's pharmacologic effects contribute, offenses motivated by the user's need for money to support continued use, and offenses connected to drug distribution itself (examples: violent behavior resulting from drug effects; stealing to get money to buy drugs; violence against rival drug dealers).

- *Drug-using lifestyle* — A lifestyle in which the likelihood and frequency of involvement in illegal activity are increased because drug users may not participate in the legitimate economy and are exposed to situations that encourage crime (example: a life orientation with an emphasis on short-term goals supported by illegal activities; opportunities to offend resulting from contacts with offenders and illegal markets; criminal skills learned from other offenders).[85]

Careful reading of ONDCP's drugs-crimes relationships shows that most types of drug-related crime are due to prohibition. For example, all drug-defined offenses are due to prohibition, for, if not illegal, these acts would not be crimes. Most drug-related offenses are also the result of prohibition. Since prohibition raises prices above what they would be if not illegal, many and probably most "offenses motivated by the user's need for money to support continued use" are due to prohibition. Most "offenses connected to drug distribution itself" are also due to prohibition, for dealers must take precautions to protect their investments, even using violence when necessary. Additionally, the drug-using lifestyle is mostly due to prohibition. It is the law that excludes drug users — even functional and recreational users — to become "exposed to situations that encourage crime." Since drugs are illegal, users are forced to make and maintain contact with criminals in order to obtain their drugs. This leads to a higher probability of criminal activity on the part of users due to the contact with the criminal world. That is, drug use is sometimes part of a criminal lifestyle, and it is so because drug use is illegal. The only type of drug offense not explicitly due to prohibition in ONDCP's categories are the "offenses to which a drug's pharmacologic effects contribute."

What is interesting is that most researchers are more cautious than ONDCP in drawing conclusions about the effects of drugs on crime. For example, in terms of research on psychopharmacological violence, one researcher concludes: "The incidence . . . is impossible to assess . . . both because many instances go unreported and because when cases are reported, the psychopharmacological state of the offended is seldom reported in official records."[86] In other words, there are no valid statistics one way or another. Likewise, with regard to the incidence of economic compulsive violence, "no national criminal justice data bases contain information on the motivations or drug-use patterns of offenders as they relate to specific crimes."[87] ONDCP ignores the absence of statistics and implies that drug use causes crime.

We can be confident that "the drug laws are themselves criminogenic. Prohibition causes crime because it enormously inflates the actual cost of producing and distributing drugs, leaves drug markets without regulation, fosters rivalries between distributors, corrupts police, and artificially enlarges demand."[88] Therefore, "most drug-related violence is actually caused by prohibition."[89]

ONDCP at times admits in the Strategy that the illicit nature of drugs produces bad outcomes for abusers. For example, the 2003 Strategy notes that "addicts must spend almost all their disposable income on illegal drugs, and a disrupted market with unreliable quality and rising prices for drugs such as cocaine and heroin does not magically enable them to earn, beg, borrow, or steal more."[90] In other words, when prices rise, drug addiction increases financial difficulties for abusers. This leads to more panhandling and criminal victimization for the rest of us when drug abusers are unable to earn enough to provide for their drug habits.

ONDCP, through its Strategy, links drugs to other problems, including increased promiscuity, sexual activity, risk of sexually transmitted diseases, unplanned pregnancies, school failure, neglectful parenting, child maltreatment, victimization, homelessness, mental illness, juvenile delinquency and criminality, and even terrorism.

The 2002 Strategy asserts that "12 of the 28 international terrorist groups listed by the U.S. Department of State are alleged to be involved to some degree in drug trafficking."[91] Versions of the Strategy, including 2003, stress the relationship between the illicit drug trade and terrorism in countries such as Colombia and Afghanistan. It should be noted that virtually all drug-funded terrorist groups rely on the illicit nature of drugs to assure their portion of the market. That is, it could also be argued that the drug war produces terrorism. ONDCP does not consider this possibility. Furthermore, ONDCP does not address the fact that drug production has been linked to U.S. allies in Colombia and Afghanistan, as well as government officials in many other countries. Not all of the drug profiteers are "bad guys" in U.S. eyes.

Finally, ONDCP's National Drug Control Strategy never has, to our knowledge, discussed all types of costs associated with the drug war. Although the Strategy formerly discussed burdens to criminal justice agencies and heightened racial disparities, these considerations are removed from the most recent versions. Further, ONDCP does not discuss erosions to civil liberties and the vast corruption allegedly caused by the war on drugs, nor does it consider threats to the sovereignty of other nations, degradation of the environment (including food and water) in countries where we spray crops with deadly chemicals, and cutbacks to social services and education that occur with increased funding for the war on drugs. In short, ONDCP's analysis of the drug war does not fully consider the many costs often associated with the policy of waging war on drugs. We turn to these in the chapter 7. For this reason, the ONDCP Strategy cannot be claimed to be a valid tool for policy analysis or evaluation of the drug war.

Part Three

Chapter Seven

A Fair Assessment of
America's Drug War

In this chapter, we conduct a fair assessment of America's drug war. We assess ONDCP's ability to reduce drug use, heal drug users, disrupt illicit drug markets, reduce drug-related crime and violence, and reduce health and social costs to the public. From the previous chapters, it is clear that America's drug war, led by ONDCP, is not achieving such goals consistently. In this chapter, our assessment focuses on a ten year period, from the year after ONDCP was created (1989) until the last year for which all statistics on drug use trends were comparable (1998). Here, we evaluate the objectives of ONDCP based on data and statistics relevant to each of these goals. We conclude with a discussion of the costs and benefits of the drug war in an effort to determine whether the benefits are worth the costs.

As noted earlier, the Office of National Drug Control Policy (ONDCP)—as the primary federal agency responsible for establishing "policies, priorities, and objectives for the Nation's drug control program . . . to reduce illicit drug use, manufacturing, and trafficking, drug-related crime and violence, and drug-related health consequences"[1]—is the one agency that can be held accountable for the effectiveness or ineffectiveness of America's drug war. Its Web site notes: "By law, the Director of ONDCP also *evaluates*, coordinates, and oversees both the international and domestic anti-drug efforts of executive branch agencies and ensures that such efforts sustain and complement State and local anti-drug activities."[2] That is, ONDCP is *legally* required to evaluate its own performance.

For example, the Office of National Drug Control Policy Reauthorization Act of 1998, passed by Congress, endorsed the ONDCP's Performance Measures of Effectiveness (PME) system. As noted in chapter 3, the PME system was "designed in 1997 to inform the drug control community about the extent to which it achieves the . . . Strategy's goals and objectives and to assist in the clarification of problem areas and the development of corrective actions." The PME system was "endorsed by Congress . . . as the vehicle by which to assess strategic progress."[3]

The 1998 law "requires ONDCP to assess federal effectiveness in achieving the Strategy's goals and objectives, the key to which is the performance measurement system. The Congress explicitly linked the PME system to agency drug control programs and budgets."[4] Further, the law increased "ONDCP congressional reporting requirements" and required "annual reports on . . . progress in achieving the goals and objectives of the PME system."[5]

In referring to the PME system, the National Academy of Sciences' Committee on Data and Research for Policy and Illegal Drugs writes that "ONDCP deserves a great deal of credit for taking the first steps to assess the impact of current policies, including enforcement, on availability, use, and consequences."[6] While this is true, so, too, is the fact that ONDCP has not been using the PME system. The only year for which the ONDCP ever used the PME system to evaluate its effectiveness was for the 1998 Strategy. It issued three reports, in which trends in drug use, availability, age of first use, and so on, were evaluated from 1998 to 2000. The statistics cited in each of the three reports show that the drug war was failing to achieve its goals across the board.

The findings of the *Final Report of the PME System for the 1998 Strategy* concludes that the goals for demand reduction and prevention were "off track" as were goals for reducing youth drug and alcohol use. Similarly, goals related to drug supply reductions were also "off track."[7]

The only drug war goals that ONDCP claimed success were related to reducing crime and violent crime. Yet, ONDCP does not present data pertaining to drug-induced crimes, but instead uses "crime rates . . . for aggravated assault, robbery, and forcible rape . . . as proxies for drug involvement."[8] We must note that criminologists claim that widespread property crime declines from the 1970s to the present day and violent crime declines in the 1990s are mostly attributable to factors beyond the control of the criminal justice system and the war on drugs. Some examples include economic improvement, an aging population, and even legalized abortion.

The 2002 Strategy claims that "ONDCP will continue to bring accountability to drug control programs through the use of the ONDCP's Performance Measures of Effectiveness System [PME] which measures the results of federal drug control programs."[9] Yet, there is no evaluation other than for one year.

According to the second of three PME reports:

> For most targets, 1996 was chosen as the base year against which progress toward achieving 2002 and 2007 end-states is measured. . . .

The year 1996 corresponds to the first introduction of the *Strategy's* five goals; 2002 corresponds to interim policy targets and 2007 corresponds to the culmination of the 10-year *Strategy* first published in February 1998 (covering 1998 through 2007). . . . However, the PME System does not begin its assessment of progress until 1998, reflecting the time at which the system became operational and the publication of the ten-year *Strategy* (1998 through 2007).[10]

It appears that ONDCP claims it began its assessment in 1998, when in fact it began *and ended* its assessment in 1998. This is strange considering that the ONDCP is expected to report every year about its effectiveness through its PME system. In the 2002 National Drug Control Strategy, the ONDCP claims that

ONDCP will *continue to bring accountability* to drug control programs through the use of the ONDCP's Performance Measures of Effectiveness System [PME] which measures the results of federal drug control programs. In so doing, the Administration will be able to make better informed management and policy decisions about resource allocation. Working from our fundamental aim — to reduce drug use in America — the Administration will measure its success, at the policy level with drug use data, and at the program level with relevant indicators. This performance management system will help direct our efforts to effective programs and point the way to improvement for programs that underperform. . . . The Administration is *committed to accountability* in government. Drug policy will be no exception.[11]

The government does not explain why it fails to use the PME. Lacking this, we provide our own assessment. We evaluate the goals of ONDCP to (1) reduce drug use; (2) heal drug users; (3) disrupt illicit drug markets; (4) reduce drug-related crime and violence; and (5) reduce health and social costs to the public. While the National Drug Control Strategy has put forth different goals over the years, these five goals consistently appeared during the time period of this analysis. We use data from 1989 (the year after ONDCP was created) through 1998 (the last year for which drug use trends from the National Household Survey on Drug Abuse are comparable). When data are unavailable from 1989, we use 1990 data.

Our assessment shows that ONDCP failed to meet its goals during the ten-year period from 1989 to 1998. This allows us to assess the effectiveness of the ONDCP over a ten-year period, the first ten years of its existence.[12]

It is important to note that an analysis of ONDCP's effectiveness must be conducted against ONDCP's expectations. In the PME reports, ONDCP makes clear what its expectations are. The thing that stands out most (aside from the finding that ONDCP clearly admits that its drug war is not achieving any of its drug-related goals) is that ONDCP expects *consistent* declines in drug use, drug availability, and health and social costs of illicit drug use, as well as *consistent* increases in average age of first use of drugs. None of these occurred in the time period of the PME study. In this chapter, we will be able to see if any of them have occurred since.

Reducing Drug Use

Figure 7.1 shows lifetime drug use trends from 1990 to 1998 as captured by the National Household Survey on Drug Abuse (NHSDA), now called the National Survey on Drug Use and Health (NSDUH).[13] This figure depicts the percentage of Americans who admitted to having ever tried an illegal drug at least once in their lives. It illustrates that, over the period of study, there clearly were no declines in lifetime drug use among Americans. This is true for marijuana, cocaine, hallucinogens, inhalants, as well as crack and heroin (not pictured).[14] Specifically, lifetime use of marijuana and hallucinogens rose, lifetime use of inhalants was steady, and lifetime use of cocaine fell, although slightly.

Figure 7.2 shows current drug use trends from 1990 to 1998 as captured by the National Household Survey on Drug Abuse (NHSDA). This figure indicts the percentage of Americans who admitted to having tried an illegal drug at least once in the past month. The figure includes measures for those over the age of 12 years, as well as for adolescents (12–17 years). This figure illustrates that,

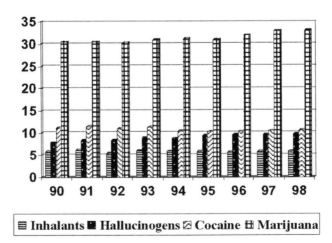

FIGURE 7.1   Lifetime Drug Use Trends, Percentages Who Used
Inhalants, Hallucinogens, Cocaine, and Marijuana (NHSDA)

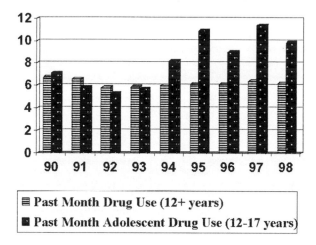

FIGURE 7.2   Current Drug Use Trends, Percentages Who Used Any Drug (NHSDA)

over the period of study, a slight decline in current drug use has occurred, but also indictes a simultaneous and larger increase for past-month drug use among adolescents.

Figure 7.3 shows the total number of new users of various illicit drugs from 1989 to 1998. While these data do not control for population growth and are thus not indicative of rate growth in drug use, they nevertheless illustrate growing numbers of new users of marijuana, hallucinogens, and inhalants. The

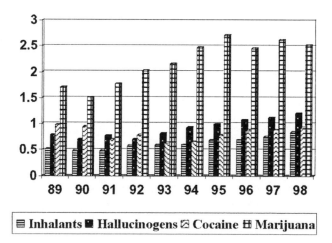

FIGURE 7.3   Total Number of New Users in Millions of Inhalants, Hallucinogens, Cocaine, and Marijuana (NHSDA)

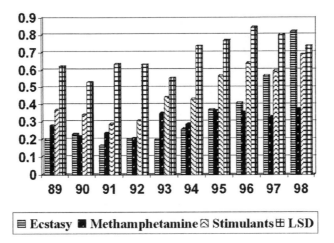

FIGURE 7.4   Total Number of New Users in Millions of Ecstasy,
Methamphetamine, Stimulants, and LSD (National Household Survey
on Drug Abuse)

number of cocaine users is virtually steady over the ten year period.
Figure 7.4 shows the total number of new users of other illicit drugs from 1989
to 1998. This figure illustrates growing numbers of new users of stimulants,
methamphetamine, LSD, and Ecstasy.

Figure 7.5 shows the total number of new users of additional illicit drugs
from 1989 to 1998. This figure illustrates growing numbers of new users of heroin, tranquilizers, sedatives, and pain relievers.

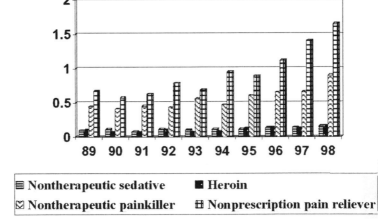

FIGURE 7.5   Total Number of New Users in Millions of Nontherapeutic Sedatives,
Nontherapeutic Painkillers, Nonprescription Pain Relievers, and Heroin (NHSDA)

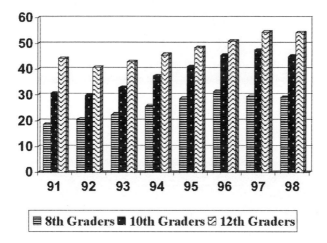

FIGURE 7.6   Lifetime Drug Use Trends, Percentages Who Used Any Drug (MTF)

The only drugs that did not see increases in new users were PCP and crack cocaine, which were both stagnant during the period (not pictured).[15]

Figure 7.6 shows lifetime drug use trends from 1991 to 1998 as captured by the Monitoring the Future Survey (MTF).[16] This figure shows the percentage of eighth, tenth, and twelfth graders who admitted to having ever tried an illegal drug at least once in their lives. It illustrates that, over the period of study, lifetime drug use among middle- and high-school age children increased. This was true for eighth, tenth, and twelfth graders.

Increases in lifetime drug use for eighth, tenth, and twelfth graders were seen for marijuana, hallucinogens, LSD, cocaine, crack cocaine, heroin, amphetamines, tranquilizers, as well as inhalants for eighth and tenth graders and several other drugs for twelfth graders.

Figure 7.7 shows current drug use trends from 1991 to 1998 as captured by the Monitoring the Future Survey (MTF). This figure shows the percentage of eighth, tenth, and twelfth graders who admitted to having tried an illegal drug at least once in the past month. It illustrates that, over the period of study, current drug use among middle- and high-school age children increased. This was true for eighth, tenth, and twelfth graders.

Increases in past-month drug use for eighth, tenth, and twelfth graders were seen for marijuana, hallucinogens, LSD, cocaine, crack cocaine, heroin, amphetamines, tranquilizers, as well as inhalants for eighth and tenth graders and several other drugs for twelfth graders.

Figure 7.8 shows the total amount of marijuana and cocaine consumed during the time period of study. While the amount of cocaine consumption

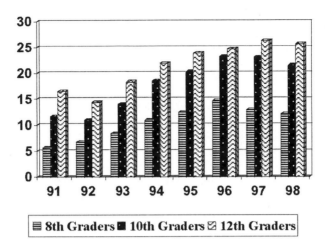

Figure 7.7   Current Drug Use Trends, Percentages Who Used Any Drug (MTF)

clearly fell, the amount of marijuana consumed rose slightly. Heroin consumption also fell during the period of study, while consumption of methamphetamine rose. Overall, drug consumption was up during the period.

In leading the nation's drug war, ONDCP would like young people to see illicit drugs as potentially (and actually) harmful to the user. It would also like

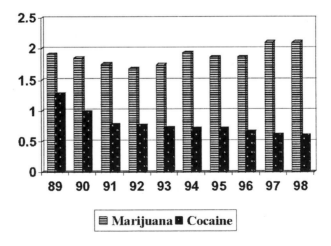

Figure 7.8   Total Amount of Marijuana and Cocaine Consumed (ONDCP)

young people to disapprove of illicit drug use. Ideally, increased perceptions of harmfulness of illicit drugs and increased disapproval of illicit drug use would lower actual use rates. Efforts to educate young people about the harmfulness of illicit drugs and to convince young people that they should disapprove of illicit drug use are part of ONDCP's effort to reduce drug use.

In terms of perceived harmfulness of illicit drugs and degree of disapproval of use of illicit drugs, the data are highly variable depending on the drug. Figure 7.9 shows trends in perceived harmfulness of various drugs for twelfth graders. First, note that there is a relatively high perception of harmfulness for occasional use of cocaine and chronic tobacco smoking, and that the trend is generally constant. Perceived harmfulness for regular use of cocaine is also very high, but declined slightly over the period of study.

Perceived harmfulness for occasional marijuana use and moderate alcohol use is much lower, and generally declined over the period of study.

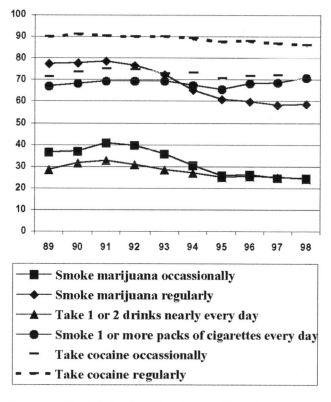

FIGURE 7.9 Trends in Perceived Harmfulness of Various Drugs for Twelfth Graders, Percentages Saying Great Risk (MTF)

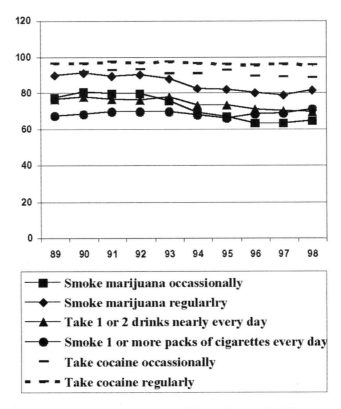

FIGURE 7.10   Trends in Disapproval of Various Drugs for Twelfth
Graders, Percentages Disapproving (MTF)

Perceived harmfulness for regular marijuana use also fell during the study.
Perceived harmfulness for LSD, PCP, crack, and barbiturates also fell during the study, whereas for heroin and amphetamines it was unchanged. The
same general trends were found for eighth and tenth graders from 1991 to
1998, as well.

Figure 7.10 shows trends in disapproval of various drugs for twelfth graders. First, note that there is a relatively high rate of disapproval for every drug
depicted in the figure. As with perceived harmfulness, trends in disapproval appear relatively constant. Disapproval of occasionally smoking marijuana declined, as did regularly smoking marijuana. Disapproval of taking one or two
drinks per day also declined, and so did disapproval of occasionally taking cocaine, although only slightly. Disapproval of regularly taking cocaine remained
constant. Disapproval of regularly smoking tobacco rose over the period of
study.

In terms of other drugs, disapproval of heroin and amphetamines remained unchanged, whereas disapproval of LSD, crack, and barbiturates declined during the period (not pictured). The same general trends were found for eighth and tenth graders from 1991 to 1998 as well.

In conclusion, the statistics show that most indicators of drug use (and likely future use) were not down during the period of 1989/1990 to 1998. Specifically:

- Lifetime use of illicit drugs by Americans did not generally decline. Lifetime use of marijuana and hallucinogens rose, while lifetime use of inhalants was steady and lifetime use of cocaine fell, although slightly.
- Current use of illicit drugs by Americans did not generally decline. Current use of illicit drugs for those twelve years and older declined slightly while there was a simultaneous and larger increase for past-month drug use among adolescents.
- New users of marijuana, hallucinogens, inhalants, stimulants, methamphetamine, LSD, Ecstasy, heroin, tranquilizers, sedatives, and pain relievers grew consistently, whereas the number of cocaine and PCP users was steady.
- Lifetime use of illicit drugs among eighth, tenth, and twelfth graders increased. This was true for marijuana, hallucinogens, LSD, cocaine, crack cocaine, heroin, amphetamines, tranquilizers, as well as inhalants for eighth and tenth graders and several other drugs for twelfth graders.
- Current use of illicit drugs by eighth, tenth, and twelfth graders increased. This was true for marijuana, hallucinogens, LSD, cocaine, crack cocaine, heroin, amphetamines, tranquilizers, as well as inhalants for eighth and tenth graders and several other drugs for twelfth graders.
- Total consumption of illicit drugs rose, as did consumption of marijuana and methamphetamine, while total consumption of cocaine and heroin fell.
- There is a relatively high perception of harmfulness for occasional use of cocaine and chronic tobacco smoking among high school students, and the trend is generally constant. Perceived harmfulness for regular use of cocaine is also very high, but slightly declined over the period of study. Perceived harmfulness for occasional marijuana use and moderate alcohol use is much lower, and generally declined over the period of study. Perceived harmfulness for regular marijuana use also fell during the study. Perceived harmfulness for LSD, PCP, crack, and barbiturates also fell during the study, whereas for heroin and amphetamines it was unchanged. The same general trends were found for eighth and tenth graders from 1991 to 1998 as well.

- There is a relatively high rate of disapproval for illicit drug use among high school students. Trends in disapproval appear relatively constant. Disapproval of occasionally smoking marijuana declined during the period of study, as did regularly smoking marijuana. Disapproval of taking one or two drinks per day also declined, and so did disapproval of occasionally taking cocaine, although only slightly. Disapproval of regularly taking cocaine remained constant. Disapproval of regularly smoking tobacco rose over the period of study. Disapproval of heroin and amphetamines remained unchanged, whereas disapproval of LSD, crack, and barbiturates declined during the period. The same general trends were found for eighth and tenth graders from 1991 to 1998 as well.

Keep in mind the limitations of drug use data discussed in chapter 3. To reiterate, the limitations to drug use data do not affect one's ability to assess long-term trends in drug use.

HEALING DRUG USERS

Recall that when ONDCP currently discusses healing drug users, it is referring to providing treatment for those drug users who need it. We already showed that ONDCP is failing to reduce deaths and illnesses associated with illicit drug use.

Little data are available with regard to the need for drug treatment in the United States, at least from ONDCP. Further, there was little emphasis placed on drug treatment by ONDCP until the 2002 National Drug Control Strategy. This flies in the face of its claim to be concerned with providing treatment to drug abuse.

Figure 7.11 shows the total number of drug admissions (including and excluding alcohol) in the United States from data provided by the Treatment Episode Data Set (TEDS), which is published by the Office of Applied Studies within the Substance Abuse and Mental Health Services Administration (SAMHSA).

The figure illustrates that the number of admissions for drug treatment, including alcohol and illicit drugs, increased during the period of study. The data do not suggest that more people sought treatment for drug problems, but rather show a slowly growing number of admissions for drug treatment over the period of study (because one person can be admitted more than one time).

It is difficult to conclude whether growth in admissions for drug treatment is a sign of success or failure. It is a sign of failure if it suggests that more

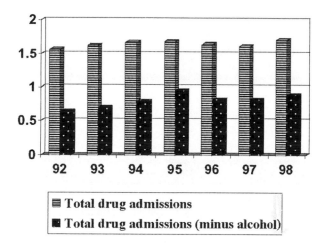

FIGURE 7.11   Total Number of Drug Admissions in Millions (Treatment Episode Data Set)

people have problems with drugs, especially illicit drugs. It is a sign of success if it means ONDCP is doing a better job at encouraging people to enter into treatment.

Although it is speculative, our educated guess is that ONDCP did not encourage more people to seek drug treatment during the late 1980s and the entire 1990s. There is simply no evidence to warrant such a conclusion. Indeed, this is perhaps the most punitive period of America's drug war. If we look at the glass as half full and conclude that growing number of admissions for drug treatment is a good sign, then the increase is far too small over a ten-year period to suggest much success at all. Indeed, the number of admissions for drug treatment was nearly stagnant.

What we do know is that, historically, there has been a "drug treatment gap" in the United States—most people who need drug treatment do not actually receive it.[17] In fact, one of the goals on ONDCP used to be to "reduce health and social costs to the public of illegal drug use by reducing the treatment gap."

Although we have no statistics to assess what was occurring during the period of our analysis, from 1989 to 1998, statistics from the 2000–2005 Strategy reports illustrate a growing number of people who need treatment for illicit drugs and no growth in the number of people who actually receive it.[18] According to the US Department of Health and Human Services, Substance Abuse and Mental Health Services Administration:

In 2003, the estimated number of persons aged 12 or older needing treatment for an alcohol or illicit drug problem was 22.2 million (9.3 percent of the total population). An estimated 1.9 million of these people (0.8 percent of the total population and 8.5 percent of the people who needed treatment) received treatment at a specialty facility. Thus, there were 20.3 million persons (8.5 percent of the total population) who needed but did not receive treatment at a specialty substance abuse facility in 2003. . . . In 2003, the estimated number of persons aged 12 or older needing treatment for an illicit drug problem was 7.3 million (3.1 percent of the total population). An estimated 1.1 million of these people (0.5 percent of the total population and 15.0 percent of the people who needed treatment) received treatment at a specialty facility for an illicit drug problem. Thus, there were 6.2 million persons (2.6 percent of the total population) who needed but did not receive treatment at a specialty facility for an illicit drug problem in 2003.[19]

It should be noted that the treatment gap is likely inflated. Two drug policy experts explain why:

The current methodology for calculating treatment gap has been in place only since 2000. From 1991 to 1998, treatment need was determined mainly from National Household Survey on Drug Abuse data on use patterns — how frequently respondents said they used drugs — rather than on indicators of a psychiatric diagnosis of dependence of abuse. Estimates of clients treated were based primarily on facility data, not NHSDA self-reports . . . one result of the methodological change has been a huge decrease in the estimated number of users receiving treatment and a correspondingly sizable increase in the treatment gap.[20]

In conclusion, the data suggest that access to drug treatment was not increased during the period of 1989/1990 to 1998. Specifically:

- The number of admissions for drug treatment, including alcohol and illicit drugs, increased only slightly during the period of study. Indeed, the number of admissions for drug treatment was nearly stagnant.
- There is a "drug treatment gap" in the United States, meaning most people who need drug treatment do not actually receive it. Only about 15% of the people who need treatment for an illicit drug receive it.

Disrupting Illicit Drug Markets

Figure 7.12 shows the total federal drug seizures and seizures of marijuana and cocaine from 1989 to 1998. Federal agencies seized more and more marijuana during that time period, but cocaine seizures were steady. Also keep in mind that the majority of marijuana being seized during this time period was ditch-weed, marijuana with so little THC that it cannot be smoked. Every year during the period of study, ditchweed made up between 94% and 99% of all marijuana seized.[21] Heroin seizures slightly increased during this period. Total pounds of drugs seized grew from 1.2 million pounds in 1989 to more than 2 million pounds in 1998.

Drug lab seizures by the Drug Enforcement Administration (DEA) from 1989 to 1998 increased during the last few years of the study, but almost all of the seizures during this time were of methamphetamine labs. Total drug lab seizures trended downward and then upward along with seizures of methamphetamine labs. The DEA made almost no seizures of labs for any other type of illicit drug during the time period.[22] Interestingly, removals from the domestic market of both marijuana and cocaine by the DEA fell during the time period. Heroin removals also fell during the time period.[23] Removals from the domestic market by the DEA of various other drugs were sporadic and generally declined. Fewer dosage units of stimulants, hallucinogens, and depressants were seized in 1998 than in 1989.[24]

However, seizures by the U.S. Customs Service increased from 1989 to 1998. Increases in seizures of marijuana were more pronounced than for

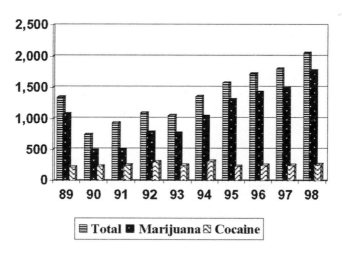

FIGURE 7.12   Total Federal Drug Seizures and Seizures of Marijuana and Cocaine (Federal-Wide Drug Seizure System)

cocaine. Seizures of heroin also grew during this period.[25] U.S. Customs (now called U.S. Customs and Border Protection, as part of the new Department of Homeland Security) was historically responsible for "ensur[ing] that all imports and exports comply with U.S. laws and regulations. The Service collects and protects the revenue, guards against smuggling, and is responsible for . . . [i]nterdicting and seizing contraband, including narcotics and illegal drugs."[26]

While federal drug control agencies, under the direction of ONDCP, seized and eradicated more drugs,[27] the key questions pertaining to disrupting illicit drug markets pertain to: (1) the availability of drugs; (2) prices of drugs; and (3) purity of drugs. That is, did all this activity make drugs less available? Did it raise the prices of drugs, thus driving down demand? And did it affect the purity of drugs? Implied in disrupting illicit drug markets are the objectives of making illicit drugs less available, raising illicit drug prices so that users will

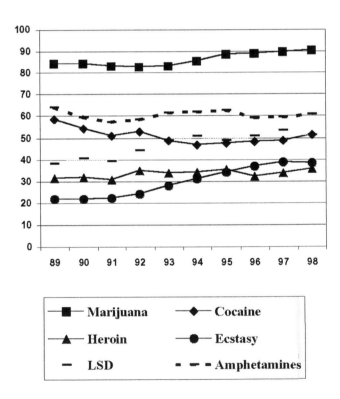

FIGURE 7.13   Trends in Perceived Availability of Drugs as Perceived by Twelfth Graders, Percentages Saying Fairly Easy or Very Easy to Obtain (MTF)

be less able to afford them, and presumably lowering the purity of illicit drugs so that they will offer less of a high to users (ONDCP also suggested that the drug war is aimed at making the purity of drugs less predictable but not necessarily lowering purity overall).

In terms of availability of illicit drugs, Figure 7.13 shows trends in availability as perceived by twelfth graders in the Monitoring the Future Survey (MTF). According to twelfth graders, the ease with which they could obtain illicit drugs in 1998 was no more difficult than in 1989. While some drugs became harder to obtain (e.g., cocaine, amphetamines), others became easier according to the data (e.g., marijuana, LSD, Ecstasy, and heroin). Generally, the availability of illicit drugs, according to the nation's twelfth graders, remains unchanged during the time period of study.

In terms of the price of illicit drugs, Figures 7.14 and 7.15 show prices for marijuana and cocaine, respectively, at various purchase levels from 1989 to 1998. Prices for marijuana and cocaine generally decreased, according to the data. Heroin prices also fell over the same period (not pictured). Overall consumer spending for marijuana and cocaine also fell during the period. Spending for heroin also fell, while spending for amphetamines increased.[28] Lower consumer spending is consistent with falling prices. Falling prices are inconsistent with disrupted markets.

In terms of purity of illicit drugs, Figures 7.16 and 7.17 depict purity trends of cocaine and marijuana, respectively, from 1989 to 1998. These figures illustrate

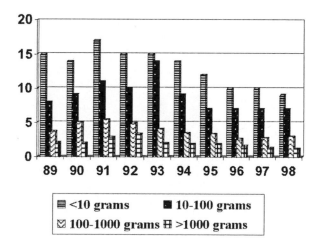

FIGURE 7.14   Trends in Prices for Marijuana at Various Purchase Levels (System to Retrieve Information from Drug Evidence)

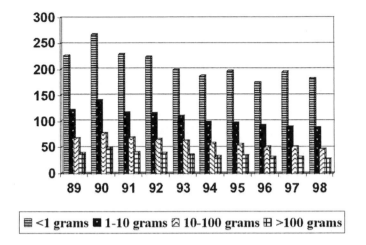

FIGURE 7.15   Trends in Prices for Cocaine at Various Purchase Levels (System to Retrieve Information from Drug Evidence)

that while the purity of cocaine generally fell during the period of study, the purity of marijuana generally rose, although not consistently. The purity of heroin also increased during the time period.

In conclusion, little in the data suggests that ONDCP is achieving its goal of disrupting illicit drug markets. Specifically:

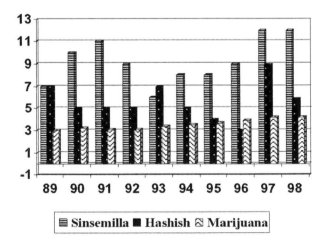

FIGURE 7.16   Trends in Purity of Marijuana, Percent THC Content (Bennett, Brian)

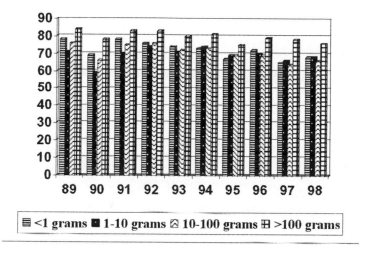

FIGURE 7.17 Trends in Purity of Cocaine, Percent Pure (Bennett, Brian)

- Federal seizures of marijuana and heroin increased, but cocaine seizures were steady.
- Drug lab seizures by the Drug Enforcement Administration (DEA) increased during the last few years of the study, but the DEA made almost no seizures of labs for any other type of illicit drug other than methamphetamine during the time period.
- Removals from the domestic market of both marijuana and cocaine by the DEA fell during the time period, as did removals of heroin.
- Removals from the domestic market by the DEA of stimulants, hallucinogens, and depressants generally declined.
- Seizures by the U.S. Customs Service increased from 1989 to 1998, especially for marijuana.
- The ease with which high school students could obtain illicit drugs in 1998 was no more difficult than in 1989. While some drugs became harder to obtain (e.g., cocaine, amphetamines), others became easier to obtain, according to the data (e.g., marijuana, LSD, Ecstasy, and heroin). Generally, the availability of illicit drugs remained unchanged during the time period of study.
- Prices for marijuana and cocaine generally decreased, as did prices for heroin.
- Overall consumer spending for marijuana and cocaine fell during the period, as did spending for heroin. Lower consumer spending is consistent with falling prices.

- While the purity of cocaine generally fell during the period of study, the purity of marijuana generally rose, although not consistently. The purity of heroin also increased during the time period.

Keep in mind the limitations of price data discussed in chapter 3. To reiterate, it is not clear whether the limitations to price data affect one's ability to assess long-term trends in drug prices. As for seizures, the National Academy of Sciences's Committee on Data and Research for Policy and Illegal Drugs affirms that "data on seizures alone should not be used to judge the effectiveness of enforcement."[29] This is because seizure data cannot tell us how much quantity of drugs are available, how much drugs are replaced when they are seized, and so forth.

Reducing Drug-Related Crime and Violence

Without a doubt, street crime declined in the period of study. Figure 7.18 shows trends in property crimes and violent crimes. Violent street crimes increased through 1994 and then declined from 1995 to 1998. There were large declines in rates of rape, robbery, and assault. Property crimes declined throughout the entire period of study, but they actually began to decline in 1975. There were large declines in burglary, theft, and motor vehicle theft.

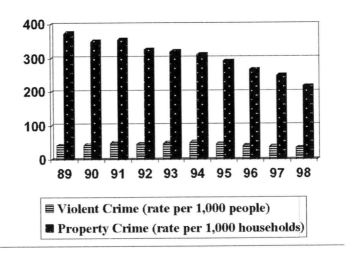

FIGURE 7.18   Trends in Property Crimes and Violent Crimes (Bureau of Justice Statistics)

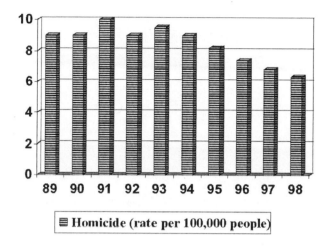

Figure 7.19   Trends in Homicide (Bureau of Justice Statistics)

Figure 7.19 illustrates the special case of homicide. Homicide rates rose from 1989 to 1991, declined in 1992, rose again in 1993, and then declined from 1994 to 1998.

The key question is to what degree did ONDCP play a role in these declines? Stated differently, to what degree is the war on drugs responsible for these declines? The answer is not clear, but logic and research suggests that the majority of the declines in street crime during the period of study were not only beyond the reach of ONDCP and the war on drugs, but were also not largely attributable to anything in criminal justice.

Several scholars have examined the causes of the crime declines in the 1990s.[30] Approximately 25% of the decline in crime in the 1990s can be attributed to the explosion in imprisonment that continued in the 1990s. More significant are such factors as improvements in the U.S. economy since the 1980s and the aging of the population. The authors of what is probably the most thorough of the books summarize what likely led to declines in street crime: "The number of very tenable explanations for the crime drop, none of which inherently excludes any of the others, leads to the conclusion that there is no single explanation but that a variety of factors, some independent and some interacting in a mutually supportive way, have been important."[31]

The factors analyzed in the book include economic improvement, an aging population, reductions in gun crimes, prison, and the stabilization of the illicit drug trade. The authors conclude that "no single factor can be invoked as *the* cause of the crime decline of the 1990s. Rather, the explanation appears to lie with a number of factors, perhaps none of which alone would have been sufficient and some of which might not have been of noticeable efficacy without reinforcement from others."[32]

The only factors reviewed that are related to the war on drugs are increasing imprisonment rates and the stabilization of the drug trade—specifically the ebbing of the crack cocaine epidemic. In terms of imprisonment rates, drug crimes were responsible for only about 20–25% of the increases in incarceration in the 1990s.[33] Therefore, the majority of incarcerations (and the subsequent reductions in crime) were for nondrug-related offenses.

In terms of stabilization, it could be argued that the drug war (and hence ONDCP) is responsible for the ebbing of the crack cocaine epidemic. As witnessed in chapter 6, ONDCP made efforts to link its drug war with falling crime rates, employing such tricks as using measures of ordinary street crime as indicators of drug-related crime, even when there was no evidence that the two were equivalent. ONDCP also showed how drugs and crime are correlated, implying that reductions in drug-related murders were related to increased drug crime arrests, even though the majority of people being arrested were arrested for possession.

As shown in chapter 2, scholarly analyses of the crack cocaine epidemic suggest that it ended in part because there never really was an epidemic, but instead the problem was blown out of proportion to the actual threat.[34] In terms of the real problem of crack, it is still there, alive and well in the nation's cities. America's focus on and concern over crack cocaine waned, in part because the violence associated with crack dealing faded.

Is ONDCP responsible for a less violent crack cocaine epidemic? The research suggests no. The available evidence suggests that when crack cocaine arrived in the nation's cities, dealers needed something to protect their investments and the enormous risk they were taking to sell the drug. Thus, guns flowed into cities and were used by dealers to protect their turf. The result was an increase in murders in the late 1980s and early 1990s.[35] As dealers were arrested, killed off, and so forth, eventually the crack cocaine market stabilized and the best dealers—the cream of the crop—rose to power and took over. As it currently stands, crack cocaine is still being sold in the nation's cities, yet the violence associated with the marketplace has greatly diminished through a process of evolution.

ONDCP and the mainstream media played a role in this by focusing the nation's attention on crack cocaine, as did the law enforcement community by focusing its resources on the problem. Yet, we should see these efforts as part of an inevitable process of reduced violence over time as the market naturally evolved for its survival. When there is a demand for a product, including crack cocaine, someone will find a way to provide it. ONDCP and mainstream media may have actually reduced demand for the drug, and the noxious nature of the drug itself also played a role in this, yet the reductions in violence were certain as the marketplace evolved.

In conclusion, there is no question that crime and violence declined during the period of study. There is great doubt, however, as to what degree ONDCP is responsible for these declines. What is clear is that most of the declines in street crime during the time period were due to changing social and economic factors that are beyond the reach of criminal justice and drug war agencies.

REDUCING HEALTH AND SOCIAL COSTS TO THE PUBLIC

We showed in chapter 6 that deaths from and emergency room mentions of illicit drugs both rose from 1989 to 1998. Assuming that dead and sick drug users are not healthy, then ONDCP is not healing drug users. Another social cost to the public is actual spending on the drug war. Figure 7.20 shows the budget of ONDCP from 1989 to 1998. As illustrated in the figure, the drug war budget has grown consistently during the period of study.

Keep in mind that during this same period of increased spending, drug use remained steady, perceived harmfulness of drugs generally fell or remained stable, disapproval of drug use generally fell or remained stable, seizures of drugs increased but drugs became no less available, drugs became less expensive, the number of admissions for drug treatment was nearly stagnant, most people who needed drug treatment did not receive it, crime and

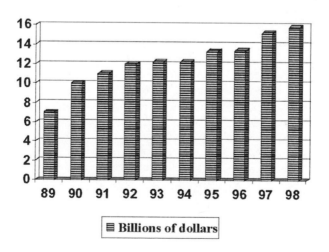

Figure 7.20   Trends in ONDCP's Budget from 1989 to 1998 (ONDCP)

violence declined but not due to the drug war, and more users died and became sick from using drugs.

In conclusion, the relevant statistics on health and social costs to the public clearly indicate that both health and social costs of the drug war have increased. This is opposite to the goals of ONDCP.

Costs of the Drug War

Analyses of the drug war almost uniformly conclude that the costs of the drug war outweigh its modest benefits.[36] The costs of the drug war include financial costs (as well as ONDCP budget and costs of criminal justice), reduced resources for social services and crime prevention, threats to civil liberties, increased violence, increased corruption, increased disrespect for the law, increased racial tensions and profiling, and increased civil unrest and terrorism.[37] Many have also suggested that since drugs are illegal, this raises prices for drugs over and above what they would be if drugs were legally available, and that the potency of drugs is heightened.[38] For example, experts with the National Academy of Sciences's Committee on Data and Research for Policy and Illegal Drugs conclude that "there is broad consensus that current enforcement policy has increased drug prices relative to what they would be otherwise."[39] Finally, it is clear that the drug war increases death and disease associated with drug use.

Further, mandatory sentencing of drug offenders can be blamed for some of the release of violent offenders from prisons each year. Because many drug offenders receive mandatory sentences, overburdened correctional facilities cannot release drug offenders early. Instead, more serious offenders must be released, including violent criminals. This is one way the war on drugs can create crime.[40]

Every resource invested into reducing drug use is a resource not invested in reducing other types of crime, including those that are the most damaging to society and the most costly to citizens—violent crimes and acts of corporate and white-collar crime. This is another cost of the drug war.

Figure 7.21 shows the percentage of all arrests for drug law violations from 1970 to 2002. Not only has the number of arrests increased, but so, too, has the percentage of all arrests that are drug-related—from 5.1% in 1970 to 11.1% in 2002. This means the war on drugs has become a larger burden on police agencies over the years.

Figure 7.22 depicts defendants charged and sentenced with drug crimes in federal courts from 1980 to 2003. The numbers have consistently increased over the years, placomg a larger burden on courts over the years.

Figure 7.23 shows the number of inmates incarcerated in federal prisons

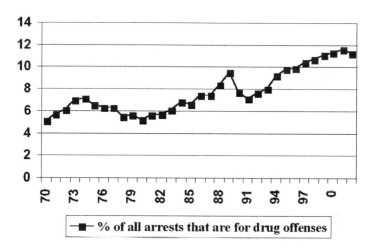

Figure 7.21 Percentage of All Arrests for Drug Law Violations (Sourcebook of Criminal Justice Statistics)

for drug offenses from 1980 to 2002. The number has consistently increased over the years, meaning the war on drugs has become a larger burden on correctional agencies over the years.

As arrests, convictions, and incarcerations have increased, the burden on criminal justice agencies and taxpayers has also increased. This leads to less

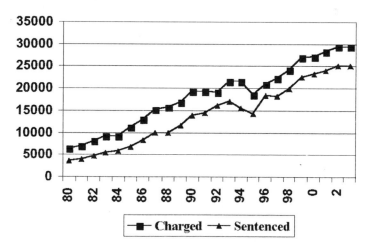

Figure 7.22 Defendants Charged and Sentenced with Drug Crimes in Federal Courts (Sourcebook of Criminal Justice Statistics)

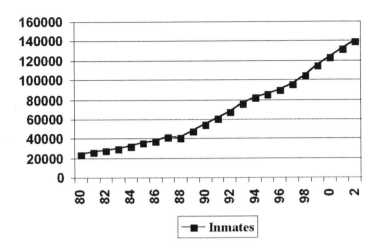

Figure 7.23   Number of Inmates Incarcerated in Federal Prisons for Drug
Offenses (Sourcebook of Criminal Justice Statistics)

effective crime prevention, less available resources of other needs, and ultimately higher state and federal taxes and budget deficits to pay for the costs
of the drug war.

There are also significant costs borne by non-U.S. citizens. For instance, strong evidence exists about the health and environmental consequences of U.S. eradication programs in Latin America (and elsewhere).
The loss of sovereignty is also of concern to many. In Mexico, U.S. agents
operate independently. In Colombia, the U.S. government is inextricably
connected to both the drug war and counterinsurgency. Countries that the
United States considers critical to drug policy must adopt programs that
satisfy the United States—or else face crippling sanctions in the drug cer-
tification process. Corruption, increased militarization, and allocation of
scarce money to American-dictated priorities are yet a few of the costs associated with the U.S. war on drugs. The cost to the United States in increased
anti-Americanism cannot be accurately calculated.

Other costs, which may or may not be important to the debate, include
threats to potential medicines such as marijuana, a marginalization of "normal" users, loss of potential tax revenue, and no employee protections for
those whose employment is provided by the illicit drug trade. While it is difficult to weigh these costs or put a dollar figure on them (other than the tens
of billions we spend each year fighting the drug war), the costs are enormous
and may outweigh the benefits of the drug war.

BENEFITS OF THE DRUG WAR

And just what are the benefits of the drug war? We have already seen that we are not achieving our goals of reducing drug use, healing drug users, or disrupting drug markets. So, what is being achieved?

Analyses of the drug war typically acknowledge that prohibition can lead to modest reductions in use.[41] That is, drug use is lower under prohibition than it would be in some other approach (e.g., legalization). Yet, as we have seen, this does not mean drug use is eliminated or even that it is consistently reduced until it reaches some minimum and acceptable level. Instead, drug use fluctuates over the years, despite what ONDCP does in the drug war. This includes rapid increases in many drugs, such as Ecstasy in the late 1990s and unprecedented increases of psychotherapeutics in the first six years of the twenty-first century.

Yet, there is some good news about drug use in the United States. In a country with more than 280 million people, there are now 19.5 million current illicit drug users, or 8.3% of the population. As shown in this chapter, there is a relatively high level of disapproval by young people of most forms of drug use. It is possible that disapproval of drug use would be lower, and that drug use and abuse would be higher, even substantially so, if drugs were legal (i.e., legal to buy, possess, and use, and marketed by private companies to consumers). It is actually quite amazing that less than 10% of Americans are current users of illicit drugs, given the wide availability of the substances, their relatively cheap prices, and that we are a free people.

Of course, another possibility is that drug use and drug abuse would not be higher even with less disapproval of use, if we pursued a policy of decriminalization or depenalization.[42] Some claim that decriminalization would actually lower rates of addiction. In this approach, possession and use of small amounts for personal use would be legal but manufacturing and selling would still be illegal, as would marketing and privatization of the drug trade.[43]

Assuming that the former is true—that drug use and abuse would be higher if there was no drug war—this still does not mean that the drug war does more good than harm. There is much evidence, even in the National Drug Control Strategy published every year by ONDCP, that costs associated with the war on drugs clearly outweigh the gains.

Other benefits of the drug war are that it provides jobs for tens or hundreds of thousands of criminal justice professionals, it gives politicians an easy issue on which to talk tough in order to get elected and reelected, and it reinforces a dominant ideology about illicit drugs and their users. The drug war may also help maintain a line between moral behavior and immoral behavior— moral people and immoral people—that is necessary for the functioning of criminal law. For example, we see very high levels of disapproval of many forms of illicit drug use by young people in Monitoring the Future (MTF) data. Arguably, this is evidence of strong moral repudiation of drugs. Finally, the drug war gives the U.S. government an "in" to countries and regions of the world to which it might not otherwise have access, particularly in Latin America.

We believe the most important question for policy-makers is this: Are modest reductions in drug use (which are not steady or even current reductions) worth the costs of the drug war? Each reader has to make up his or her own mind, and this can be a difficult decision since no one really knows what would happen if drug use was allowed (either legalized or decriminalized). Yet it is clear that the drug war provides little tangible benefit, that ONDCP does not meet its goals, and that the costs of the drug war are enormous.

Our review of the annual editions of the National Drug Control Strategy also shows that ONDCP does not conduct a fair assessment of its drug war. It does not weigh the significant costs of the drug war against its modest benefits. This is an important finding for it suggests that ONDCP is really not interested in whether the drug war is a sound policy.

Chapter Eight

Conclusions and
Policy Recommendations

In this chapter, we summarize our book, including lessons from America's drug war history, the findings of our study of claims-making by ONDCP in the areas of reducing drug use, healing drug users, disrupting markets, and costs of drug use and abuse and the drug war. We also summarize our main conclusions from our own assessment of the effectiveness of ONDCP between 1989 and 1998. Finally, we discuss policy implications aimed at changing the course of the way ONDCP uses, presents, and discusses statistics, as well as fights the nation's drug war.

LESSONS FROM HISTORY

As we showed in chapter 2, America has a long and sordid history with "fighting" drugs and drug users. Since at least 1875, when the city of San Francisco, California, passed an ordinance prohibiting the smoking or possession of opium, the operation of opium dens, or the possession of opium pipes, governments at the local, state, and federal levels have made it their goal to eradicate drugs from their jurisdictions. Among the many lessons we should have learned from this history are:

- Drug laws often are not really about drugs but instead about who is using them. At various times throughout our history—even our recent history—laws have banned certain drugs in part because of concerns over who was using them.

- Many of America's drug wars have been inspired by racist sentiment or ethnocentrism.
- It is not the nature of the drug that determines its legal or criminal status. At one time, both alcohol and tobacco were illegal drugs, whereas cocaine, heroin, morphine, and other drugs were once legal.
- America's drug laws are not necessarily in place to reduce illicit drug use for the sake of reducing drug use. Ulterior motives also operate.
- One priority of government often takes precedence over another, and even interferes with it. This makes fighting drugs in other countries and even at home more difficult, as we create and pursue policies aimed at other outcomes.
- In a capitalistic marketplace where drugs are advertised and sold freely to willing users, use grows and becomes problematic. When cocaine, heroin, morphine, and other similar substances were once legal and widely marketed, use became problematic.
- Drug prohibition produces a black market that can survive and even thrive, despite the best efforts of criminal justice agencies to deny the opportunities.
- Alcohol prohibition was promoted by several ideological groups, including the Women's Christian Temperance Union (WCTU), which was motivated not only by concern over alcohol consumption but also by anti-immigrant fever. Similarly, several ideological groups have influenced how and why governments pursue wars on other drugs.
- Alcohol prohibition reduced cirrhosis death rates by 10 to 20% and simultaneously reduced alcohol use a modest amount. Yet, it also caused great costs, including corrupted enforcement, overly aggressive enforcement, increases in organized crime, increases in homicide, an enormous growth in opportunities for illegal profiting through crime and violence, and an expansion of criminal justice. Experts widely agree that the costs of prohibition outweighed its benefits.
- Evidence and expert opinion about the true nature of a drug and use of the drug have mattered less than politics in the nation's drug war. That is, drug wars throughout our history have been about creating and maintaining the dominant ideology of the time.
- The drug war, prior to 1988 when ONDCP was created, was not a clearly formulated and carefully planned policy of the U.S. government.
- ONDCP was created in the wake of a moral panic about crack cocaine in the 1980s. This suggests the possibility that its creation was not well thought out and based on empirical evidence suggesting the office would be effective or even necessary.

- ONDCP has offered different goals of the drug war over the years. The shifting of these goals also raises the real possibility that the ONDCP's National Drug Control Strategy is not carefully planned.
- The majority of funding in America's drug war has always been, and remains, intended for reactive measures aimed at supply reduction rather than proactive and preventive measures aimed at demand reduction. The drug war is not, nor has it ever been, balanced as ONDCP claims.

FINDINGS

Our study of claims-making by ONDCP discovered overwhelming evidence of consistently false and dishonest claims by ONDCP, as well as inappropriate and dishonest uses of statistics to prove its case. Among our most significant findings, presented in chapters 4–6, are:

General Findings

- The contents and appearance of the 2000 and 2001 annual Strategy reports are very different from the 2002, 2003, 2004, and 2005 versions of the Strategy reports. Beginning with the 2002 Strategy, ONDCP changed the format of its annual report, providing less data and subsequent analysis of drug use trends. No explanation is offered by ONDCP.
- ONDCP claims that recent drug use declines among youth are attributable to its "balanced approach" to the drug war. Statistics on drug war spending show that the drug war is not balanced, but instead is mostly reactive and focused on criminal justice and military strategies.
- Beginning with the 2003 Strategy, ONDCP changed its budgeting technique to exclude costs associated with drug use and abuse and the drug war (including law enforcement and corrections costs). ONDCP claims the change more accurately captures the amount of money spent fighting the war on drugs, and that it increases accountability and provides a better guide to drug control policy-makers. Two effects of the budgeting changes include the appearance of lessening the total amount of federal dollars requested to fight the drug war (without actually changing the amount of money spent fighting the drug war) and the appearance of increasing the proportion of funding for treatment in the drug war budget (without substantially increasing the availability of drug treatment for those in need).

- ONDCP has offered different goals of the drug war over the years. The 1995 Strategy stated fourteen goals. From 1996 to 2001, ONDCP stated five goals, including to: educate and enable America's youth to reject illegal drugs as well as tobacco and alcohol; increase the safety of America's citizens by substantially reducing drug-related crime and violence; reduce health and social costs to the public of illegal drug use; shield America's air, land, and sea frontiers from the drug threat; and break foreign and domestic drug sources of supply.
- In the 2000 Strategy, ONDCP claimed that its previous five goals and thirty-two related objectives would be used through 2004, but this is not the case. Beginning with the 2002 Strategy, new goals of the drug war are offered. In the 2002 Strategy, new goals related to reducing drug use are stated, including two-year and five-year objectives. Two-year goals include: "A 10 percent reduction in current use of illegal drugs by 8th, 10th, and 12th graders" and "A 10 percent reduction in current use of illegal drugs by adults aged 18 and older." Five-year goals include: "A 25 percent reduction in current use of illegal drugs by 8th, 10th, and 12th graders" and "A 25 percent reduction in current use of illegal drugs by adults aged 18 and older." No explanation is offered by ONDCP as to why it shifts and drops goals over the years.
- The 2005 National Drug Control Strategy states three goals of the drug war, including: stop use before it starts through education and community action; heal America's drug users by getting treatment resources where they are needed; and disrupt the market by attacking the economic basis of the drug trade.
- ONDCP generally does not readily admit failure in meeting any of its goals. Instead, it uses its own failures to call for stepped up efforts in the drug war.
- Across the 2000–2005 versions of the Strategy, ONDCP shifts years and data sources for evaluating drug use trends. Originally, drug use trends were to be evaluated beginning in 1996, then in 2000, and then in 2002. Originally, drug use trends for youth were to be evaluated using the National Household Survey on Drug Abuse (NHSDA), but ONDCP changed to Monitoring the Future Survey (MTF) data. ONDCP explains that shifting evaluation periods and data sets are necessary due to changes in the NHSDA (which is now called the National Survey on Drug Use and Health or NSDUH). ONDCP does not discuss its role, if any, in changing the methodology of the NHSDA.

Findings Regarding Claims to Reduce Drug Use

- Across the 2000–2005 versions of the Strategy, ONDCP claims success in reducing drug use when the statistics warrant it and also when they do not.
- To create the impression of declines in drug use, ONDCP begins trend analysis in 1979 (the peak of drug use) and 1985 (prior to the establishment of ONDCP in 1988). ONDCP thus claims and shows visually that drug use is down when it has actually not decreased during its existence. Using statistics from 1979 and 1985 as initial statistics in trend analyses assures ONDCP that it can demonstrate it has met its goal of reducing drug use, even though it has not.
- ONDCP uses positive language to "spin" drug use trends into patterns that are consistent with its goal of reducing drug use even when the statistics suggest overall increases in drug use. For example, ONDCP characterizes unchanging drug use rates as consistent with its goal of reducing drug use, focuses only on recent declines of data that overall are trending upward, and isolates limited successes and treats them as typical of overall trends.
- ONDCP makes numerous statements of failure throughout each of the yearly editions of the Strategy, but never does it relate such statements to its goals or admit failure in achieving any of its goals. For example, ONDCP admits that widespread and consistent declines in drug use are rare, but then uses recent such declines as clear proof of success despite long-term trends to the contrary.
- Typically, ONDCP downplays or ignores entirely statistics that depict a failure to achieve drug war goals. When it does admit failure, it typically does so in a very mild or subtle way. When ONDCP's admissions of failures are rarely clear and honest, they are used to cause alarm and justify a continuation of the drug war.
- Even when claims of success are made by ONDCP, clear evidence indicates long-term failure in the claims (and in the statistics presented to back up those claims).
- ONDCP's general approach to interpreting drug use trend statistics is to celebrate declines even when they are short term or occurred in the past and downplay increases unless they are being used to create alarm.
- ONDCP ignores trend data that run counter to its goals even when the statistics are included in the Strategy reports as supplemental tables. ONDCP selectively chooses which data to present visually and the data nearly always support its case. Other statistics are simply ignored. No explanation is offered by ONDCP.

- ONDCP ignores clear evidence of substitution from some illicit drugs to others when claiming declines in drug use, even though statistics indicating such substitution can be found in the text of the Strategy reports. For example, recent declines in Ecstasy and LSD use are countered by recent increases in use of psychotherapeutic drugs. Since use of some of these drugs has increased, it suggests that ONDCP is attempting to hide the evidence from readers of its Strategy.
- In the 2004 and 2005 Strategy reports, ONDCP combines MTF data for eighth, tenth, and twelfth graders to report overall declines in past-month drug use consistent with its goal of reducing use by youth by 10% over two years. Yet, the goal stated in the 2002 Strategy was "A 10 percent reduction in current use of illegal drugs by 8th, 10th, and 12th graders." MTF data indicate past-month drug use for twelfth graders did not decline 10% over two years. Youth use is also on the rise, according to the NSDUH. No explanation is offered by ONDCP.
- ONDCP implies things have occurred that have not. In the 2004 and 2005 Strategy reports, ONDCP implies that recent drug use data indicate lifetime use by twelfth graders had finally fallen below 50%, even though it had not.
- The contents and appearance of the 2000 and 2001 annual Strategy reports are very different from the 2002, 2003, 2004, and 2005 versions of the Strategy reports. Beginning with the 2002 Strategy, ONDCP changed the format of its annual report, providing less data and subsequent analysis of drug use trends. Virtually no trend data are presented in the 2002, 2003, 2004, and 2005 versions of the Strategy for individual drugs such as marijuana, cocaine, heroin, methamphetamine, LSD, Ecstasy, or other drugs. No explanation is offered by ONDCP.
- ONDCP claims success on at least one occasion in meeting a goal that it has never formally stated, to get "drug use by our young people moving downward."
- ONDCP takes credit when drug use trends decline, but assumes no responsibility when drug use trends increase.
- At times, ONDCP purposely presents inappropriate statistics to prove that getting serious about drug use works. For example, ONDCP presents a figure showing trends among only 18–25 year olds (rather than all users) to prove that the "Just Say No" campaign of First Lady Nancy Reagan caused drug use to decline. A cursory review of statistics for drug use trends among youth proves that this conclusion is not warranted. ONDCP selectively uses statistics to prove a point, even when an examination of all drug use statistics (and especially the most relevant) does not warrant the conclusion.

- ONDCP makes false and unsupportable claims regarding the ability of human beings to force drug use down. For example, visual evidence and verbal claims suggest that Nancy Reagan's "Just Say No" campaign caused drug use to decline starting in 1985, when in fact drug use trends had been declining since 1979.
- Confronted with statistics that show first-time use of illicit drugs increasing, past-month of illicit drugs steady, and age of first use decreasing, ONDCP does not consider the implications of these trends for its drug war goals.
- ONDCP generally mischaracterizes trend data. For example, in the 2004 and 2005 Strategy reports, ONDCP focuses on the final years of statistics pertaining to Ecstasy use, and celebrates the rapid declines. Yet, ONDCP ignores that the trend first increased rapidly, suggesting steady use over the long run.
- Even when ONDCP acknowledges increases in the use of some drugs, it generally does not present figures to illustrate these increases.
- ONDCP claims that drug testing programs in schools work, even though national data show they do not. In the 2004 and 2005 Strategy reports, ONDCP selectively chooses a handful of evaluations to show the effectiveness of school drug testing programs even although national data lead to different conclusions.
- ONDCP claims that its Media Campaign works to save lives by increasing the likelihood that youth see drugs in a negative light. Yet, ONDCP ignores the rising death toll attributable to drug abuse and also does not present trend data with regard to youth disapproval of drugs. MTF data also show disapproval of drug use generally unchanged or down since ONDCP was created.
- Research on anti-drug ads shows that most will not work to reduce drug use by youth and that many may even increase drug use in the long run. For ONDCP to claim otherwise is dishonest and inconsistent with the evidence.
- Despite the lack of actual strategies aimed at prevention pursued by ONDCP in the drug war, ONDCP begins to emphasize prevention in the 2002 Strategy.
- ONDCP stresses the importance of prevention, yet admits prevention is not well funded and that no specific programs exist aimed at prevention. ONDCP asserts that responsibility for prevention rests with informal sources such as parents, teachers, and peers.
- No explanation is given as to why prevention does not receive the majority of the ONDCP budget, or at least a more sizable portion.
- For most forms of illicit drug use for most grade levels, disapproval of drug use and perceived harmfulness of drug use has gone down or

remains unchanged. These outcomes are inconsistent with ONDCP's drug war goals. ONDCP does not acknowledge this.

Findings Regarding Claims to Heal Drug Users

- Across the 2000–2005 versions of the Strategy, ONDCP generally does not claim success in healing America's drugs users. Simply stated, relevant statistics do not warrant such claims.
- ONDCP makes few statements of any kind regarding treatment in the 2000 and 2001 versions of the Strategy. ONDCP claims regarding the importance of drug treatment begin in the 2002 Strategy and become more common in the 2003 and 2004 versions of the Strategy. Yet, funding for treatment as a portion of actual drug war spending remains relatively small and only one in seven people in need of drug treatment receive it.
- ONDCP admits that most people who need drug treatment do not get it. ONDCP claims this is the fault of the users who are simply in denial and suggests it is the responsibility of average citizens to coerce people who need it into treatment.
- Even though ONDCP admits that the United States fails to actually provide drug treatment for the vast majority of the people who need it, ONDCP makes optimistic claims and stresses the importance of healing drug users through treatment.
- ONDCP's statistics on the ability to provide treatment to those who need it suggest that, as the years go by, the drug war is less and less able to provide treatment. In the 2002 Strategy, ONDCP reported that 18.6% of drug users who needed treatment got it, while in the 2003 Strategy, the number fell to 16.6%. In the 2004 Strategy, only 14.3% of drug users who needed treatment got it. This is clearly not consistent with ONDCP's goal of healing drug users through treatment.
- ONDCP does not present a clear picture of the actual need for drug treatment. ONDCP's claims of the extent of drug treatment need vary significantly across different versions of the Strategy and even within individual versions of the Strategy.
- ONDCP characterizes drug use as a harmful disease and drug users as bad people. It never acknowledges possible positive, social, recreational, and harmless nature of much drug use, even though several of its claims show ONDCP knows that most users do not become abusers or dependent users.
- ONDCP blurs the boundaries between drug use and drug abuse. ONDCP characterizations about the inevitability of drug use are

refuted by its own claims that only a fraction of drug users go on to need drug treatment.

- The 2003, 2004, and 2005 Strategy reports contain more rhetoric related to the dangers of drug use than previous years, further obfuscating the clear lines between use and abuse.

- ONDCP promotes the regulation of prescription drugs to reduce abuse because of the legitimate medical uses of these substances. ONDCP claims that such regulation works, yet this begs the question of whether regulation of illicit substances might also work. ONDCP simultaneously ignores the medicinal value of marijuana.

- ONDCP's promotion of prescription monitoring programs in the 2004 Strategy is based on a single, misleading statistic that supposedly shows that the number of OxyContin prescriptions was related to the presence or absence of PMPs. In the 2005 Strategy, ONDCP also claims PMPs helped bring about declines in drug use of all kinds in rural areas.

Findings Regarding Claims to Disrupt Drug Markets

- Across the 2000–2005 versions of the Strategy, ONDCP generally does not claim successes in disrupting drug markets. The relevant statistics do not warrant such claims. ONDCP claims are in the area of needing to better attack the drug market as a business.

- ONDCP makes optimistic claims about future successes and stresses the importance of disrupting drug markets, even though its own data show it has not been effective.

- The contents and appearance of the 2000 and 2001 annual Strategy reports are very different from the 2002, 2003, and 2004 versions of the Strategy reports. Beginning with the 2002 Strategy, ONDCP changed the format of its annual report, providing less data and subsequent analysis of drug availability, drug prices, and drug purity. No explanation is offered by ONDCP.

- ONDCP admits that most illicit drugs are still widely available. ONDCP spins its ability to disrupt drug markets and claims it is close to making a difference, yet the 2000 and 2001 Strategy reports show that drug prices are generally down, drug purity is generally up, and young people report they can still easily obtain drugs. The 2002, 2003, 2004, and 2005 Strategy reports do not discuss drug prices, drug purity, or drug availability. The statistics are simply left out. Other data sources suggest that the 2000 and 2001 findings continue to hold true.

- ONDCP mischaracterizes trend statistics by claiming prices for illicit drugs are steady when in fact they are generally declining. Further, ONDCP does not discuss the implications of falling prices of illicit drugs for its drug war goals, even though it argues elsewhere that higher prices lead to decreased demand.
- ONDCP argues the effectiveness of interdiction based on faith (without evidence), yet simultaneously admits its focus has been episodic and ineffective. ONDCP claims progress on all fronts of drug interdiction, but does not explain or offer evidence in support.
- In the 2003 Strategy, ONDCP admits that its focus on disruption if the market has not been consistent. ONDCP also notes a "lack of collaboration" between law enforcement agencies and a failure to agree on "a set of trafficker targets." ONDCP also admits that its High Intensity Drug Trafficking Areas (HIDTA) program has not demonstrated adequate results and that over time the initial focus of the program has been diluted. ONDCP admits the failure but does not consider the possibility that such findings prove interdiction may be futile.
- In the 2004 Strategy, ONDCP claims that current interdiction rates are within reach of the 35 to 50% seizure rate that is estimated would prompt a collapse of profitability for drug smugglers. Yet this same claim proves that, even after decades of interdiction, government agencies have not been able to seize enough drugs to make a real difference.
- In the 2005 Strategy, ONDCP claims to be seizing 50% of all cocaine worldwide. However, data on drug trends, drug prices, and drug purity do not indicate the collapse of the market, as ONDCP argues will occur with a 50% interdiction rate. This implies that either the claim about the level of interdiction is wrong or the prediction about the impact of 50% is inaccurate.
- ONDCP's interpretation of statistics dealing with interdiction rates suggest it is close to making a difference. Strangely, the statistics actually show the opposite, that we are not close to making a difference.
- ONDCP notes that many illicit drugs are widely available, but it never admits that the widespread availability of drugs indicates a failure to meet its goal of disrupting drug markets. Further, it overstates the rise in THC content.
- ONDCP highlights rising levels of THC content in marijuana, but does so to cause concern about the nature of the drug. It never discusses the implications of rising THC content in marijuana for its goal of disrupting drug markets.
- ONDCP notes increased seizures of drugs over the years, but does not admit that these seizures have not had the intended effect on drug prices and drug purity.

- Aggressive eradication programs in Latin America have not translated into higher drug prices, lower drug purity, or less drug availability.
- Data from ONDCP's Pulse Check reports, its report titled The Price and Purity of Illicit Drugs, the Drug Enforcement Administration's Illegal Drug Price and Purity Report, and the National Drug Intelligence Center's National Drug Threat Assessment show that interdiction efforts have not been successful.

Findings Regarding Claims of Costs of Drug Use and Abuse and the Drug War

- The contents and appearance of the 2000 and 2001 annual Strategy reports are very different from the 2002, 2003, 2004, and 2005 versions of the Strategy reports. Beginning with the 2002 Strategy, ONDCP changed the format of its annual report, providing less data and subsequent analysis of costs associated with the drug war. No explanation is offered by ONDCP. It simply removes the costs and presents them in a separate report.
- ONDCP's report, titled The Economic Costs of Drug Abuse in the United States 1992–1998, shows that the costs of drug abuse rose significantly, inconsistent with its goal of reducing health and social costs to the public, and indicates that most of the costs are due to prohibition.
- Beginning with the 2003 Strategy, no consideration whatsoever is given to costs of the drug war. While the 2000 and 2001 versions of the Strategy contain data and analysis of social and economic costs of the drug war, including increasing deaths attributable to drug use, increasing mentions of drug use in emergency rooms, increasing costs of imprisonment, and increasing racial disparities, the 2002 Strategy contains only one small box pertaining to such costs. The 2003 and 2004 versions of the Strategy include no information about such costs and the 2005 Strategy contains only a brief and limited discussion of costs. No explanation is offered by ONDCP.
- ONDCP counts components of the drug war—law enforcement, incarceration, and treatment—as part of the costs of drug use and abuse.
- ONDCP statistics on the costs of drugs are misleading because they suggest that it is drug use and abuse per se that is costly.
- ONDCP statistics on financial costs of illicit drugs are false— ONDCP invents figures for financial costs due to premature deaths, financial costs of illnesses, and financial costs of crime careers.

- ONDCP admits that the economic costs to society of drug use and abuse have grown 57% from 1992 to 2000. Since one of ONDCP's goals through the 2002 Strategy included reducing health and social costs to the public of illegal drug use, rising economic costs are a sign of failure not success.
- Cumulative evidence indicates that the costs of the drug war outweigh costs of drug use and abuse.
- ONDCP claims that medical research on treatment and prevention is unsurpassed and outweighs the amounts spent on enforcement- and interdiction-related research. Yet, statistics are not presented here about actual dollars spent overall on all aspects of the drug war rather than just research dollars. ONDCP misleads the public through use of statistics by reporting only on research dollars spent on the war on drugs rather than on all dollars spent on the war on drugs.
- Statistics show health and social costs of drug use are up since the creation of ONDCP. Such costs were removed from the Strategy beginning in 2002. ONDCP does not consider the implications of these growing costs for its drug war goal of reducing costs of drug use and abuse.
- A steady climbing of drug-related deaths in the United States in the 1990s and emergency room mentions of illicit drugs is inconsistent with ONDCP's goal of reducing health and social costs to the public of illegal drug use and its objective to reduce drug-related health problems. Yet, ONDCP does not admit or even address this.
- Current drug users in 2000 were four times more likely in 2000 to die from a drug-induced death than current drug users in 1979. This is inconsistent with ONDCP's goal of making drug users healthy.
- ONDCP claims its drug war is not punitive. For example, in the 2004 Strategy, ONDCP presents data with regard to research funding to prove that research funding for law enforcement is virtually nonexistent while research funding for treatment and prevention is much higher. Yet, ONDCP does not present data with regard to actual spending on law enforcement and punishment that show the punitive nature of the drug war.
- ONDCP claims drug arrests represent a small portion of all arrests and that most incarcerations are for trafficking rather than possession. ONDCP presents only federal statistics and ignores local level data, where the bulk of arrests for drug crimes occur. These data show that approximately 80% of all arrests for drug crimes are for possession.
- ONDCP admits that the drug war is responsible for about one-fifth of the costs of state prisons in the 1990s and 60% of federal prison costs in at least one year in the 1990s.

- ONDCP notes increased costs associated with incarceration and greater national spending on incarceration than on education. Evidence is also presented showing clear evidence of racial disparities in incarceration. Yet, ONDCP attempts to minimize such statistics. In fact, no discussion of these facts occurs after the 2001 Strategy.
- In the 2004 Strategy, ONDCP denies that most incarcerations are for possession. It attempts to prove this by offering statistics from the U.S. Sentencing Commission to prove its claim, reporting average quantities of drugs involved in federal drug trafficking cases. Since the vast majority of drug cases are handled by local police (e.g., city police and county sheriffs), the majority of drug cases are handled by state courts, and the majority of drug incarcerations are at the state level, ONDCP statistics about federal cases are misleading. ONDCP providees no local or state level statistics.
- ONDCP shows that drug use correlates with crime. ONDCP does not explain that this does not mean that drug use causes criminality, or that a person can test positive for some drugs for a significant period of time after use.
- ONDCP claims a large percentage of the property crimes and violent crimes committed each year in America are drug related.
- ONDCP reports that drugs are involved in many crimes, yet its data on illicit drugs and alcohol are combined, thereby distorting the relationship between illicit drugs and crime. ONDCP ignores that alcohol use is responsible for a greater share of criminality than use of all illicit drugs combined.
- ONDCP implies that increased drug abuse arrests led to declines in drug-related murders. Yet, ONDCP does not explain whether there is a meaningful relationship between drug arrests and drug murders.
- ONDCP implies that drug use causes crime, and to show this it includes statistics on alcohol (a legal drug) and criminality.
- ONDCP notes that a portion of jail inmates committed their offenses in order to obtain money to buy drugs. Yet, ONDCP does not consider the possibility that the illicit nature of drugs increases prices over what they would cost if legally available, thereby producing greater likelihood that people will commit crimes to obtain money for drugs.
- Most drug crimes are not caused by the effects of the drugs themselves, but instead by their illicit nature.
- ONDCP's discussion of three types of drugs-crimes relationships proves that prohibition accounts for most types of drug-induced crimes.
- ONDCP at times admits in the Strategy that the illicit nature of drugs produces bad outcomes for abusers.

- ONDCP, through its Strategy, links drugs to other problems, including increased promiscuity, sexual activity, risk of sexually transmitted diseases, unplanned pregnancies, school failure, neglectful parenting, child maltreatment, victimization, homelessness, mental illness, juvenile delinquency and criminality, and even terrorism. However, ONDCP fails to provide evidence of causation.
- ONDCP's National Drug Control Strategy never has discussed all types of costs associated with the drug war. ONDCP does not discuss erosions to civil liberties and the vast corruption allegedly caused by the war on drugs, nor does it consider threats to the sovereignty of other nations, degradation of the environment (including food and water) in countries where we spray crops with deadly chemicals, and cutbacks to social services and education that occur with increased funding for the war on drugs. In short, ONDCP's analysis of the drug war does not fully consider the many costs often associated with the policy of waging war on drugs.

Taken together, these findings of the Office of National Drug Control Strategy's National Drug Control Strategy share at least one thing in common — they suggest that ONDCP does not present accurate, honest, transparent, and justifiable claims in its annual National Drug Control Strategy reports. This does not mean the drug war is a failure. Our analysis of ONDCP claims-making does not warrant this conclusion, although the our findings at least call into question the efficacy of the drug war since ONDCP was created. The findings of what we call our fair assessment of America's drug war, however, lead to stronger conclusions.

A Fair Assessment of America's Drug War

Our assessment of ONDCP's drug war from 1989 (the year after ONDCP was created) until 1998 (the last year for which statistics from the National Household Survey on Drug Abuse are comparable) shows clear evidence of an inability of ONDCP to achieve its goals. This suggests a failed drug war for the first decade under the leadership of ONDCP. Among our findings, presented in chapter 7, are:

- ONDCP is the primary federal agency responsible for establishing "policies, priorities, and objectives for the Nation's drug control program . . . to reduce illicit drug use, manufacturing, and trafficking, drug-related crime and violence, and drug-related health consequences." Thus, it is the one agency that can be held accountable for the effectiveness or ineffectiveness of America's drug war.

- There is clear evidence of failure in the drug war led by ONDCP (from 1989 to 1998) to achieve its goals of reducing drug use, healing America's drug users, disrupting illicit drug markets, and reducing health and social costs to the public. Crime is down in line with ONDCP goals, but there is little evidence that this is attributable to the drug war. No straightforward admission of this failure is offered by ONDCP.
- ONDCP is legally required to evaluate its own performance. Yet, ONDCP has not dedicated itself to regular and fair assessment of the drug war. The Performance Measures of Effectiveness (PME) system, intended to be used to evaluate the efficacy of the drug war, was used to evaluate only one year (1998) of the National Drug Control Strategy. No explanation is offered by ONDCP.
- ONDCP says it will "continue to bring accountability" and that it is "committed to accountability" yet there is no evaluation other than for the 1998 Strategy.
- ONDCP never assesses its actual role in influencing drug use trends versus competing explanations such as changes in social, demographic, moral, economic, criminal justice, and other factors. ONDCP consistently claims, based on faith (without evidence), that the drug war is responsible for declines in drug use since 1979, even though there has been no decline in overall drug use since ONDCP was founded in 1988. While ONDCP claims credit for overall drug use decline, it does not accept responsibility for increases during the 1990s.
- Statistics show that most indicators of drug use (and likely future use) were not down during the period of 1989 to 1998.
- Lifetime use of illicit drugs by Americans did not generally decline. Lifetime use of marijuana and hallucinogens rose, while lifetime use of inhalants was steady and lifetime use of cocaine fell, although slightly.
- Current use of illicit drugs by Americans did not generally decline. Current use of illicit drugs for those twelve years and older declined slightly while there was a simultaneous and larger increase for past-month drug use among adolescents.
- New users of marijuana, hallucinogens, inhalants, stimulants, methamphetamine, LSD, Ecstasy, heroin, tranquilizers, sedatives, and pain relievers grew consistently, whereas the number of new users of cocaine and PCP were steady.
- Lifetime use of illicit drugs among eighth, tenth, and twelfth graders increased. This was true for marijuana, hallucinogens, LSD, cocaine, crack cocaine, heroin, amphetamines, tranquilizers, as well as inhalants for eighth and tenth graders and several other drugs for twelfth graders.

- Current use of illicit drugs by eighth, tenth, and twelfth graders increased. This was true for marijuana, hallucinogens, LSD, cocaine, crack cocaine, heroin, amphetamines, tranquilizers, as well as inhalants for eighth and tenth graders and several other drugs for twelfth graders.
- Total consumption of illicit drugs rose, as did consumption of marijuana and methamphetamine, while total consumption of cocaine and heroin fell.
- There is a relatively high perception of harmfulness for occasional use of cocaine and chronic tobacco smoking among high school students, and the trend is generally constant. Perceived harmfulness for regular use of cocaine is also very high, but slightly declined over the period of study. Perceived harmfulness for occasional marijuana use and moderate alcohol use is much lower, and generally declined over the period of study. Perceived harmfulness for regular marijuana use also fell during the study. Perceived harmfulness for LSD, PCP, crack, and barbiturates also fell during the study, whereas for heroin and amphetamines it was unchanged. The same general trends were found for eighth and tenth graders from 1991 to 1998, as well.
- There is a relatively high rate of disapproval for illicit drug use among high school students. Trends in disapproval appear relatively constant. Disapproval of occasionally smoking marijuana declined during the period of study, as did regularly smoking marijuana. Disapproval of taking one or two drinks per day also declined, and so did disapproval of occasionally taking cocaine, although only slightly. Disapproval of regularly taking cocaine remained constant. Disapproval of regularly smoking tobacco rose over the period of study. Disapproval of heroin and amphetamines remained unchanged, whereas disapproval of LSD, crack, and barbiturates declined during the period. The same general trends were found for eighth and tenth graders from 1991 to 1998 as well.
- Statistics suggest that access to drug treatment was not increased during the period of 1989/1990 to 1998.
- The number of admissions for drug treatment, including for alcohol and illicit drugs, increased only slightly during the period of study. Indeed, the number of admissions for drug treatment was nearly stagnant.
- There is a "drug treatment gap" in the United States—most people who need drug treatment do not actually receive it. Only about 15% of the people who need treatment for an illicit drug receive it, according to statistics, although this is likely an overstatement of the problem.
- ONDCP is not achieving its goal of disrupting illicit drug markets.
- Federal seizures of marijuana and heroin increased, but cocaine seizures were steady.

- Drug-lab seizures by the Drug Enforcement Administration (DEA) increased during the last few years of the study, but the DEA made almost no seizures of labs for any other type of illicit drug other than methamphetamine during the time period.
- Removals from the domestic market of both marijuana and cocaine by the DEA fell during the time period, as did removals of heroin.
- Removals from the domestic market by the DEA of stimulants, hallucinogens, and depressants generally declined.
- Seizures by the U.S. Customs Service increased from 1989 to 1998, especially for marijuana.
- Eradication programs were expanded in the 1990s, but drug availability did not decrease, purity did not decrease, and prices did not rise.
- The ease with which high school students could obtain illicit drugs in 1998 was no more difficult than in 1989. While some drugs became harder to obtain (e.g., cocaine, amphetamines), others became easier, according to the data (e.g., marijuana, LSD, Ecstasy, and heroin). Generally, the availability of illicit drugs remained unchanged during the time period of study.
- Prices for marijuana and cocaine generally decreased, as did prices for heroin.
- Overall consumer spending for marijuana and cocaine fell during the period, as did spending for heroin. Lower consumer spending is consistent with falling prices.
- While the purity of cocaine generally fell during the period of study, the purity of marijuana generally rose, although not consistently. The purity of heroin also increased during the time period.
- Street crime declined in the 1980s and 1990s. Violent street crimes increased through 1994 and then declined from 1995 to 1998. There were large declines in rates of rape, robbery, and assault. Homicide rates rose from 1989 to 1991, declined in 1992, rose again in 1993, and then declined from 1994 to 1998. Property crimes declined throughout the entire period of study, but they actually began to decline in 1975. There were large declines in burglary and motor vehicle theft.
- The majority of the declines in street crime during the period of study were not only beyond the reach of ONDCP and the war on drugs, but were also not largely attributable to anything in criminal justice.
- The costs of the drug war include financial costs (along with ONDCP budget and costs of criminal justice), reduced resources for social services and crime prevention, threats to civil liberties, increased violence, increased corruption, increased disrespect for the law, increased racial tensions and profiling, rising anti-Americanism, and increased civil unrest and terrorism. The illicit nature of drugs also raises prices for

drugs over and above what they would be if drugs were legally available, and the potency of drugs is uncertain and appears to be heightened. The drug war also increases death and disease associated with drug use.

- Statistics show that arrests for drug offenses have increased over the years, placing a larger burden on police agencies over the years.
- Statistics show consistently increasing court caseloads for drug offenders, meaning the war on drugs has become a larger burden on courts over the years.
- Statistics show consistently increasing numbers of inmates incarcerated in federal prisons for drug offenses, causing a larger burden on correctional agencies over the years.
- As arrests, convictions, and incarcerations have increased, the burden on criminal justice agencies and on taxpayers has also increased. This leads to less effective crime prevention, less available resources of other needs, and ultimately higher state and federal taxes and budget deficits to pay for the costs of the drug war.
- The benefits of the drug war are modest, and include modest reductions in use and strong disapproval ratings of many illegal drugs.
- The war on drugs also provides jobs for tens or hundreds of thousands of criminal justice professionals, gives politicians an easy issue on which to talk tough in order to get elected and reelected, and reinforces a dominant ideology about illicit drugs and their users.

Taken together, all these findings suggest the Office of National Drug Control Policy (ONDCP) failed from 1989 to 1998 to achieve its goals of reducing drug use, healing drug users, disrupting drug markets, and reducing health and social costs to the public. Yet, during this same time period, funding for the drug war grew tremendously and costs of the drug war expanded as well. Further, despite its manifest failure, ONDCP was reauthorized in 1994, 1998, and 2003.

A RATIONAL RESPONSE TO ONDCP FAILURE

In theory, one would expect that policies that do not achieve their objectives (such as the drug war) would be discontinued. Furthermore, when the costs of policies exceed the benefits (such as with the drug war), one would anticipate policy termination. The Anti-Drug Abuse Act of 1988 specifically set a time limit for the existence of ONDCP. Additional laws specified that the agency should be evaluated and held accountable for its policy progress or failure. This has not happened. Our assessment reveals that ONDCP has not achieved its goals in the years since its creation. Thus, a rational response to this situation would be to terminate ONDCP. This would save tax money, alleviate government inefficiency, and reduce the size of government. If accompanied by a reassessment of U.S. policy toward drugs, it might even result in better outcomes with regard to drug use and abuse in the United States.

Further justification for the termination of ONDCP is the General Accounting Office (GAO) conclusion that ONDCP illegally spent $155,000 on propaganda "video news releases" (VNRs) that aired on 300 television stations and were seen by 22 million American households over 56 days around the time of the 2004 Super Bowl.[1] This was part of ONDCP's National Youth Anti-Drug Media Campaign. The video segments, which appeared to be actual news reports, were actually produced by ONDCP and sent to hundreds of news stations along with instructions on how to use them. Unseen narrators of the videos, none of which were actual journalists, reported on supposed "press conferences and other activities of ONDCP and other government officials regarding ONDCP's anti-drug campaign." Moreover, "each story is accompanied by proposed 'lead-in' and 'closing' remarks to be spoken by television station news anchors" thereby linking the fictional stories to real newscasts.[2] Viewers thought they were watching news. Instead they were watching covert propaganda from ONDCP.

The GAO report concluded:

> While ONDCP is authorized by the Drug-Free Media Campaign Act of 1998 to engage in "news media outreach," ONDCP is also required to comply with applicable appropriations act publicity or propaganda prohibitions. Those prohibitions require ONDCP to disclose to the television viewing audience ONDCP's role in the production and distribution of its news stories. There is no reasonable basis in the law to find that Congress exempted ONDCP from these prohibitions. Since ONDCP did not provide the required disclosures, ONDCP's prepackaged news stories constituted covert propaganda in violation of publicity or propaganda prohibitions of the fiscal year 2002, 2003, and 2004 appropriations acts. Moreover, because ONDCP had no appropriation available to produce and distribute materials in violation of each of these publicity or propaganda prohibitions, ONDCP also violated the Antideficiency Act . . . ONDCP must report these violations to the Congress and the President, and submit a copy of that report to this Office.[3]

Despite its failures and illegal use of propaganda to sell the drug war to citizens, history suggests that a rational response such as shutting down ONDCP is too radical for government, which tends toward bureaucratic inertia and agency persistence. At the very least, if ONDCP continues to coordinate policy, changes in ONDCP and its actions are in order.

Policy Implications:
Evaluating the Drug War and Using Statistics

Given the absence of evaluations by ONDCP of its own drug war, we firmly believe that ONDCP must commit itself to regular evaluations of its ability to meet its goals. Relevant questions would be what works, what doesn't work, what is promising, and why? This is a format established by researchers at the University of Maryland who evaluated federally funded crime prevention programs.[4]

ONDCP should also conduct regular costs-benefits analyses of the drug war. Relevant questions would be what are the benefits of various aspects of the drug war, what are the costs, and why? This is a format used effectively by researchers who have already analyzed the drug war.[5] Further, ONDCP ought to seriously consider alternatives to its current drug war strategies, paying special attention to those strategies that appear to be more effective based on the empirical evidence.[6]

These evaluations should be done fairly and honestly, in a transparent way. Claims-making by ONDCP also should be accurate, honest, transparent, and justifiable based on the data on which they are based. Simply stated, ONDCP should tell the truth. If ONDCP does not tell the truth, this is another reason for Congress to pull the plug on ONDCP.

In its evaluations, ONDCP must present all the relevant statistics to the consumers of its data, not just those that support its case. ONDCP also ought to be less concerned with justifying how it allocates the drug war budget and more concerned with critical analyses of how drug war money is spent.

Not only has ONDCP not committed itself to regularly assessing the drug war, at times it behaves in way that appears to purposefully inhibit evaluations. For example, its PME system, described in chapter 7, has only been used to assess one year of the National Drug Control Strategy (1998). Further, it either requested or allowed the National Household Survey on Drug Abuse (NHSDA) to be redesigned twice—once in 1999 and again in 2002—during a period of supposed evaluation. Thus, ONDCP's two objectives stated in the 1998 Strategy of reducing drug use and drug availability by 50% by 2007 cannot be assessed. We shouldn't tolerate such behavior, given the hundreds of billions of dollars and the countless lives at stake when it comes to the war on drugs.

The findings of our analysis also lead us to concur with some of the policy implications of the National Academy of Sciences' Committee on Data and Research for Policy and Illegal Drugs. For example: "Statistical results should be released without prior political or administrative review" and prior access should be limited "to the President and his or her immediate staff . . . [which] would help to reduce or eliminate departmental and White House 'spin' of data releases."[7]

To achieve this, we believe that if ONDCP is not terminated, then ONDCP should be removed as an Executive Agency of the White House. That is, it should exist as a stand-alone, independent agency responsible for assessment of the nation's drug war goals. Under this approach, the White House would ask ONDCP for its reports and would have no power to review them or change them prior to publication. It is simply unacceptable that Congress would allow ONDCP to operate as it does, leading a budget of tens of billions of dollars each year that is largely inefficient.

The findings of our study of ONDCP claims-making suggest that it is predominantly acting as a generator and defender of a given ideology in the drug war. This ideology asserts that illicit drugs are always bad, never acceptable, supply-driven, and must be fought through an ongoing war. This ideology asserts that fighting a "war" on drugs is the only way to reduce drug use and achieve related goals. Further, it maintains that the drug war actually works. As shown in this book, ONDCP uses several methods of statistical manipulation, inappropriate presentations of statistics and figures, and false and faulty claims-making to convince the reader that the drug war is effective at achieving ONDCP's drug war goals and that the benefits of the drug war outweigh its costs. Its National Drug Control Strategy, therefore, is fundamentally flawed as a mechanism for achieving a sound analysis of the drug war policy.

The National Academy of Science's Committee on Data and Research for Policy and Illegal Drugs also characterizes the ONDCP Strategy reports as insufficient for sound policy analysis. It asserts that the Strategy reports "are largely concerned with setting policy and describing the results of federal activities." Further, they "focus on policy goals and implementation strategies, and there is relatively little analysis of the underlying trends and data sources."[8] We concur that "it would be useful to have an annual report on illegal drugs in the United States that presents and assesses the most important statistical series" on "health, law enforcement, international, and economic facets of illegal drugs and related issues along with an appropriate commentary."[9] Our simple analysis of the drug war, presented in chapter 7, could be replicated each year by ONDCP and expanded to include all relevant statistics.

Amazingly, even the agencies leading the war on drugs and evaluating its effectiveness have always known of the threat of misusing statistics to support the prevailing ideology. For example, in 1973, the National Commission on Marijuana and Drug Abuse wrote:

the Commission cautions against research that points only in one direction. In the past, government agencies have sometimes used drug research to support policy rather than shape it. Studies that produced the answers they wanted were promoted and publicized; projects which appeared to document the 'wrong' results were quietly buried and not released. [New research] should specifically include studies that examine without bias alternate hypotheses and approaches.[10]

It is one thing to honestly examine and present statistics/data to evaluate a policy along the lines identified in chapter 1—either through an assessment of goals and outcomes or costs and benefits. It is an entirely different thing to intentionally examine and present statistics/data to serve ideological functions. The practice of using statistics/data to prove an effective drug war, typically despite the evidence, is intolerable.

Policy Implications: Drug War

Based on the findings of our study and our analysis of the drug war from the founding of the Office of National Drug Control Policy (ONDCP) to the present day, we concur with an ONDCP statement from its 2005 Strategy: "Programs and efforts that do not reduce drug use must be restructured or eliminated, an effort to use taxpayer money wisely that this Administration takes seriously."[11] We believe there is ample evidence to turn this logic on the drug war itself. Those elements that do not work should be restructured (if they are logical and based on strong theory) or eliminated (if they are not logical and are not based on strong theory).

Our analysis of the drug war during the first ten years of its existence under the leadership and direction of ONDCP—from 1989 to 1998—suggesting that the drug war was a massive failure. Not only did ONDCP not achieve it goals, but the evidence suggests the costs outweighed the modest benefits achieved.

The National Academy of Sciences Committee on Data and Research for Policy and Illegal Drugs report on drug war data and statistics reached a different conclusion that "an absence of evidence about the merits of current drug policy implies neither that this policy should be abandoned nor that it should be retained. An absence of evidence implies only uncertainty about the merits of current policy relative to possible alternatives."[12] We do not promote any particular alternative to the war on drugs, as our analysis does not warrant any particular alternative. Yet, we are confident, given our findings about ONDCP's inability to achieve its drug war goals that *any* alternative other than pure legalization would be more effective at reducing harms associated with both drug use and abuse and the war on drugs.

What are we to do? The findings of our study on ONDCP claims-making and our analysis of the drug war from 1989 to 1998 do not justify any particular policy alternative. Yet, assuming that reducing drug use, healing drug users, and disrupting drug markets remain the goals of America's drug control policies, we first would suggest investing greater resources into strategies that have been proven more effective than fighting a "war" on drugs — most notably, prevention.

The National Academy of Sciences' Committee on Data and Research for Policy and Illegal Drugs concludes that "at least 20 reviews and meta-analyses of drug prevention programs were published during the 1980s and 1990s. The most recent of these generally conclude that substance abuse prevention efforts are 'effective' for preventing substance use."[13] Criminal justice research also suggests that crime prevention is a more fruitful strategy than traditional means of control such as law enforcement, courts, and corrections.[14]

These conclusions do not apply to the prevention approaches historically used by ONDCP. According to research, the following approaches tend to be ineffective:

1. Information dissemination approaches that teach about the effects of drug use.
2. Fear arousal approaches that focus on risks and harms of various drugs.
3. Moral appeal approaches that appeal to people's morality to reject the evils of drug use.
4. Affective education approaches that attempt to build self-esteem and promote adaptive forms of behavior.

These are all approaches pursued by ONDCP. In other words, most of ONDCP's prevention efforts also are inconsistent with empirical evidence about which prevention efforts are effective.

The one approach that ONDCP uses that appears to be effective is the resistance-skills approach that teaches people about the influences that likely lead to drug use and those that can be employed to resist using drugs.[15] According to the evidence, the most effective prevention programs "pay attention to the social context of drug use, which is related to many other aspects of the individual's life and setting."[16] ONDCP should focus on such programs, rather than continuing to push school programs and media ad programs, the vast majority of which simply fail.[17]

We recommend utilizing the risk factor/protective factor approach to address the situations in people's lives that make them more or less like to use and abuse drugs. Risk factors are those that increase one's risk of using and abusing drugs, and protective factors are those that reduce one's risk of using and abusing drugs.[18] As noted in chapter 5, these factors include genetic, individual, group, community, organization, and society level factors. Many of these are simply beyond the scope of criminal justice and any war on drugs. ONDCP has admitted in its Strategy that factors producing drug use are beyond the control of criminal justice intervention. For example, in the 2000 Strategy, ONDCP claims:

> Risk factors include a chaotic home environment, ineffective parenting, anti-social behavior, drug-using peers, general approval of drug use, and the misperception that the overwhelming majority of one's peers are substance users; Protective factors include: parental involvement; success in school; strong bonds with family, school, and religious organizations; knowledge of dangers posed by drug use; and the recognition by young people that substance use is not acceptable behavior.[19]

Our review of the past six versions of the National Drug Control Strategy suggests that not many of these risk and protective factors are even addressed in America's drug war. Perhaps this is why the drug war is not effective.

Second, we believe ONDCP ought to invest more money in treatment. According to the experts, many forms of treatment are highly effective, and are more cost-effective than crime control mechanisms such as arresting, convicting, and punishing drug users and abusers.[20] For example, two drug policy experts assert that treatment programs "have shown both effectiveness, as measured by reductions in crime and illness associated with their clients, and cost-effectiveness."[21] This is true, even when clients are coerced into programs, such as through criminal justice referrals.[22] Ironically, treatment programs receive only modest funds and public expenditures on drug treatment have slowed down since the early 1990s.[23] As we showed in our study of ONDCP claims-making, ONDCP also believes in treatment. It has simply yet to invest enough resources in it relative to the supply reduction efforts it pursues (that mostly do not work).

Third, ONDCP and Congress should take a hard look at alternatives to prohibition, particularly approaches that are aimed not just at reducing drug use but especially at reducing harm. *Harm reduction* approaches are not necessarily aimed at reducing drug use. Based on the realization that some drug use is inevitable, harm reduction strategies are simply aimed at reducing harms associated with recreational drug use and especially drug abuse, as well as harms associated with prohibition efforts. We showed in chapter 2 that ONDCP's goals are not aimed at harm reduction, but instead revolve around the overall goal of reducing the prevalence of drug use.

Some alternative harm reduction programs have proven to be effective in other nations. These include *needle exchange programs*, which save lives by reducing HIV and AIDS infections, but do not seem to lead to increased use. Needle exchange programs are endorsed by the Centers for Disease Control and Prevention, the National Academy of Sciences, and numerous health and medical organizations. Other successful programs include *methadone maintenance programs*, which allow drug users to lead functional lives with a much lower risk of overdose or death as a result of their use, and *depenalization* of marijuana, which has kept use rates lower in the Netherlands than the United States. The Dutch have saved money by not incarcerating marijuana offenders while *not* witnessing increases in the use of harder drugs.[24]

There is fear among policy-makers that harm reduction approaches might increase drug use and abuse. There is some evidence that legalization would increase use and abuse, as noted in chapter 2. Yet, there is no such evidence that a policy of depenalization would lead to more use. In this approach, possession of small amounts for personal use would be legal, but manufacturing and selling would still be illegal, as would marketing and privatization of the drug trade.

Even assuming that drug use and abuse would be higher if the United States pursued alternatives to its drug war, this does not mean that the policy would do more harm than good. There is much evidence, even in ONDCP's annual National Drug Control Strategy, that harms associated with the war on drugs clearly outweigh gains. Some of these harms would be eliminated through the pursuit of alternatives to the drug war. That is, since many of the harms associated with the prohibition of drugs would be eliminated or reduced, we still would witness greater overall savings in financial costs, social costs, criminal justice costs, and so forth.[25]

In the 2003 Strategy, ONDCP claims that alternatives to the drug war are not acceptable: "No policy can seriously be considered in the public good if it advances the contagion of drug use. Yet that is precisely the effect of harm reduction actions such as marijuana decriminalization: as the drug becomes more available, acceptable, and cheap, it draws in greater numbers of vulnerable youth."[26] While the accuracy of this statement is beyond the scope of this book, we simply want to point out that data presented in the Strategy show that the drug war itself has not consistently made illicit drugs less available, acceptable, or expensive. It also has not stopped the rise in new users of illicit drugs.

Drug policy experts now consistently say the drug war is "unconvincing" and "deserves low marks."[27] So, it is time for the government to answer the critique. As noted by two drug war experts: "It is surely reasonable to ask that those who would maintain the status quo offer some basis for believing the additional expense and suffering are justified."[28] We cannot know for sure what would happen in an alternative regime to prohibition, unless of course we try it. The burden is on ONDCP to explain why we should not.

Another option would be to carefully weigh the evidence on all sides and make informed policy judgments based on this evidence. This is what we'd hope to have found about the approach of ONDCP in evaluating its drug policies annually through the National Drug Control Strategy. Instead, we found ONDCP manipulates evidence and presents faulty evidence to justify the nation's drug war. This is inconsistent with fair policy analysis and should be stopped by Congress.

ONDCP is quite good at reinforcing symbols related to drug use and drug users and thereby strengthening state power in its "fight" against drugs. Through its annual claims-making activities of the National Drug Control Strategy, ONDCP characterizes drug use and abuse as bad and dangerous, and drug users as evil, dangerous, and the enemy. The annual reports of the Strategy thereby serve as a means of assuring the continuation of the drug war and the dominant ideology on which it is based, despite the growing empirical evidence illustrating the futility of the drug war. And therein lies the danger.

American citizens expect accuracy, honesty, transparency, and efficacy from government agencies. And citizens deserve more from government than their opposite.

Postscript

In February 2006, after the study reported in this book was completed, the White House released the most recent edition of "The President's National Drug Control Strategy." This most recent Strategy, like previous versions of the Strategy discussed in the book, inappropriately utilizes and presents information in the form of statistics and visual graphs.

As in previous versions of the Strategy, the 2006 Strategy:

- Claims to be balanced when it is not (the budget is clearly titled in favor of reactive and supply side tactics rather than proactive and demand side methods).
- Reports combined drug use statistics for eighth, tenth, and twelfth graders from the Monitoring the Future (MTF) study to show declines consistent with its new short-term goals.
- Reports and focuses almost exclusively on short-term declines in reported use by young people, using only MTF data.
- Fails to report and focus on long-term increases in reported use by people twelve years and older according to National Survey on Drug Use and Health (NSDUH) data.
- Focuses on those drugs (and visually depicts trends) where data show recent declines in use.
- Downplays and ignores those drugs (and fails to visually depict trends) where data show increases in use.
- Fails to explain the significance of long-term drug use trends that have increased overall under ONDCP's tenure (in spite of recent declines), and the meaning of high drug use rates relative to earlier time periods.
- Advocates regulation approaches rather than prohibition to reduce prescription drug abuse.
- Characterizes drug use as a disease that is transmitted by unsuspecting users in their "honeymoon period" of use.
- Links illicit drugs to all kinds of bad outcomes, including terrorism.

- Presents the faulty "Just Say No" argument in the form of a figure that is noticeably different from one used in a previous Strategy report.
- Examines trends in legal drug use to suggest that legalization of illicit drugs would be a mistake.
- Sells policies such as drug testing in schools using anecdotal evidence from select schools rather than evidence from national studies.
- Speaks about the benefits of treatment but fails to adequately fund it.
- Claims to be winning the drug war through effective drug market disruption while simultaneously failing to report the most relevant statistics.
- Fails to present any data whatsoever about costs of drug use and abuse, or the drug war itself.

In this Postscript, we briefly discuss some of these issues. We also summarize some new drug war approaches introduced in the 2006 Strategy and show how the 2006 Strategy is the most war-like drug war strategy laid out in some time.

A Balanced Strategy?

ONDCP writes, "This year's *National Drug Control Strategy* seeks to build on the progress that has already been made by outlining a balanced, integrated plan aimed at achieving the President's goal of reducing drug use. Each pillar of the strategy is crucial, and each sustains the others."[1] One expects that each pillar of the strategy will be appropriately and roughly equally funded. Yet, this is not the case. Instead, examination of fiscal year 2007 (FY 2007) drug war funding requests shows:

- Funding for efforts aimed at stopping use has decreased (e.g., prevention with research now makes up only 11.7% of FY 2007 budget requests). The largest decline is found in funding for drug abuse prevention activities, shrinking from $1.54 billion in FY 2001 to $1.06 billion in FY 2007.
- Funding for efforts aimed at disrupting the market has simultaneously increased (e.g., domestic law enforcement now makes up 18.3% of FY 2007 requests, interdiction makes up 24.6% of FY 2007 requests, and international efforts now make up 11.5% of FY 2007 requests). The largest increases are found in domestic law enforcement, growing from $2.51 billion in FY 2001 to $3.59 billion in FY 2007, interdiction, growing from $1.90 billion in FY 2001 to $3.12 billion in FY 2007, and international spending, growing from $617 million in FY 2001 to $1.46 billion in FY 2007.[2]
- ONDCP claims that prevention is important, but its budget requests do not effectively demonstrate its commitment to prevention. ONDCP

discusses its new "Strategic Prevention Framework" (SPF) in the 2006 Strategy, which "creates an infrastructure that ties together prevention efforts at Federal, state, and local levels and within communities" to develop "a prevention strategy that is tailored to local needs." All of this is aimed at reducing "factors that put communities at risk for drug abuse, while strengthening protective factors that can result in healthy outcomes for individuals of all ages—particularly our Nation's youth."3

- There is a stable but small devotion to treatment in the drug war budget (making up only 23.8% of the overall FY 2007 budget request). Treatment research funding grew only slightly from $489 million in FY 2001 to $605 million in FY 2007, and funding for treatment activities grew only slightly from $2.09 billion in FY 2001 to $2.41 billion in FY 2007. In spite of these small changes, ONDCP claims that it has "made healing drug users a priority—a testament to the fact that American is the land of second chances."4

The outcome of these budget adjustments is that the portion of the drug war budget devoted to supply side approaches grew from 53.1% in FY 2001 to 64.5% in FY 2007. The portion of the budget devoted to demand side approaches shrank from 46.9% in FY 2001 to 35.5% in FY 2007. Thus, less money is devoted to the Department of Education and more is allocated to the Department of Homeland Security (Customs and Border Protection, Immigration and Customs Enforcement, and U.S. Coast Guard), Department of Justice (Bureau of Prisons, Interagency Crime and Drug Enforcement, Office of Justice Programs), and the Department of State (Bureau of International Narcotics and Law Enforcement Affairs).

These figures and facts, as in previous years, illustrate the imbalanced nature of the drug war budget and the disproportionate focus on criminal justice responses to illicit drug use in America's drug war. The drug war in FY 2007 is even more imbalanced and punitive than in previous years.

Short-Term Focus

The 2006 Strategy clearly makes the drug war about President George W. Bush and his plan to achieve three "priorities" of the drug war. This is perhaps the first time a Strategy has ever been framed this way. For example, the document begins:

> When President George W. Bush took office in 2001, drug use had risen to unacceptably high levels. Over the past decade, drug use by young people had nearly doubled, as measured by those who reported

having used drugs in the past month: 11 percent of young people had
used drugs in the past month in 1991, and 19 percent had done so in
2001. Indeed, *in 2000, over half of all 12th graders in the United States
had used an illicit drug at least once in his or her life before graduation. . . .*
Determined to fight this trend, the President set aggressive goals to
reduce drug use in the United States, including reducing youth drug
use by 10 percent in two years. That goal has been met and exceeded.[5]

The implication that less than half of high school seniors now report using
illegal drugs appears again in the 2006 Strategy. In fact, the 2005 Monitoring
the Future (MTF) study on which almost all of the 2006 Strategy is based,
shows that 50.4% of high school seniors in 2005 indicated that they had tried
an illegal drug at least once in their lives.[6]

Framing America's drug war goals as the President's responsibility is consistent with claims from earlier Strategy reports reviewed in the book that
ONDCP would be accountable for achieving its goals, as well as comments by
ONDCP Director John Walters that the Bush Administration would hold itself accountable by stating short-term goals that could be achieved on President Bush's watch (see the Appendix). Viewed from this perspective, only ex-
amining in detail drug use trends over the Bush Administration's term in office
makes sense. Yet, the larger question of whether the drug war has generally
been effective since implemented is not addressed.

One figure in the 2006 Strategy shows progress toward achieving two-
and five-year goals in reducing drug use (10% reductions after two years and
25% reductions after five years). In this figure, data are presented only from
2001 (when President Bush took office) to 2005 (the last year for which data
are available). The figure shows "special tabulations" from the 2005 MTF
study, illustrating the percentage of teens that used any illicit drug in the past
month. The figure demonstrates that 19.4% of teens used an illicit drug in
2001, followed by 18.2% in 2002, 17.3% in 2003, 16.1% in 2004, and 15.7% in
2005. Thus, between 2001 and 2005, during the Presidency of George W.
Bush, there was a 19% reduction in current drug use among eighth, tenth, and
twelfth graders combined.

This allows ONDCP to claim that its drug war is effective, at least
under President Bush. That drug use has been assessed among only young
people using MTF and not among all age groups using NSDUH is not mentioned by ONDCP. Though the 2005 NSDUH had not been released at the
time of the release of the 2006 Strategy, data from the 2004 NSDUH were
available, including long-term drug use trend data for various types of drugs
and across various age groups. Figures in the report clearly illustrate that current drug use is higher in 2004 than in 1988, when ONDCP was created, for
marijuana and psychotherapeutics, and is generally unchanged for cocaine.

Data pertaining to long-term trends for other drugs are not presented in figure or table format.[7]

Additionally, that illicit drug use by young people according to MTF is still higher than it was in 1991, 1992, and 1993, is also not highlighted by ONDCP, although a figure in the 2006 Strategy shows this to be the case. ONDCP does note that "overall illicit drug use remains too high among America's young people."[8]

Limited Focus on Only Some Drug Use Trends

The 2006 Strategy highlights that use of many kinds of illicit drugs has declined for students, including methamphetamine, steroids, marijuana, LSD, Ecstasy, other club drugs (i.e., rohypnol, GHB, and ketamine), and even consumption of alcohol and tobacco by young people. According to the Strategy report, only one drug showed an increase among all three grade levels—Oxycontin.[9] Similar to previous versions of the Strategy, the 2006 Strategy does not illustrate increasing trends in Oxycontin use in a figure. In fact, every figure pertaining to drug use in the 2006 Strategy depicts declines in use, including among all drugs,[10] methamphetamine,[11] steroids,[12] and Ecstasy.[13]

While there were only increases among all three grade levels for Oxycontin, several other drugs showed increases from 2004 to 2005 in past-month use for at least one grade level, including marijuana by eighth graders, inhalants by twelfth graders, hallucinogens by eighth graders, PCP by twelfth graders, Ecstasy by tenth graders, cocaine by eighth graders, heroin by twelfth graders, methamphetamine by eighth graders, ice by twelfth graders, barbiturates by twelfth graders, tranquilizers by eighth graders, cigarettes by eighth graders, and smokeless tobacco by tenth and twelfth graders.[14]

While most of these increases were tiny and not statistically significant, the point is that there are plenty of data about which to be concerned that counter ONDCP's claims of success, and that show that decreasing drug use trends are slowing. Consistent with its historical treatment of statistics, ONDCP mentions none of this.

Ignore Adult Drug Use

The 2006 Strategy also presents no data whatsoever with regard to adult drug use trends, which is strange considering that ONDCP has stated two- and five-year goals for both youth and adults in several consecutive years of the Strategy.[15] Thus, ONDCP writes that "drug use is down, particularly by young people." In fact, the only mention of the NSDUH in the report says that there has been "reduced past-year consumption of crack cocaine between 2002 and 2004." ONDCP does not discuss NSDUH data for any other drug.

Prescription Drug Abuse

ONDCP discusses prescription drug abuse in the 2006 Strategy, again pointing out that it is the second highest form of illicit drug use in the United States behind marijuana. ONDCP asks:

> How do individuals who abuse prescription drugs get them? Data of this sort are hard to obtain, but experience suggests that it largely occurs in six ways (in no particular order): illegal purchases without a prescription over the Internet; so-called doctor shopping; theft or other diversion directly from pharmacies; unscrupulous doctors who—knowingly at worst, carelessly at best—overprescribe medications; traditional street-level drug dealing; and receiving prescription drugs for no cost from family and friends. The illegal use of pharmaceuticals is one of the fastest growing forms of drug abuse.[16]

As in previous versions of the Strategy, ONDCP discusses few statistics about prescription drug abuse and illustrates no data in figures.

Further, ONDCP again advocates regulation rather than prohibition to solve the problem: "The Administration's strategy in this area focuses on preventing diversion and getting users into treatment where necessary." It notes that prescription-drug monitoring programs (PMPs) assist "doctors, pharmacists, and, when appropriate, law enforcement with information about patient prescriptions." PMPs do this by helping "prevent doctors and pharmacists from becoming unwitting accessories to the abuse of these prescription drugs by showing information on other prescriptions given to, or filled by, the individual within the preceding weeks or months. In addition, identifying the abuser can help medical professionals recommend appropriate treatment."[17]

With prescription drug abuse, ONDCP is advocating compassionate regulation. Yet, as in the past, ONDCP fails to consider this approach for all illicit drugs.

Drug Use as a Disease

Throughout the 2006 Strategy, ONDCP links drug use to various kinds of bad outcomes, including addiction. ONDCP writes: "Drug addiction can . . . be seen as a threat to individual freedom in that it can reduce people to a single, destructive desire."[18] This links the war on drugs to another war that is often justified in the name of freedom — the war on terror.

Just Say No?

One interesting thing about the 2006 Strategy that jumped out at us was the use of the Nancy Reagan "Just Say No" figure that was used previously in the 2003 Strategy. In the 2003 Strategy, the figure showed trends in illicit drug use among those aged 18–25 years from 1974 to 1998. The 2006 figure shows trends in illicit drug use among those aged 18–25 years from 1974 to 2004.[19] Amazingly, whereas the 2003 Strategy figure showed that cocaine use began to decline in the year of the initiation of the Just Say No campaign (1985), the 2006 Strategy figure (which is based on the same data) shows that cocaine use had already begun to decline in 1979 with no noticeable increase prior to 1985. In other words, the two figures, each based on the same statistics, show two different trends and lead to two very different conclusions.

In the 2003 Strategy, ONDCP commented on its figure and claimed that the "Just Say No" campaign caused drug use to go down. In the 2006 Strategy, ONDCP merely presents the figure but makes no such claim (probably because the data don't, and never did, justify this conclusion). The discrepancy in the two figures is deeply troubling given that ONDCP used the figure in the 2003 Strategy to try to prove the effectiveness of the "Just Say No" educational campaign.

Legalization?

The 2006 Strategy discusses trends in legal drug use (i.e., alcohol and tobacco) to illustrate the importance of . . .

> cultural changes regarding perceptions of risk and the social acceptability of substance use, as well as the impact of effective policies that affect the availability of, and demand for, harmful substances . . . As substance abuse became socially acceptable in the 1970s, use increased. Likewise, when social norms changed and people became more aware of the dangers of substance abuse, use declined.[20]

ONDCP's point is that when drugs are disapproved and more difficult to attain (as in the case of tobacco and alcohol in some circumstance), use declines. Ironically, both of these drugs are legal. ONDCP appears to prove the point of some legalization proponents who argue that even if illicit drugs were legalized, use might not increase as long as serious efforts were implemented to restrict and discourage use.

Drug Testing

The 2006 Strategy again sells the effectiveness of drug testing in schools, saying that it "deters young people from initiating drug use; it identifies those who have initiated drug use so that parents and counselors can intervene early; and it helps identify those who have a dependency on drugs so that they can be referred for treatment."[21] Further, it "helps prepare students for the workforce . . . that is increasingly insistent on maintaining a drug free environment."[22] ONDCP notes that "[m]any schools across the country have instituted student testing as a way to maintain drug free schools and ensure that students who use drugs get the help they need" and then utilizes results from one school system in North Carolina to prove the effectiveness of drug testing.[23] Yet, again, ONDCP fails to even mention the evidence from national studies showing the ineffectiveness of drug testing.

Drug Treatment

ONDCP again notes the importance of drug treatment in its 2006 Strategy and claims it is "cost effective."[24] Yet, only one-quarter of FY 2007 drug war funds are requested for drug treatment. Amazingly, in only two places in the 2006 Strategy does ONDCP provide data with regard to the number of people who received treatment for a drug problem. First, when discussing market disruption of Colombian heroin, ONDCP claims:

> The resulting shortfall in the supply of Colombian heroin has led to a decline in use. Heroin-treatment admissions reflect this decline. Admissions for heroin use reached a peak in 2002, with 289,056 recorded entries. Entries into treatment institutions declined in the following years, to 272,815 in 2003 (a 6 percent decrease from 2002) and an estimated 254,181 in 2004 (a 12 percent decrease from 2002). This data represents [sic] a summation of 2004 state data from Substance Abuse and Mental Health Services Administration's Treatment Episode Data Set.[25]

Second, ONDCP writes: "In the past decade and a half, methamphetamine use has gradually spread eastward across the United States. Between 1992 and 2002, the treatment admission rate for methamphetamine/amphetamine has increased from 10 to 52 admissions per 100,000 population age 12 or older (an increase of over 500 percent)."[26]

With no systematic data on the number of people who need treatment or the number of people who receive it, it is impossible with the 2006 National Drug Control Strategy to assess the ability of the drug war to provide treatment for those who need it and thus "heal America's drug users"—a long standing goal of the drug war and ONDCP. If ONDP has prioritized treatment in its balanced drug war, we do not understand the failure to present data to demonstrate the effectiveness of its drug treatment efforts.

Market Disruption

In the 2006 Strategy, ONDCP again thoroughly explains the logic of market disruption:

> The policies and programs of the *National Drug Control Strategy* are guided by the fundamental insight that the illegal drug trade is a market, and both users and traffickers are affected by market dynamics. By disrupting this market, the US Government seeks to undermine the ability of drug suppliers to meet, expand, and profit from drug demand. When drug supply does not fully meet drug demand, changes in drug price and purity support prevention efforts by making initiation to drug use more difficult. They also contribute to treatment efforts by eroding the abilities of users to sustain their habits.[27]

Citing an "increasingly diverse body of scientific evidence [that] underscores the significance of drug price and purity to the habits of drug users," ONDCP claims that the "sensitivity of users to drug price and purity is a durable relationship that can be influenced to help achieve America's national drug control goals."[28]

Yet, as in previous strategies, ONDCP fails to provide any meaningful statistics with regard to drug use prices and drug purity. One figure in the Strategy illustrates decreasing purity of Colombian heroin from 2001–2004 and corresponding declines in chronic use between 2001 and 2003.[29] Interestingly, Colombian heroin is a drug that is rarely used in the United States. Similarly, in a box titled "Changes in Retail Price and Purity of Cocaine," ONDCP claims that beginning in "February 2005, retail-level cocaine price and purity showed evidence of *reversing a three-year trend of increasing purity and decreasing prices*."[30] Here, ONDCP suggests effective market disruption based on only four years of data and only one year of a decline (after three years of increasing purity and decreasing prices!).

ONDCP again goes back only to 2001, writing: "Potential production of co-caine in South America has declined steadily since 2001, and worldwide cocaine seizures reached record levels in the past four years. Moreover, no 'balloon effect' has occurred in Bolivian and Peruvian cultivation that would offset the dramatic year-over-year decreases in Colombia."[31] Yet, ONDCP admits that "[r]etail price and purity data are just now showing the effects of our supply-side suc-cesses, partly because there is a lag between when leaf is harvested in Colombia and a US retail sample is collected and analyzed by the Drug Enforcement Ad-ministration (DEA)."[32] Further, ONDCP admits: "Our supply-side constriction of US-bound cocaine appears to have now outpaced the decline in demand, and we are witnessing the early stages of a change in cocaine availability."[33]

These kinds of claims do not suggest long-term or consistent success in drug market disruption—which is clearly ONDCP's goal—but rather some-thing that is only recently different about drug market disruption outcomes. ONDCP admits as much when it writes:

> We are *beginning to see the results of our market disruption strategy* in the United States. Cocaine price and purity at the retail level have re-versed a three year trend of increasing purity and decreasing price. Continued declines in the potential production of cocaine in South America and record worldwide cocaine seizures have gradually re-duced global supply . . . unprecedented removals of cocaine from glo-bal distribution, combined with the diminished ability of the source countries to replenish worldwide supply, is *beginning to have an effect in the United States*. Between February and September 2005, retail co-caine purity dropped by 15 percent. Retail cocaine prices increased during the same period, suggesting the *beginnings of a disruption of the cocaine market*.[34]

Given ONDCP's past willingness to claim success in numerous years of the Strategy, we do not understand how it can now claim that its efforts are only now just beginning to work.

In addition to the recent reductions in cocaine purity and increases in co-caine prices, ONDCP suggests some other successes. They include reductions in Colombian heroin cultivation and purity and increases in heroin prices.[35] ONDCP offers figures showing increased eradication of hectares sprayed with herbicide in Colombia and declines in potential production of pure Colombian heroin.[36] Other good news includes a reduction in methamphetamine labs and "superlabs" in the United States, attributable in part to the 35 states that "have passed legislation to impose new regulations on the retail sale of the metham-phetamine precursor pseudoephedrine."[37] Additionally, ONDCP reports a large decline in the Ecstasy market caused in part due to a major initiative between the United States and Dutch governments. Unfortunately, ONDCP provides no long-term data or figures depicting such data in order to assess the overall effectiveness of market disruption efforts.

Further, ONDCP uses statistics related to process-oriented outcomes such as the number of extraditions achieved from Colombia, amount of drugs eradicated and seized, number of high priority targets disrupted, and so forth, to claim U.S. drug control efforts are responsible for recent drug use declines, ignoring the possibility of spuriousness due to uncontrolled confounding factors. ONDCP also ignores the issue of replacement (e.g., when one individual or organization is removed, another takes over), substitution (e.g., when one drug becomes less available, users may change drugs), and to a lesser degree, displacement (e.g., when efforts to disrupt supply in one place are counteracted by increased production in other areas). This is inconsistent with thorough and fair policy analysis.

Finally, in the 2006 Strategy, ONDCP links successful market disruption to the "Global War on Terrorism," claiming that it helps sever "links between drug traffickers and terrorist organizations in countries such as Afghanistan and Colombia, among others."[38] This again ignores the fact that, without prohibition, terrorists could not so greatly profit from the drug market.

New Parts of the Strategy

New parts of the nation' drug control efforts are introduced in the 2006 Strategy. For example, the Major Cities Drug Initiative aims to target drug problems in the nation's largest cities where they are often greatest. The initiative "brings together Federal, state, and local officials working in drug prevention, treatment and law enforcement to identify the unique challenges drugs pose to each community."[39] ONDCP notes efforts in Miami, Baltimore, Washington D.C., and Denver. Interestingly, citizens of the city of Denver, Colorado recently voted to allow adults 21 years and older to possess up to an ounce of marijuana without any penalty.[40] ONDCP does not mention this.

Another new part of the Strategy is Screening, Brief Intervention, Referral and Treatment (SBIRT) that aims to stop people who have starting using drugs from becoming drug abusers and to help those who have already developed drug abusing habits. It attempts to achieve these goals by screening patients in hospitals and other medical settings for drug use. Although ONDCP calls the system "cost effective" it offers no evidence that this is the case.[41] Instead, it writes, "This program is built on a body of research showing that simply by asking questions regarding unhealthy behaviors and conducting a brief intervention, patients are more likely to avoid the behavior in the future and seek help if they believe they have a problem."[42]

An additional part of the Strategy is the "National Synthetic Drugs Action Plan" — "the first comprehensive national plan to address the problems of synthetic and pharmaceutical drug trafficking and abuse. The Action Plan outlines current Federal and state efforts in the areas of prevention, treatment, regulation, and law enforcement and made concrete recommendations for enhancing government efforts to reduce synthetic drug abuse."[43]

ONDCP also describes a new prevention advertisement program — the "above the influence" campaign — that targets youth aged 14–16 years old to encourage them to "live 'above the influence' and to reject the use of illicit drugs and other negative pressures."[44] A series of ads via television, print media, and web sites tells teenagers that drugs stand in the way of their aspirations, abilities, and full potential. Based on the literature reviewed in the book, this approach may prove more effective than those employed previously by ONDCP such as the Media Campaign. Only time (and honest policy evaluation) will tell if this is the case.

More Like a War

More than any of the other Strategy reports reviewed in this book, the 2006 Strategy lays out approaches that "feel" like a true drug war. The great bulk of the document deals with market disruption efforts. In fact, twenty-four of the forty pages (60%) of the 2006 Strategy are devoted to market disruption. This clearly illustrates the imbalanced nature of the Strategy.

Market disruption efforts include targeting Consolidated Priority Organizations Targets (CPOTS), "the highest level of criminal organizations in the drug trade,"[45] disrupting violent drug gangs,[46] interrupting money laundering efforts of drug trafficking organizations,[47] interdicting transit zones,[48] increasing border security along the Mexican border,[49] breaking up Mexican drug trafficking organizations (DTOs) within the United States,[50] and fighting the war on terrorism in Afghanistan.[51]

The latter effort is summarized by ONDCP:

> The strategy for attacking the economic basis of the drug trade in Afghanistan reinforces other priorities in the US Global War on Terror. We are committed to a counternarcotics strategy that aims to enhance stability in this fledgling democracy by attacking a source of financial and political support for terrorist organizations that threaten the United States and our allies. Our strategic objectives are to (1) build Afghan institutional capacity to sustain the battle against narcotics; (2) assist Afghan authorities to arrest, prosecute, and punish drug traffickers and corrupt Afghan officials; (3) increase the risk and

provide economic alternatives to the illegal narcotics trade; and (4) support Afghan Government efforts to make the narcotics trade culturally unacceptable.[52]

When discussing opium poppy cultivation in Afghanistan, ONDCP highlights a decline between 2004 and 2005; yet , a figure on the same page shows that poppy cultivation is up overall from 2000 to 2005.[53]

Conclusion

The 2006 Strategy is more of the same from ONDCP—a dishonest, incomplete report that is ill-suited to assist in a truthful assessment of the nation's drug control efforts. While ONDCP highlights the good news in the nation's drug control efforts—and there is much good news—it continues to produce a flawed assessment of the nation's drug war. The National Drug Control Strategy appears to be little else than a document that is intended to reinforce the dominant ideology of the drug war regardless of what the relevant data show.

Appendix

ONDCP Director John Walters Responds

On March 11, 2004, John Walters, Director of the Office of National Drug Control Policy (ONDCP), addressed attendees of the annual meeting of the Academy of Criminal Justice Sciences (ACJS), who were convened in Las Vegas, Nevada. His presentation focused on the 2004 Strategy and the recent efforts of ONDCP.

Mr. Walters made several startling admissions of failure in his presentation and one of the authors (Robinson) had the opportunity to ask him a question related to the findings of the study in this book. This is a brief summary of the admissions of Mr. Walters and his response.

In his presentation, Director Walters claimed that ONDCP is "the government" and is thus responsible for "doing things" including "making problems smaller." He noted that the problem of drug use is down since its peak in 1979, acknowledged that youth drug use increased in the 1990s, and stated that overall youth drug use is lower today than in 1979. Given that "prevention does not work," once kids start drug use, according to Walters, and that those who are already using "resent it" when they are encouraged not to use drugs, Walters maintained that the most important goal is to stop kids from starting to use drugs -- to get the message to them before they start because "we don't want them to resent us."

Walters admitted that ONDCP has not been effective in disrupting markets, that it has not left a "big enough footprint" in this area. He asserted that ONDCP must redefine and rethink its federal level activities to intervene in illicit markets, to more effectively work with businesses, economics, public health and social science experts, and foreign intelligence to "begin to have an effect" on market disruption. He also noted that ONDCP needs to be more effective at going after drugs "as a business."

Walters also explained that ONDCP has few tools to assess what is happening now ("real-time data") in the drug war, and that its "dated" data from long-term studies are not well suited to inform policy. The Director asserted that the drug war is not managed as if we really expect the policy to make a difference, and that this needs to change.

Walters noted successes in reducing drug use based on very specific interventions in LSD and Ecstasy markets and said that the "greatest barrier to success [in the drug war] is cynicism." The notion that "since drug use is still around, the drug war is a failure" is an example of the cynical attitude that Walters feels is held by many.

After the presentation, Robinson asked Mr. Walters a question about the findings of the study reported in this book. Robinson indicated that he taught a course called "The War on Drugs" and that he wanted to make sure he was imparting to his students a fair assessment of the drug war since the founding of ONDCP. Robinson asked Walters to respond to the assessment of the relative degree of effectiveness of ONDCP since its creation in 1988--that ONDCP was not meeting any of its three goals of reducing drug use, healing drug users, or disrupting drug markets. Specifically, Robinson asked Walters if the following was an accurate and fair assessment of ONDCP's performance:

1. Since 1989, the year after ONDCP was founded, adult drug use overall is up, youth drug use overall is up, and recent declines in some drug use have been offset by increases in others, therefore ONDCP is not meeting its goal of reducing drug use;

2. Since 1989, need for drug treatment is up, availability of drug treatment is only slightly up, and most people who need treatment do not get it; and since 1989, emergency room mentions of drug use are up and deaths attributable to drug use are up, therefore ONDCP is not meeting its goal of healing drug users.

3. Since 1989, students indicate that drugs are slightly less available, but that they are still widely available, prices for drugs are down meaning they are cheaper to buy, and purity of most drugs is up, therefore ONDCP is not meeting its goal of disrupting drug markets.

Director Walters responded that ONDCP is not the only agency involved in the drug war and is not solely responsible for increases and decreases in drug use. Yet, ONDCP provides accountability in the drug war--that is, it is fair to see the ONDCP as "the accountable agency." Walters indicated that the new two- and five-year goals of the drug war increase accountability because ten-year goals (and longer) assure that no one will be held accountable for drug war policies. That is, previously, a president could set long-term goals and never be evaluated on performance in meeting the goals because he or she would not longer be in office, whereas, with short-term goals, a president can be held accountable during the term of office.

Walters noted that the term "war on drugs" was well intentioned, based on the notion that there was a consensus that drugs posed a threat to the well-being of the nation, "like a foreign enemy." He did suggest that perhaps it was time to stop using the term because of its negative implications.

With regard to the specific question, Director Walters said he would not use the founding of ONDCP as a baseline for evaluation of the effectiveness of the drug war because it "does not capture our national efforts in the drug war." Walters maintained that the drug war has still reduced drug use because it is lower than it was in the 1979 and early 1980s. Yet, he admitted that, although drug use continued to fall until the early 1990s, it then increased through the 1990s. In essence, this is an admission that if one does begin an evaluation of the drug war since 1988, drug use trends would be inconsistent with the goals of the drug war.

It is safe to conclude that even John Walters, Director of ONDCP, is aware that, during the existence of ONDCP, trends in drug use, drug treatment, deaths attributed to drug use, emergency room mentions of drug use, drug availability, drug purity, and drug prices are inconsistent with the goals of ONDCP. Yet, Walters would not use the founding of ONDCP in 1989 to evaluate the effectiveness of ONDCP in its drug war because 1989 is an "arbitrary" starting point.

Notes

Preface

1. Former British Prime Minister Benjamin Disraeli actually said this first, but the quote became well known in the United States because of Mark Twain.

2. Actually, the net worth of Bill Gates was $48 billion in 2004. See Armstrong, D., & Newcomb, P. (2004). *Special report: The 400 richest Americans.* Retrieved May 31, 2004, from http://www.forbes.com/2004/09/22/rlo4land.html.

3. U.S. Census Bureau. (2003). New worth and asset ownership of households: 1998 and 2000. Retrieved May 31, 2004, from http://www.census.gov/prod/2003pubs/p70-88.pdf

4. The White House later corrected this figure to $1,586! See Factcheck.org. (2004). Here we go again: Bush exaggerates tax cuts. Retrieved May 31, 2004, from http://www.factcheck.org/article145.html.

5. Ibid.

6. Drug policy experts acknowledge that "'war' is not an apt metaphor when identified with policy seeking to control drug use . . . the campaign against drugs includes the expenditure of substantial sums of such non-war like activities as drug abuse treatment and prevention." Nevertheless, given that the terms "war on drugs" and "drug war" are commonly used to refer to America's efforts to reduce drug use and abuse, we use these terms throughout the book. See, for example, Caulkins, J., Reuter, P., & Iguchi, M. (2005). *How goes the "war on drugs"? An assessment of US drug problems and policy.* Santa Monica: RAND Drug Policy Research Center, p. 3.

7. Office of National Drug Control Policy. (2003). About ONDCP. Retrieved January 13, 2005, from http://www.whitehousedrugpolicy.gov/about/index.html.

Chapter 1

1. Office of National Drug Control Policy. (2004). About ONDCP. Retrieved January 13, 2005, from http://www.whitehousedrugpolicy.gov/about/index.html.

2. The slide show is no longer available online but can be requested from the primary author.

3. Walters, J. (2004). Comments of the Director of the Office of National Drug Control Policy (ONDCP) to the attendees of the annual meeting of the Academy of Criminal Justice Sciences (ACJS), Las Vegas, Nevada, March 11.

4. U.S. Department of Health and Human Services (2004). 2001 National Household Survey on Drug Abuse. Section 9.2. Long-term trends in illicit drug use. Retrieved February 13, 2005, from http://www.drugabusestatistics.samhsa.gov/nhsda/2k1nhsda/vol1/chapter9.htm.

5. Manski, C., Pepper, J., & Petrie, C. (2001). *Informing America's policy on illegal drugs: What we don't know keeps hurting us.* Committee on Data and Research for Policy on Illegal drugs. Washington DC: National Academy Press, p. 7.

6. We are indebted to Professor Ruth Ann Strickland of Appalachian State University for this definition.

7. See, for example, Bagdikian, B. (2000). *The media monopoly* (6th ed.). Boston: Beacon Press.

8. Discussions of ideology in the operation of criminal justice agencies can be found in Merlo, A., & Benekos, P. (2000). *What's wrong with the criminal justice system: Ideology, politics and the media.* Cincinnati: Anderson; Robinson, M. (2005). *Justice blind? Ideals and realities of American criminal justice* (2nd ed.), Upper Saddle River, NJ: Prentice-Hall.

9. Merriam-Webster OnLine (2004). Ideology, Retrieved February 10, 2005, from http://m-w.com/cgi-bin/thesaurus?book=Thesaurus&va=ideology.

10. Gaines, L., & Kraska, P. (1997). *Drugs, crime, and justice.* Prospect Heights, IL: Waveland Press, p. 4.

11. Best, J. (1989). *Random violence.* Hawthorne, NY: Aldine de Gruyter, p. 144.

12. Mauss, A. (1975). *Social problems as social movements.* New York: Lippincott.

13. Jensen, E., Gerber, J., & Babcock, G. (1991). The new war on drugs: Grass roots movement or political construction? *The Journal of Drug Issues, 21(3),* 651–667.

14. Mauss (1975), p. 62.

15. Ibid., p. 63.

16. Jensen, Gerber, & Babcock (1991).

17. Mauss (1975); Mauss, A. (1989). Beyond the illusion of social problems theory. In J. Holstein & G. Miller (Eds.), *Perspectives on Social Problems* (Vol. 1). Greenwich, CT: JAI Press; Spector, M., & Kitsuse, J. (1987). *Constructing social problems.* Hawthorne, NY: Aldine de Gruyter.

18. Cohen, S. (1972). *Folk devils and moral panics: The creation of the Mods and the Rockers.* London: MacGibbon and Kee, p. 9.

19. Escholtz, S. (1997). The media and fear of crime: A survey of research. *University of Florida Journal of Law and Public Policy, 9(1),* 48.

20. Suratt, H., & Inciardi, J. (2001). Cocaine, crack, and the criminalization of pregnancy. In J. Inciardi & K. McElrath (Eds.), *The American drug scene*. Los Angeles: Roxbury.

21. Jensen, E., & Gerber, J. (1998). *The new war on drugs: Symbolic politics and criminal justice policy*. Cincinnati: Anderson, p. ix.

22. Robinson (2005).

23. Best (1989).

24. Jensen & Gerber (1998), p. 5.

25. Some of these ads can be viewed on the Internet. See Office of National Drug Control Policy (2004). Ad gallery. Retrieved February 17, 2005, from http://www.mediacampaign.org/mg/.

26. Jensen & Gerber (1998), p. 8.

27. Quoted in Bonnie, R., & Whitebread, C. (1974). *Marihuana conviction: A history of Marihuana prohibition in the United States*. Charlottesville: University of Virginia, p. 109.

28. Kappeler, V., Blumberg, M., & Potter, G. (2000). *The mythology of crime and criminal justice* (3rd ed.). Prospect Heights, IL: Waveland Press, p. 9.

29. For a summary of this evidence, see Vankin J., & Whalen, J. (2004). *The 80 greatest conspiracies of all time*. New York: Citadel Press; J. Herer (1998). *The emperor wears no clothes: The authoritative historical record of cannabis and the conspiracy against marijuana* (11th ed.). Van Nuys, CA: Ah Ha Publishing.

30. To read some of Anslinger's words, see: Anslinger, H., & Cooper, C. (2001). Marijuana: Assassin of youth." In J. Inciardi & K. McElrath (Eds.), *The American drug scene*. Los Angeles: Roxbury.

31. Webb, G., & Brown, M. (1998). United States drug laws and institutionalized discrimination. In E. Jensen & J. Gerber (Eds.), *The new war on drugs: Symbolic politics and criminal justice policy*. Cincinnati: Anderson, p. 45.

32. Jensen & Gerber (1998).

33. Sandor, S. (1995). Legalizing / decriminalizing drug use. In R. Coombs & D. Zeidonis (Eds.), *Handbook on drug abuse prevention: A contemporary strategy to prevent the abuse of alcohol and other drugs*. Boston: Allyn & Bacon, p. 48.

34. Belenko, S. (1993). *Crack and the evolution of the anti-drug policy*. Westport, CT: Greenwood Press, p. 9.

35. Becker, H. (1963). *Outsiders*. New York: Free Press.

36. Beckett, K., & Sasson, T. (2000). *The politics of injustice: Crime and justice in America*. Thousand Oaks, CA: Pine Forge Press, p. 37.

37. Reinarman, C., & Levine, H. (1989). Crack in context: Politics and media in the making of a drug scene. *Contemporary Drug Problems, 16*, 116-129.

38. Beckett, K. (1997). *Making crime pay: Law and order in contemporary American politics*. New York: Oxford University Press.

39. Potter, G., & Kappeler, V. (1998). *Constructing crime: Perspectives on making news and social problems*. Prospect Heights, IL: Waveland Press.

40. Beckett (1997).

41. Reinarman, C. (1995). Crack attack: America's latest drug scare, 1986–1992. In J. Best (Ed.), *Typifying contemporary social problems*. New York: Aldine de Gruyter.

42. Robinson (2005).

43. Reinarman & Levine (1989), pp. 541–542.

44. Orcutt, J., & Turner, J. (1993). Shocking numbers and graphic accounts: Quantified images of drug problems in print media. *Social Problems, 6*, 217–232; Walker, S. (1998). *Sense and nonsense about crime and drugs, A policy guide* (4th ed.). Belmont, CA: Wadsworth.

45. Jensen & Gerber (1998), p. 14.

46. U.S. Department of Health and Human Services (2000). 1999 National Household Survey of Drug Abuse. Table 4.2a. Estimated numbers (in thousands) of persons who first used cocaine during the years 1965 to 1999, their mean age at first use, and annual age-specific rates of first use (per 1,000 person-years of exposure): Based on 1999 and 2000 NHSDAs. Retrieved February 20, 2005, from http://oas.samhsa.gov/ nhsda/2kdetailedtabs/Vol_1_Part_3/sect3_5v1.htm#4.2a.

47. U.S. Department of Health and Human Services (2000). 1999 National Household Survey of Drug Abuse. Table 4.3a. Estimated numbers (in thousands) of persons who first used crack during the years 1965 to 1999, their mean age at first use, and annual age-specific rates of first use (per 1,000 person-years of exposure): Based on 1999 and 2000 NHSDAs. Retrieved February 10, 2005, from http://oas.samhsa.gov/ nhsda/2kdetailedtabs/Vol_1_Part_3/sect3_5v1.htm#4.3a.

48. Beckett & Sasson (2000), p. 28.

49. Reinarman (1995).

50. Jensen & Gerber (1998), p. 17.

51. Clymer, A. (1986). Public found ready to sacrifice in drug fight. *New York Times*, September 2, A1, D 16.

52. Sourcebook of Criminal Justice Statistics (2005). Table 2.1. Attitudes toward the most important problem facing the country. Retrieved March 30, 2005, from http:// www.albany.edu/sourcebook/pdf/t21.pdf.

53. Jensen, Gerber, & Babcock (1991).

54. Bertram, E., Blachman, M., Sharpe, K., & Andreas, P. (1996). *Drug war politics: The price of denial*. Berkeley: University of California Press.

55. Johns, C. (1992). *State power, ideology and the war on drugs: Nothing succeeds like failure*. New York: Praeger.

56. See, for example, Gray, J. (2001). *Why our drug laws have failed and what we can do about it.* Philadelphia: Temple University Press; Miron, J. (2004). *Drug war crimes: The consequences of prohibition.* Oakland, CA: The Independent Institute; Reiman, J. (1998). *The rich get richer and the poor get prison: Ideology, class, and criminal justice* (5th ed.). Boston: Allyn & Bacon; Walker (1998).

57. These include Change the Climate, the Coalition for Compassionate Leadership on Drug Policy, Common Sense for Drug Policy, the Drug Policy Alliance, the Drug Reform Coordination Network, Drug Sense, Law Enforcement Against Prohibition (LEAP), the National Organization for the Reform of Marijuana Laws (NORML), the November Coalition, The Sentencing Project, Students for Sensible Drug Policy, and the American Civil Liberties Union (ACLU).

58. Carson, G. (1999). Making claims against the war on drugs in the United States: A look at the emergence of Internet sites. Retrieved April 20, 2004, from http://www.angelfire.com/pa/sergeman/issues/drugs/main.html.

59. Office of National Drug Control Policy (2003). *2003 President's national drug control strategy.* Retrieved February 13, 2004, from http://www.whitehousedrugpolicy .gov/publications/pdf/strategy2003.pdf, p. 9.

60. At the same time, the General Social Survey shows that the percentage of Americans with a "great deal" of confidence in the executive branch of the U.S. government has remained below 30% since 1973. See Kearl, M. (2004). Political sociology. Retrieved February 14, 2004, from http://www.trinity.edu/~mkearl/polisci.html.

61. Jones, C. (1970). *An introduction to the study of public policy.* Belmont, CA: Wadsworth; Anderson, J. (1975). *Public policy making.* New York: Praeger; Brewer, G., & DeLeon, P. (1983). *The foundations of policy analysis.* Monterey, CA: Brooks/Cole; Brewer, G. (1974). The policy sciences emerge: To nurture and structure a discipline. *Policy Sciences, 5(3),* 239–244.

62. Manski et al. (2001), p. 1.

63. Ibid., pp. 15–16.

64. Boyum, D., & P. Reuter (2005). *An analytic assessment of US drug policy.* Washington, DC: AIE Press, p. 10.

65. Caulkins, J., Reuter, P., & M. Iguchi (2005). *How goes the "war on drugs"? An assessment of US drug problems and policy.* Santa Monica, CA: RAND Drug Policy Research Center, p. 23.

66. See, for example, Alder, M., & Posner, E. (2001). *Cost-benefit analysis: Legal, economic, and philosophical perspectives.* Chicago: University of Chicago Press.

67. Sunstein, C. (1999). From consumers sovereignty to cost-benefit analysis: An incompletely theorized agreement? *Harvard Journal of Law & Public Policy, 23(1),* 203–211.

CHAPTER 2

1. Jensen, E., & Gerber, J. (1998). *The new war on drugs: Symbolic politics and criminal justice policy.* Cincinnati: Anderson, p. 6.

2. Eddy, M. (2003). War on drugs: Legislation in the 108th Congress and related developments. *CRS Issue Brief for Congress.* Washington, DC: Library of Congress, p. ii.

3. MacCoun, R., & Reuter, P. (2001). *Drug war heresies: Learning from other vices, times & places.* New York: Colombia University Press, p. 199.

4. Jensen & Gerber (1998), p. 6.

5. Inciardi, J. (2002). *The war on drugs III.* Boston: Allyn & Bacon.

6. Ibid., pp. 17-18.

7. Hamid, A. (1998). *Drugs in America: Sociology economics, and politics.* Gaithersburg, MD: Aspen.

8. MacCoun & Reuter, p. 183.

9. Ibid.

10. Ibid., p. 195.

11. Gray, J. (2001). *Why our drug laws have failed and what we can do about it: A judicial indictment of the war on drugs.* Philadelphia: Temple University Press.

12. Hamid (1998), p. 85.

13. Ibid., p. 186.

14. Ibid., p. 188.

15. Ibid., p. 193

16. Ibid., p. 184.

17. Inciardi (2002), p. 21.

18. Ibid., p. 22.

19. Ibid., p. 20

20. Ibid., p. 24.

21. Ibid., p. 29

22. MacCoun & Reuter (2001).

23. Ibid., p. 199.

24. Ibid., p. 200.

25. Ibid., p. 201.

26. Jensen & Gerber (1998), p. 7.

27. Hamid (1998), p. 86.

28. Brecher, E. (1972). *Licit and illicit drugs.* Boston: Little, Brown, p. 49

29. Inciardi (2002), p. 173.

30. Jensen & Gerber (1998), pp. 8-9.

31. Gray (2001), p. 22.

32. Inciardi (2002), p. 29.

33. Miron, J. (2004). *Drug war crimes: The consequences of prohibition*. Oakland, CA: The Independent Institute, p. 26.

34. Ibid.; MacCoun & Reuter (2001). p. 158.

35. MacCoun & Reuter (2002), pp. 159-160.

36. Hamid (1998), p. 88.

37. Inciardi (2002), p. 32.

38. Gray (2001), p. 25.

39. Jensen & Gerber (1998), p. 48.

40. Jensen & Gerber (1998), p. 11.

41. Gray (2001), p. 27.

42. British League Cannabis Campaigns (2004). Single convention on narcotics drugs. Retrieved November 30, 2004, from http://www.ukcia.org/pollaw/lawlibrary/singleconventiononnarcoticdrugs1961.html.

43. International Narcotics Control Board (2004). Introduction. Retrieved November 30, 2004, from http://www.incb.org/e/.

44. See, for example, Drug Policy Alliance (2005). Marijuana: The facts. Retrieved March 31, 2005, from http://www.drugpolicy.org/marijuana/factsmyths/.

45. Boaz, D., & Lynch, T. (2004). *CATO handbook on policy* (Sixth ed.). Retrieved February 17, 2005, from http://www.cato.org/pubs/handbook/.

46. Manski, C., Pepper, J., & Petrie, C. (2001). *Informing America's policy on illegal drugs: What we don't know keeps hurting us*. Committee on Data and Research for Policy on Illegal drugs. Washington, DC: National Academy Press, p. 271.

47. PBS *Frontline* (2000). Thirty years of America's drug war: A chronology. Retrieved February 10, 2004, from http://www.pbs.org/wgbh/pages/frontline/shows/drugs/cron/.

48. Eddy (2003), p. 1.

49. Bryant, L. (1990). The posse comitatus act, the military, and drug interdiction: Just how far can we go? *Army Law, 3*, December, 1990.

50. Elliot, J. (1995). Drug prevention placebo: How DARE wastes time, money, and police. *Reason, March*. Retrieved February 10, 2004, from http://www.drugpolicy.org/library/tlcdare.cfm.

51. Hanson, D. (2004). Effectiveness of DARE. Retrieved February 10, 2004, from http://www2.potsdam.edu/alcohol-info/YouthIssues/1059145293.html, emphasis in original featured in italics.

52. Gray (2001), p. 27.

53. Ibid.

54. Ibid.

55. Manski et al. (2001), p. 195.

56. Ibid., p. 196.

57. Thomas Legislative Information on the Internet (2004). Bill summary & status for the 100th Congress. H.R.5210. A bill to prevent the manufacturing, distribution, and use of illegal drugs, and for other purposes. Retrieved February 13, 2005, from http://thomas.loc.gov/cgi-bin/bdquery/z?d100:HR05210:@@@L&summ2=m&.

58. Eddy (2003), p. 4.

59. Office of National Drug Control Policy (2004). Enabling legislation. Retrieved February 6, 2005, from http://www.whitehousedrugpolicy.gov/about/legislation.html.

60. Bush, G. (1989). Speech to the nation about the invasion of Panama. Weekly Compilation of Presidential Documents, Wednesday, December 20, 1989, emphasis added.

61. Borger, J., & Hodgson, M. (2001). A plane is shot down and the U.S. proxy war on drugs unravels. *The Guardian*, June 2, 2001.

62. Office of National Drug Control Policy (2004). Enabling legislation. Retrieved February 6, 2005, from http://www.whitehousedrugpolicy.gov/about/legislation.html.

63. Eddy, M. (2003), p. 6.

64. Hornik, R. et al. (2002). *Evaluation of the national youth anti-drug media campaign: Fifth semi-annual report of findings executive summary*. Rockville, MD: Westat, p. xi.

65. Eddy (2003), p. i.

66. Perl (2004), p. 11.

67. Ibid., p. 16.

68. Ibid., p. 9.

69. Eddy (2001), p. 13.

70. Piper, B., Briggs, M., Huffman, K., & Lubot-Cook, R. (2003). *State of the states: Drug policy reforms: 1996-2002*. New York: Drug Policy Alliance, p. 1.

71. Office of National Drug Control Policy (2005). *President's national drug control strategy*. Retrieved March 5, 2005, from http://www.whitehousedrugpolicy.gov/publications/policy/ndcs05/ndcs05.pdf, p.4.

72. Caulkins, J., Reuter, P., & M. Iguchi (2005). *How goes the "war on drugs"? An assessment of US drug problems and policy*. Santa Monica, CA: RAND Drug Policy Research Center, p. 4.

73. Ibid., p. 5.

74. Boyum, D., & P. Reuter (2005). *An analytic assessment of US drug policy*. Washington, DC: AIE Press, p. 10.

75. Caulkins et al. (2005), pp. 26–27.

76. Office of National Drug Control Policy (1995). *National drug control policy: Strengthening Communities' response to drugs*. Retrieved April 5, 2005, from http://www.ncjrs.org/pdffiles/strat95b.pdf, p. 10.

77. Office of National Drug Control Policy (1998). *National drug control strategy, 1998: A ten year plan*. Retrieved February 15, 2005, from http://www.ncjrs.org/ondcppubs/pdf/strat_pt1.pdf, p. 1.

78. Welsh, W., & Harris, P. (1999). *Criminal justice policy and planning*. Cincinnati: Anderson.

79. Office of National Drug Control Policy (2000). *President's national drug control strategy*. Retrieved March 12, 2002, from http://www.ncjrs.org/ondcppubs/publications/policy/ndcs00/strategy2000.pdf, p. 4.

80. Office of National Drug Control Policy (2004). National drug control strategy FY 2005 budget summary. Retrieved March 4, 2005, from http://www.whitehousedrugpolicy.gov/publications/policy/budgetsum04/budgetsum05.pdf, p. 10.

81. U.S. Department of Health & Human Services, Substance Abuse & Mental Health Services Administration (2005). About SAMHSA. Retrieved February 6, 2005, from http://www.samhsa.gov/Menu/Level2_about.aspx.

82. Office of National Drug Control Policy (2004), p. 37.

83. Ibid., p. 38.

84. Ibid., p. 47.

85. Ibid., p. 54.

86. Ibid., p. 59

87. Ibid., pp. 65–66.

88. Ibid., pp. 73–73.

89. Ibid., p. 98.

90. Office of National Drug Control Policy (2004). National drug control strategy FY 2005 budget summary. Retrieved March 4, 2005, from http://www.whitehousedrugpolicy.gov/publications/policy/budgetsum04/budgetsum05.pdf.

91. Office of National Drug Control Policy (2005). National drug control strategy FY 2006 budget summary. Retrieved March 10, 2005, from http://www.whitehousedrugpolicy.gov/publications/policy/06budget/06budget.pdf.

92. Robinson (2005).

93. Office of National Drug Control Policy (2002). *President's national drug control strategy*. Retrieved March 24, 2003, from http://www.whitehousedrugpolicy.gov/publications/pdf/Strategy2002.pdf, p. 33.

94. Office of National Drug Control Policy (2003). *President's national drug control strategy*. Retrieved March 11, 2004, from http://www.whitehousedrugpolicy.gov/publications/pdf/strategy2003.pdf. p. 6.

95. Office of National Drug Control Policy (2002). *President's national drug control strategy*. Retrieved March 24, 2003, from http://www.whitehousedrugpolicy.gov/publications/pdf/Strategy2002.pdf, p. 33.

96. Drug Policy Alliance (2003). Drug czars office tries to mask true costs of the drug war. Retrieved December 24, 2003, from http://www.drugpolicy.org/news/press room/pressrelease/pr020703.cfm.

97. Drug Policy Alliance (2003). Fuzzy math in new ONDCP report. Retrieved December 24, 2003, from http://www.drugpolicy.org/news/02_12_03fuzzy.cfm.

98. Drug Policy Alliance (2003). Drug czars office masks true costs of war on drugs in federal budget released today. Retrieved December 24, 2003, from http://www.drug policy.org/news/pressroom/pressrelease/pr021203.cfm.

99. Office of National Drug Control Policy (2005). National drug control strategy FY 2006 budget summary. Retrieved March 10, 2005, from http://www.whitehouse drugpolicy.gov/publications/policy/06budget/06budget.pdf.

100. Caulkins et al. (2005), p. 15.

101. Boyum & Reuter (2005), p. 38.

102. Ibid., p. 39

103. Caulkins et al. (2005), p. 16.

104. Ibid., p. 17.

105. Boyum & Reuter (2005), pp. 39, 42.

CHAPTER 3

1. For examples of others who have challenged specific claims by ONDCP, see Common Sense for Drug Policy (2004). Drug war distortions. Retrieved May 29, 2004, from http://www.drugwardistortions.org/; Compassionate Leadership for Drug Policy (2004). Urban myths. Retrieved May 29, 2004, from http://www.ccldp.org/myths.html.

2. National Criminal Justice Reference Service. Drugs and crime. Retrieved May 25, 2004, from http://virlib.ncjrs.org/DrugsAndCrime.asp.

3. ONDCP still provides data on prices, purity, deaths, emergency room mentions, drug arrests, costs to society, drug seizures, asset forfeiture, and so forth. The are contained in ONDCP's fact sheet titled *Drug data summary*. This fact sheet is located at the very bottom of one of ONDCP's Web sites titled "Federal Drug Data Sources." Retrieved March 10, 2005, from http://www.whitehousedrugpolicy.gov/drugfact/sources.html. The location of the fact sheet is: http://www.whitehousedrugpolicy.gov/publications/factsht/drugdata/index.html.

4. Office of National Drug Control Policy (2001). *The economic costs of drug abuse in the United States 1992–1998*. Retrieved January 13, 2005, from http://www.whitehouse drugpolicy.gov/publications/pdf/economic_costs98.pdf.

5. Office of National Drug Control Policy (2005). *President's national drug control policy*. Retrieved March 10, 2005, from http://www.whitehousedrugpolicy.gov/publications/policy/ndcs05/ndcs05.pdf, p.8.

6. Bennett, B. (2004). truth: the Anti-drug war. Retrieved March 3, 2004, from

http://www.briancbennett.com.

7. Office of National Drug Control Policy (2004). Federal drug data sources. Retrieved February 4, 2005, from http://www.whitehousedrugpolicy.gov/drugfact/sources.html.

8. For a summary of the changes and why data should not be compared, see U.S. Department of Health and Human Services Office of Applied Statistics (2004). Appendix C: NSDUH changes and their impact on trend measurement. Retrieved August 30, 2004 from http://www.oas.samhsa.gov/nhsda/2k2nsduh/Results/appC.htm.

9. Manski, C., Pepper, J., & Petrie, C. (2001). *Informing America's policy on illegal drugs: What we don't know keeps hurting us*. Committee on Data and Research for Policy on Illegal drugs. Washington DC: National Academy Press, p. 131.

10. Office of National Drug Control Policy (2002). *2002 final report on the 1998 national drug control strategy performance measures of effectiveness*. Retrieved November 30, 2004, from http://www.whitehousedrugpolicy.gov/publications/policy/02pme/index.html, p. viii.

11. Manski, et al. (2001).

12. Ibid., p. 11.

13. Ibid., p. 124.

14. Ibid., p. 3.

15. Ibid., p. 87.

16. Ibid., p. 93.

17. Ibid., p. 4.

18. Ibid., p. 109.

19. Ibid., p. 44.

20. Boyum, D., & P. Reuter (2005). *An analytic assessment of US drug policy*. Washington, DC: AIE Press, pp. 17–18.

21. Ibid., p. 18.

Chapter 4

1. Office of National Drug Control Policy (2000). *President's national drug control strategy*. Retrieved March 12, 2001, from http://www.ncjrs.org/ondcppubs/publications/policy/ndcs00/strategy2000.pdf, p. 7.

2. Ibid., p. 8.

3. Office of National Drug Control Policy (2001). *President's national drug control strategy*. Retrieved March 12, 2001, from http://www.ncjrs.org/ondcppubs/publications/policy/ndcs01/strategy2001.pdf, p. 9.

4. Office of National Drug Control Policy (2000), p. 8.

5. Ibid., p. 9.

6. Office of National Drug Control Policy (2001), p. 11.

7. Office of National Drug Control Policy (2002). *President's national drug control strategy*. Retrieved March 16, 2002, from http://www.whitehousedrugpolicy.gov/publications/policy/03ndcs/pages1_30.pdf, p. 3.

8. U.S. Department of Health and Human Services Office of Applied Statistics (2004).

Overview of findings from the 2002 national survey on drug use and health. Chapter 10, discussion. Retrieved September 14, 2004, from http://www.oas.samhsa.gov/nhsda/2k2nsduh/Overview/2k2Overview.htm#chap10.

9. Office of National Drug Control Policy (2002), p. 1.

10. Ibid., emphasis added.

11. Ibid., p. 4.

12. Office of National Drug Control Policy (2003). *President's national drug control strategy*. Retrieved April 14, 2003, from http://www.whitehousedrugpolicy.gov/publications/pdf/strategy2003.pdf, p. 4.

13. Ibid., p. 4.

14. Ibid., p. 1, emphasis added.

15. Ibid.

16. Ibid., p.2.

17. Ibid., emphasis added.

18. U.S. Department of Health and Human Services Office of Applied Statistics (2004). Trends in lifetime prevalence of substance abuse. Retrieved November 30, 2004, from http://www.oas.samhsa.gov/nhsda/2k2nsduh/Results/2k2Results.htm#chap5.

19. Office of National Drug Control Policy (2003). Table 5. Trends in 30-day prevalence of selected drugs among 8th graders, Monitoring the Future study, 1991–2002 (percent prevalence). Retrieved November 16, 2003, from http://www.whitehousedrug policy.gov/publications/policy/ndcs03/table5.html; Office of National Drug Control Policy (2003). Table 6. Trends in 30-day prevalence of selected drugs among 10th graders, Monitoring the Future study, 1991–2002 (percent prevalence) Retrieved November 16, 2003, from http://www.whitehousedrugpolicy.gov/publications/policy/ndcs03/table6.html; Office of National Drug Control Policy (2003). Table 7. Trends in 30-day prevalence of selected drugs among 12th graders, Monitoring the Future study,

1991–2002 (percent prevalence). Retrieved November 16, 2003, from http://www.white housedrugpolicy.gov/publications/policy/ndcs03/table7.html.

20. Office of National Drug Control Policy (2003), p. 2.

21. Ibid., p. 4.

22. See, for example, U.S. Department of Health and Human Services Office of Applied Statistics (2004). Figure 5.1 lifetime marijuana use among persons aged 12 to 25, by age group: 1965–2002. Retrieved November 27, 2004, from http://www.oas.samhsa .gov/nhsda/2k2nsduh/Results/2k2Results.htm#chap5.

23. Office of National Drug Control Policy (2003), p. 10.

24. Ibid., p. 11.

25. To review the evidence and long-term drug use according to the NHSDA, see: U.S. Department of Health and Human Services Office of Applied Statistics (2004). Trends in lifetime prevalence of substance abuse. Retrieved November 21, 2004, from http://www.oas.samhsa.gov/nhsda/2k2nsduh/Results/2k2Results.htm#chap5.

26. Office of National Drug Control Policy (2004). Table 2. Percentages reporting use of selected illicit drugs 1979–2002. Retrieved December 17, 2004, from http:// www.whitehousedrugpolicy.gov/publications/policy/ndcs04/table2.doc.

27. Ibid.

28. Office of National Drug Control Policy (2003), p. 10.

29. Monitoring the Future (2004). Table 14. Long-term trends in thirty-day prevalence of use of various drugs for twelfth graders. Retrieved December 30, 2004, from http://www.monitoringthefuture.org/data/04data/pro4t16.pdf.

30. Office of National Drug Control Policy (2003), p. 10.

31. Office of National Drug Control Policy (2002), p. 3.

32. To review evidence of long-term drug use according to the MTF, see Monitoring the Future (2004). Figure 1. Trends in annual prevalence of an illicit drug use index. Retrieved December 30, 2004, from http://monitoringthefuture.org/data/02data/fig02_1.pdf.

33. For discussions of the evidence of the "Just Say No" campaign and other efforts to reduce youth drug use, such as Drug Abuse Resistance Education (DARE), see Engs, R., & Fors, S. (1988). Drug abuse hysteria: The challenge of keeping perspective. Retrieved November 16, 2003, from http://www.indiana.edu/~engs/articles/drug hysteria.html; Lynam, D., Milich, R., Zimmerman, R., Novak, S., Logan, T., Martin, C., Leukefeld, C., & Clayton, R. (1999). Project DARE: No effects at 10-year follow-up. Retrieved November 16, 2003, from http://www.apa.org/journals/ccp/ccp674590 .html; and Moilanen, R. (2004). Just say no again: The old failures of new and improved anti-drug education. Retrieved November 16, 2003, from http://reason.com/0401/ fe.rm.just.shtml.

34. Office of National Drug Control Policy (2002), p. 3, emphasis added.

35. See, for example, MacCoun, R., Reuter, Jr. P., & Wolf, C. (2001). *Drug war heresies: Learning from other vices, times, and places.* New York: Cambridge University Press.

36. Office of National Drug Control Policy (2004). *President's national drug control strategy.* Retrieved March 15, 2004, from http://www.whitehousedrugpolicy.gov/publications/policy/ndcs04/2004ndcs.pdf, p. 1, emphasis added.

37. Monitoring the Future (2004). Table 1. Trends in lifetime prevalence of use of various drugs for eighth, tenth, and twelfth graders. Retrieved December 20, 2004, from http://www.monitoringthefuture.org/data/03data/pro3t1.pdf.

38. Office of National Drug Control Policy (2004), p. 1.

39. Monitoring the Future (2004). Table 2. Trends in annual and 30-day prevalence of use of various drugs for eighth, tenth, and twelfth graders. Retrieved December 20, 2004, from http://www.monitoringthefuture.org/data/03data/pro3t2.pdf.

40. Monitoring the Future (2004). Table 6. Long-term trends in thirty day prevalence of use of various drugs for twelfth graders. Retrieved December 20, 2004, from http://www.monitoringthefuture.org/data/03data/pro3t6.pdf.

41. Office of National Drug Control Policy (2004), p. 1.

42. Monitoring the Future (2004). Table 3. Trends in 30-day prevalence of use of various drugs for eighth, tenth, and twelfth graders. Retrieved December 20, 2004, from http://www.monitoringthefuture.org/data/04data/pro4t3.pdf.

43. White House (2002). President delivers state of the union address. Retrieved December 20, 2004, from http://www.whitehouse.gov/news/releases/2002/01/20020129 11.html.

44. Office of National Drug Control Policy (2004), pp. 1-2.

45. Ibid., p. 3.

46. Ibid.

47. Ibid.

48. Ibid.

49. Ibid., p. 3.

50. Ibid., p. 4.

51. Office of National Drug Control Policy (2005), p. 19.

52. Ibid., p. 6.

53. Ibid., p. 2.

54. U.S. Department of Health & Human Services, Substance Abuse & Mental Health Administration, Office of Applied Statistics (2004). National survey on drug use and health. Table 1.3b. Illicit drug use in lifetime, past year, and past month among persons aged 18-25. Retrieved December 20, 2004, from http://www.oas.samhsa.gov/nhsda/2k3tabs/sect1petabs1to66.htm#tab1.1B.

55. U.S. Department of Health & Human Services, Substance Abuse & Mental Health Administration, Office of Applied Statistics (2004). National survey on drug use and health. Table 1.10. Illicit drug use in lifetime, past year, and past month among persons aged 26-34. Retrieved December 20, 2004, from http://www.oas.samhsa.gov/nhsda/2k3tabs/sect1petabs1to66.htm#tab1.10.

56. U.S. Department of Health & Human Services, Substance Abuse & Mental Health Administration, Office of Applied Statistics (2004). National survey on drug use and health. Table 1.11b. Illicit drug use in lifetime, past year, and past month among persons aged 35 and older [online]. Available: http://www.oas.samhsa.gov/nhsda/2k3tabs/sect1petabs1to66.htm#tab1.11B.

57. Office of National Drug Control Policy (2005). *The president's national drug control Strategy.* Retrieved March 5, 2005, from http://www.whitehousedrugpolicy.gov/publications/policy/ndcs05/ndcs05.pdf, p. 1.

58. Ibid.

59. Monitoring the Future (2005). Table 1. Trends in lifetime prevalence of use of various drugs for eighth, tenth, and twelfth graders. Retrieved March 25, 2005, from http://www.monitoringthefuture.org/data/04data/pro4t1.pdf.

60. Office of National Drug Control Policy (2005), p. 1.

61. Ibid., p. 2.

62. Office of National Drug Control Policy (2000), p. 12.

63. Office of National Drug Control Policy (2001), p. 14.

64. Office of National Drug Control Policy (2000), p. 14.

65. Office of National Drug Control Policy (2001), p. 16.

66. Ibid., p. 16.

67. Office of National Drug Control Policy (2000), p. 16.

68. Office of National Drug Control Policy (2001), p. 18.

69. Office of National Drug Control Policy (2000), p. 21.

70. Office of National Drug Control Policy (2001), p. 23.

71. Ibid.

72. Office of National Drug Control Policy (2003), p. 3; Office of National Drug Control Policy (2004), p. 2.

73. Office of National Drug Control Policy (2001), p. 21.

74. Office of National Drug Control Policy (2000), p. 19.

75. Office of National Drug Control Policy (2001), p. 25.

76. Ibid., p. 25.

77. Office of National Drug Control Policy (2004), pp. 22-23.

78. Ibid., p. 23.

79. Ibid., pp. 23–24.

80. Ibid., p. 26.

81. Ibid., p. 27

82. Ibid., p. 28.

83. See, for example, Marijuana as Medicine (2004). Retrieved June 5, 2004, from http://www.marijuana-as-medicine.org/; The Science of Medical Marijuana (2004). Retrieved June 5, 2004, from http://www.medmjscience.org/; Marijuana: The Forbidden Medicine (2004). Retrieved June 5, 2004, from http://www.rxmarihuana.com/index2.htm; National Academy of Science Institute of Medicine (2004). Marijuana and medicine: Assessing the science base. Retrieved June 5, 2004, from http://books.nap.edu/html/marimed/; Marijuana Policy Project (2003). Medical marijuana briefing paper—2003: The need to change state and federal law. Retrieved June 5, 2004, from http://www.mpp.org/medicine.html.

84. A similar example comes from another criminal justice policy—the death penalty. The ten states with the highest murder rates have the death penalty, whereas of the ten states with the lowest murder rates, eight do not have the death penalty. Does this simple statistic mean the death penalty is not a deterrent to murder? See Death Penalty Information Center (2004). States with the death penalty and states without. Retrieved June 5, 2004, from http://www.deathpenaltyinfo.org/article.php?scid=12&did=167#STATES%20WITH%20THE%20DEATH%20PENALTY%20V.%20STATES %20WITHOUT.

85. For more on PMPs, see Drug Enforcement Administration Diversion Control Program (2004). Frequently asked questions. Retrieved June 5, 2004, from http://www.deadiversion.usdoj.gov/faq/rx_monitor.htm.

86. Office National Drug Control Policy (2005), p. 3.

87. Ibid., p. 36.

88. Ibid., pp. 36–37.

89. Ibid., p. 37.

90. Office of National Drug Control Policy (2002), p. 9.

91. See, for example, Robinson, M. (2004). *Why crime? An integrated systems theory of antisocial behavior.* Upper Saddle River, NJ: Prentice-Hall.

92. Office of National Drug Control Policy (2003), p. 9.

93. Office of National Drug Control Policy (2004), p. 4.

94. See Monitoring the Future (2004). Drug and alcohol press release and tables. Retrieved May 15, 2004, from http://monitoringthefuture.org/data/03data.html#2003 data-drugs. See also Sourcebook of Criminal Justice Statistics (2004). Table 2.82. High school seniors disapproving of drug use, alcohol use, and cigarette smoking. Retrieved May 15, 2004, from http://www.albany.edu/sourcebook/1995/pdf/t282.pdf; Table 2.83. Eighth and tenth graders disapproving of drug use, alcohol use, and cigarette smoking. Retrieved May 15, 2004, from http://www.albany.edu/sourcebook/1995/pdf/t283.pdf.

The percentage of 12th graders who think drug use in private should be illegal has also fallen. See Sourcebook of Criminal Justice Statistics (2004). Table 2.84. High school seniors approval of prohibition of drug use, alcohol use, and cigarette smoking. Retrieved May 15, 2004, from http://www.albany.edu/sourcebook/1995/pdf/t284.pdf.

95. Monitoring the Future (2004). Table 1. Trends of lifetime prevalence of use of various drugs for eighth, tenth, and twelfth graders. Retrieved December 30, 2004, from http://www.monitoringthefuture.org/data/04data/pro4t1.pdf.

96. U.S. Department of Health and Human Services, Substance Abuse Administration & Mental Health Services, Office of Applied Statistics (2003). NSDUH. Table 1.1B Illicit drug use in lifetime, past year, and past month among persons aged 12 or older: percentages, 2002 and 2003. Retrieved December 19, 2003, from http://www.oas.samhsa.gov/nhsda/2k3tabs/Sect1peTabs1to66.htm#tab1.1b.

97. National Institute on Drug Abuse (2003). *Evaluation of the national youth anti-drug media campaign: 2003 report of findings executive summary*. Retrieved April 6, 2004, from http://www.nida.nih.gov/PDF/DESPR/1203report.pdf.

98. Office of National Drug Control Policy (2005), p. 3.

99. Ibid., pp. 18–19.

100. See, for example, Robinson, M. (2004), chapter 7.

CHAPTER 5

1. Office of National Drug Control Policy (2000). *President's national drug control strategy*. Retrieved March 12, 2001, from http://www.ncjrs.org/ondcppubs/publications/policy/ndcs00/strategy2000.pdf, p. 4.

2. Office of National Drug Control Policy (2001). *President's national drug control strategy*. Retrieved March 12, 2001, from http://www.ncjrs.org/ondcppubs/publications/policy/ndcs01/strategy2001.pdf, p. 4.

3. Ibid., p. 9.

4. Office of National Drug Control Policy (2002). *President's national drug control strategy*. Retrieved March 16, 2002, from http://www.whitehousedrugpolicy.gov/publications/policy/03ndcs/pages1_30.pdf, p. 2.

5. Ibid., p. 13.

6. Ibid.

7. Office of National Drug Control Policy (2003). *President's national drug control strategy*. Retrieved April 14, 2003, from http://www.whitehousedrugpolicy.gov/publications/pdf/strategy2003.pdf, p. 19.

8. Ibid., pp. 2–3.

9. Ibid., p. 14.

10. Ibid., p. 14.

11. Ibid.

12. Ibid.

13. Caulkins, J., Reuter, P., & M. Iguchi (2005). *How goes the "war on drugs"? An assessment of US drug problems and policy.* Santa Monica, CA: RAND Drug Policy Research Center, p. 11.

14. Boyum, D., & P. Reuter (2005). *An analytic assessment of US drug policy.* Washington, DC: AIE Press, p. 23.

15. Ibid., p. 23.

16. Ibid., pp. 23–24.

17. Ibid., p. 1.

18. Ibid., p. 14.

19. Eddy (2003), p. 4.

20. Ibid.

21. Office of National Drug Control Policy (2003), p. 20.

22. Lyman, M., & Potter, G. (1998). *Drugs in society* (3rd ed.). Cincinnati: Anderson.

23. Caulkins et al. (2005), p. 9.

24. Lyman & Potter, G. (1998).

25. Manski, C., Pepper, J., & Petrie, C. (2001). *Informing America's policy on illegal drugs: What we don't know keeps hurting us.* Committee on Data and Research for Policy on Illegal drugs. Washington, DC: National Academy Press, p. 37.

26. Ibid., p. 38.

27. Office of National Drug Control Policy (2004). *President's national drug control strategy.* Retrieved March 15, 2004, from http://www.whitehousedrugpolicy.gov/ publications/policy/ndcs04/2004ndcs.pdf, p. 19.

28. Ibid., pp. 19–20.

29. Ibid., p. 21.

30. Hamid (1998), p. vii.

31. Office of National Drug Control Policy (2005). *The president's national drug control Strategy.* Retrieved March 5, 2005, from http://www.whitehousedrugpolicy.gov/ publications/policy/ndcs05/ndcs05.pdf, p. 25.

32. Ibid.

33. Ibid., p. 7.

34. Office of National Drug Control Policy (2004), pp. 21–22.

35. Ibid., p. 26.

36. For a complete discussion of drug courts in the United States, including tests of their effectiveness, see National Criminal Justice Reference Service (2004). In the spotlight: Drug courts — summary. Retrieved November 10, 2004, from http://www.ncjrs .org/drug_courts/summary.html.

37. Office of National Drug Control Policy (2005), p. 30.

38. Ibid., p. 31.

39. Office of National Drug Control Policy (2004), p. 13.

40. Ibid.

41. Ibid., p. 14.

42. Manski et al. (2001), p. 33.

43. Monitoring the Future (2004). New information. Retrieved April 17, 2004, from http://monitoringthefuture.org/new.html.

44. University of Michigan News and Information Services (2004). Student drug testing not effective at reducing drug use. Retrieved April 17, 2004, from http:// monitoringthefuture.org/pressreleases/03testingpr.pdf, p.1.

45. Office of National Drug Control Policy (2004), p. 13.

46. Office of National Drug Control Policy (2005), p. 16.

47. Ibid., pp. 17-18.

48. Ibid., p. 18.

49. Ibid., p. 19.

50. Jack Cole, Director of Law Enforcement Against Prohibition, personal communication, April 7, 2004.

51. Ibid.

52. Ibid., p. 20.

53. As we pointed out in chapter 3, drug policy experts believe that the treatment gap is likely overstated.

54. See, e.g., Kandel, D, & Chen, K. (2000). Extent of smoking and nicotine dependence in the United States: 1991-1993. *Nicotine & Tobacco Research, 2(3)*, 263-274.

55. Office of National Drug Control Policy (2005), p. 20.

56. Ibid., p. 10.

57. Based on the number of deaths attributed to each drug per the number of users of each drug. Cigarette smokers are between 4.7 and 45.8 times more likely to die in any given year from tobacco use than a user of illicit drugs is likely to die from illicit drugs in any given year, depending on which figure you use for drug death induced deaths. We believe cigarette users are closer to 45 times more likely to die in any given year than illicit drug users. The death rate in 2000 for tobacco was 67.9 deaths per 100,000 smokers (430,000 deaths of 56 million users). The death rate for illicit drug users was 16.4

deaths per 100,000 users (2,300 deaths of 14 million users). Even if we use the government's figure of 19,000 illicit drug induced deaths, the death rate would still be less than for cigarettes at 135.7 per 100,000 users (19,000 deaths of 14 million users). See U.S. Department of Health and Human Services Office of Applied Statistics (2001). Highlights. Retrieved March 21, 2004, from http://www.oas.samhsa.gov/NHSDA/2kNHSDA/highlights.htm.

58. Boyum & Reuter (2005), p. 82.

59. Office of National Drug Control Policy (2000), p. 12.

60. Ibid., p. 13.

61. Ibid.

62. Office of National Drug Control Policy (2000), p. 15.

63. Ibid., p. 17.

64. Ibid., p. 20.

65. Ibid., p. 22.

66. Ibid., p. 15.

67. Office of National Drug Control Policy (2001), pp. 14–15.

68. See, for example, Drug Policy Alliance (2005). Marijuana: The facts. Retrieved March 31, 2005, from http://www.drugpolicy.org/marijuana/factsmyths/.

69. Office of National Drug Control Policy (2001), p. 15.

70. Ibid., p. 16.

71. Ibid., p. 17.

72. Office of National Drug Control Policy (2000), p. 17.

73. Office of National Drug Control Policy (2001), p. 18.

74. Ibid., p. 22.

75. Ibid., p. 24.

76. Ibid.

77. To review government data on purity of drugs and drug prices, see Bennett, B. (2004). Quick links to data and statistics. Retrieved January 20, 2005, from http://www.briancbennett.com/quick-look.htm.

78. Office of National Drug Control Policy (2004). Federal drug data sources. Retrieved March 31, 2005, from http://www.whitehousedrugpolicy.gov/drugfact/sources.html. The location of the fact sheet is: http://www.whitehousedrugpolicy.gov/publications/factsht/drugdata/index.html.

79. See, for example, Boulmetis, J., & Dutwin, P. (1999). *The ABCs of evaluation 6" x 9": Timeless techniques for program and project managers.* New York: Jossey-Bass; Mark, M., Henry, G., & Julnes, G. (2000). *Evaluation: An integrated framework for understanding, guiding, and improving policies and programs.* New York: Jossey-Bass.

80. Office of National Drug Control Policy (2002), p. 21.

81. Office of National Drug Control Policy (2003), p. 13.

82. Ibid., p. 15.

83. Drug Policy Alliance (2005).

84. Walters, J. (2002). The myth of "harmless" marijuana. *Washington Post*, May 1, p. A25.

85. Bennett, B. (2005). Marijuana overview. Retrieved January 10, 2005, from http://www.briancbennett.com/marijuana.htm, emphasis in original.

86. Bennett, B. (2005). Modern day "super weed." Retrieved January 10, 2005, from http://www.briancbennett.com/charts/fed-data/stronger-weed.htm.

87. Office of National Drug Control Policy (2003), p. 30.

88. Ibid., p. 31, emphasis added.

89. This was calculated as 1 minus [28/50] (1 minus the percentage of cocaine entering the country that is seized divided by the percentage of cocaine entering the country that must be seized to make a difference). This gives us 44%, or how far away we are from seizing enough cocaine to make a difference. If we only need to seize 35% of the cocaine entering the country, then we are still coming up 20% short by seizing 28% of it.

90. Office of National Drug Control Policy (2003), pp. 27-28.

91. Ibid., p. 28.

92. Ibid., p. 29.

93. Office of National Drug Control Policy (2004), p. 31.

94. Manski et al. (2001), p. 32.

95. Ibid., p. 150.

96. Ibid., p. 177.

97. Office of National Drug Control Policy (2004), p. 31.

98. Ibid., p. 32.

99. Ibid., p. 32, emphasis added.

100. For a discussion of the meaning of this figure, see U.S. Drug Enforcement Administration (2002). Plan Columbia and regional "spill-over." In *The drug trade in Colombia: A threat assessment*. Retrieved January 2, 2005, from http://www.usdoj.gov/dea/pubs/intel/02006/index.html#4d.

101. Office of National Drug Control Policy (2005). *Source countries and transit zones*. Retrieved March 24, 2005, from http://www.whitehousedrugpolicy.gov/international/afghanistan.html/.

102. For figures pertaining to these data, see Monitoring the Future (2004). Figure 13. Cocaine powder: Trends in annual use, risk, disapproval, and availability. Retrieved December 30, 2004, from http://www.monitoringthefuture.org/data/03data/fig03 _13.pdf.

103. Perl, R. (2004). Drug control: International policy and approaches. *CRS Issue Brief for Congress*. Washington, DC: Library of Congress.

104. Boyum & Reuter (2005), pp. 73–74.

105. Ibid., pp. 75–76.

106. Ibid., p. 77.

107. Ibid.

108. Ibid., p. 78.

109. Office of National Drug Control Policy (2005), p. 39.

110. Ibid.

111. Office of National Drug Control Policy (2004). *Pulse check*. Retrieved March 30, 2005, from http://www.whitehousedrugpolicy.gov/drugfact/pulsecheck.html.

112. Office of National Drug Control Policy (2004). About pulse check. Retrieved March 30, 2005, from http://www.whitehousedrugpolicy.gov/drugfact/aboutpc.html.

113. See Office of National Drug Control Policy (2004). National snapshot. Retrieved March 30, 2005, from http://www.whitehousedrugpolicy.gov/publications/drugfact/pulsechk/january04/national_snapsht.pdf.

114. Office of National Drug Control Policy. (2004). *The price and purity of illicit drugs: 1981 through the second quarter of 2003*. Retrieved March 30, 2005, from http://www.whitehousedrugpolicy.gov/publications/price_purity/price_purity.pdf, p. vii.

115. Ibid., p. 20.

116. Drug Enforcement Administration (2005). *Illegal drug price and purity report*. Retrieved March 30, 2005, from http://www.usdoj.gov/dea/pubs/intel/02058/02058.html.

117. National Drug Intelligence Center (2004). *National drug threat assessment*. Retrieved March 30, 2005, from http://www.usdoj.gov/ndic/pubs8/8731/index.htm.

118. Office of National Drug Control Policy (2005), p. 41.

119. Ibid., p. 42.

120. Cable News Network (2005). Report: Colombia drug war failing. April 1, 2005. Retrieved April 1, 2005, from http://www.cnn.com/2005/WORLD/americas/04/01/colombia.coca.ap/index.html.

121. Office of National Drug Control Policy (2005), p. 42.

122. Ibid., p. 6.

123. Ibid., p. 7.

124. Ibid., pp. 44–45.

125. Ibid., p. 44.

126. Ibid., p. 45.

127. Ibid., p. 48.

128. Ibid.

129. Ibid., p. 49.

130. Ibid., p. 50.

131. Ibid., p. 52.

132. Ibid., p. 53.

133. Ibid., p. 50.

134. Ibid., p. 51.

135. Ibid.

136. Ibid., p. 52.

137. Ibid.

138. Ibid.

139. Ibid., p. 53.

140. Ibid., p. 54.

141. Ibid., p. 55.

142. Ibid., p. 57.

143. Ibid.

CHAPTER 6

1. Boulmetis, J., & Dutwin, P. (1999). *The ABCs of evaluation 6" x 9": Timeless techniques for program and project managers*. New York: Jossey-Bass; Mark, M., Henry, G., & Julnes, G. (2000). *Evaluation: An integrated framework for understanding, guiding, and improving policies and programs*. New York: Jossey-Bass.

2. Office of National Drug Control Policy (2000). *President's national drug control strategy*. Retrieved March 12, 2001, from http://www.ncjrs.org/ondcppubs/publications/policy/ndcs00/strategy2000.pdf, p. 28.

3. Ibid., p. 27.

4. Ibid., p. 28 (emphasis added).

5. Ibid., pp. 28–29.

6. Office of National Drug Control Policy (2001). *President's national drug control strategy*. Retrieved March 12, 2001, from http://www.ncjrs.org/ondcppubs/publications/policy/ndcs01/strategy2001.pdf, p. 30.

7. Office of National Drug Control Policy (2002). *President's national drug control strategy*. Retrieved March 16, 2002, from http://www.whitehousedrugpolicy.gov/publications/policy/03ndcs/pages1_30.pdf, p. 25, emphasis added.

8. Office of National Drug Control Policy (2001). *The economic costs of drug abuse in the United States 1992–1998.* Retrieved March 21, 2005, from http://www.whitehouse drugpolicy.gov/publications/pdf/economic_costs98.pdf.

9. Ibid., p. 10.

10. Office of National Drug Control Policy (2005). *The president's national drug control Strategy.* Retrieved March 5, 2005, from http://www.whitehousedrugpolicy.gov/publications/policy/ndcs05/ndcs05.pdf, p. 6.

11. Ibid., p. 8.

12. Ibid., p. 9.

13. Ibid., p. 7.

14. Ibid.

15. The main page of the Web site of the Office of National Drug Control Policy contains a link to "Drug Data Sources." From that page, one can select "Economic Cost of Drug Abuse in the United States." The link brings up a report titled *The economic costs of drug abuse in the United States 1992–1998.* Retrieved March 21, 2005, from http://www.whitehousedrugpolicy.gov/publications/pdf/economic_costs98.pdf. No updated figures pertaining to costs of the drug war since 1998 are available from the ONDCP Web site.

16. Office of National Drug Control Policy (2004), p. 40.

17. Ibid., emphasis added.

18. Manski, C., Pepper, J., & Petrie, C. (2001). *Informing America's policy on illegal drugs: What we don't know keeps hurting us.* Committee on Data and Research for Policy on Illegal drugs. Washington, DC: National Academy Press, p. 6.

19. Office of National Drug Control Policy (2003), p. 40.

20. Manski et al. (2001), p. 26.

21. Office of National Drug Control Policy (2005), pp. 3–4.

22. Ibid., p. 4.

23. Bennett, B. (2004). Exposing the myths about the "costs" of drug use. Retrieved January 11, 2005, from http://www.brianbennett.com/charts/fed-data/costs/costs.htm.

24. Office of National Drug Control Policy (2001). *The economic costs of drug abuse in the United States 1992–1998.* Retrieved March 21, 2005, from http://www.whitehouse drugpolicy.gov/publications/pdf/economic_costs98.pdf.

25. Bennett, B. (2004). "Exposing the myths about the 'costs' of drug use." Retrieved January 11, 2005, from http://www.brianbennett.com/charts/fed-data/costs/costs.htm, emphasis in original.

26. Ibid.

27. Ibid.

28. Ibid.

29. Manski et al. (2001), p. 54.

30. Ibid., p. 63.

31. Office of National Drug Control Policy (2000), p. 29.

32. Office of National Drug Control Policy (2001), p. 31.

33. Ibid.

34. Office of National Drug Control Policy (2002), p. 29.

35. Bennett, B. (2004). Overview of drug induced deaths. Retrieved January 11, 2005, from http://www.briancbennett.com/charts/death/drug-death.htm (emphasis in original).

36. Office of National Drug Control Policy (2003). *National drug control strategy, Update 2003*. Table 24. Number of deaths from drug-induced causes, by sex and race: U.S., 1979–2002. Retrieved March 12, 2004, from http://www.whitehousedrugpolicy .gov/publications/policy/ndcs03/table24.html.

37. See, for example, MacCoun, Reuter, Jr., & Wolf, C. (2001).

38. Information Please [2004]. Retrieved September 30, 2004, from http://www.info please.com/year/2000.html#us and http://www.infoplease.com/year/1979.html#us.

39. Boyum, D., & P. Reuter (2005). *An analytic assessment of US drug policy*. Washington, DC: AIE Press, p. 20.

40. Office of National Drug Control Policy (2000), p. 30.

41. Ibid., p. 32.

42. Office of National Drug Control Policy (2001), p. 31.

43. Office of National Drug Control Policy (2002), p. 2.

44. Office of National Drug Control Policy (2003), p. 13.

45. Office of National Drug Control Policy (2003). *National drug control strategy, Update 2003*. Table 26. Trends in drug-related emergency room episodes and selected drug mentions, 1988–2001. Retrieved March 12, 2004, from http://www.whitehouse drugpolicy.gov/publications/policy/ndcs03/table26.html.

46. Office of National Drug Control Policy (2000), p. 5.

47. Ibid., p. 26.

48. Bennett, B. (2004). Crime & mayhem: Alcohol leads the pack. Retrieved January 11, 2005, from http://www.briancbennett.com/charts/fed-data/crime/arrest overview.htm.

49. Jack Cole, Director of Law Enforcement Against Prohibition, suggests that since a person can test positive for marijuana for up to a month, some marijuana users may switch to harder drugs because they remain in the body for far shorter periods of time, especially if faced with random drug tests. Personal communication, April 7, 2004.

50. Office of National Drug Control Policy (2001), p. 26.

51. Office of National Drug Control Policy (2000), p. 26.

52. Caulkins, J., Reuter, P., & M. Iguchi (2005). *How goes the "war on drugs"? An assessment of US drug problems and policy*. Santa Monica, CA: RAND Drug Policy Research Center, p. 10.

53. Office of National Drug Control Policy (2001), p. 27.

54. Office of National Drug Control Policy (2004), p. 6.

55. We are not referring to individual cities or states here. We mean that ONDCP does not offer national data from the local and state levels of government. Such statistics pertaining to drug offenses are available through the Bureau of Justice Statistics. See U.S. Department of Justice Office of Special Programs Bureau of Justice Statistics (2004). Retrieved December 13, 2004, from http://www.ojp.usdoj.gov/bjs/.

56. For the data in table format, see Sourcebook of Criminal Justice Statistics (2004). Table 4.29. Percent distribution of arrests for drug abuse violations. Retrieved March 18, 2004, from http://www.albany.edu/sourcebook/1995/pdf/t429.pdf.

57. For a summary of these statistics, see The Sentencing Project (2002). *Distorted priorities: Drug offenders in state prisons*. Retrieved February 11, 2004, from http://www.sentencingproject.org/pdfs/9038.pdf.

58. Office of National Drug Control Policy (2000), p. 27.

59. Ibid.

60. Office of National Drug Control Policy (2001), p. 27.

61. Ibid., p. 29.

62. Gray (2001).

63. Office of National Drug Control Policy (2001), p. 27.

64. Ibid., p. 29.

65. Hamid (1998), pp. 123-124.

66. Manski et al. (2001), p. 57.

67. Hamid (1998), pp. 139-140.

68. Ibid., pp. 132-133.

69. Robinson, M. (2004). *Why crime? An integrated systems theory of antisocial behavior*. Upper Saddle River, NJ: Prentice Hall.

70. Hamid (1998), p. 147.

71. Goldstein, P. (2001). The drugs violence nexus: a tripartite conceptual framework. In J. Inciardi & K. McElrath (Eds.), *The American drug scene: An anthology* (3rd ed.). Los Angeles: Roxbury, p. 344.

72. Ibid., p. 345.

73. Ibid., p. 343.

74. Hamid (1998), pp. 125–126.

75. Ibid., p. 148.

76. Ibid., pp. 127–128.

77. Caulkins et al. (2005), pp. 10–11; Boyum & Reuter (2005), p. 25.

78. Boyum & Reuter (2005), pp. 25–26.

79. Hamid (1998), p. 140.

80. Goldstein, P. (2001), p. 344.

81. Hamid (1998), p. 130.

82. Nurco, D., T. Kinlock, & Hanlon, T. (2001). The drugs-crime connection. In J. Inciardi & K. McElrath (Eds.). *The American drug scene: An anthology* (3rd ed.). Los Angeles: Roxbury, p. 309.

83. Manski et al. (2001), p. 43.

84. Office of National Drug Control Policy (2005). Fact sheet. *Drug-related crime*. Retrieved March 28, 2005, from http://www.whitehousedrugpolicy.gov/publications/ factsht/crime/index.html.

85. Ibid.

86. Goldstein, P. (2001), p. 344.

87. Ibid., p. 345.

88. Hamid (1998), p. 133.

89. Ibid., p. 155.

90. Office of National Drug Control Policy (2003), p. 27.

91. Office of National Drug Control Policy (2002), p. 26.

CHAPTER 7

1. Office of National Drug Control Policy (2003). About ONDCP. Retrieved January 13, 2005, from http://www.whitehousedrugpolicy.gov/about/index.html.

2. Ibid. Emphasis added.

3. Office of National Drug Control Policy (2002). *2002 final report on the 1998 national drug control strategy performance measures of effectiveness*. Retrieved November 30, 2004 from http://www.whitehousedrugpolicy.gov/publications/policy/02pme/ index.html, p. viii. The ONDCP issued three reports as part of an evaluation of the 1998 Strategy goals, the last in February 2002. The final report says that the PME system "should be viewed as a rough gage of the national drug control community's progress toward the desired end states" or, in other words, whether the drug war is meeting its goals.

4. Office of National Drug Control Policy (1998). Factsheet. Office of National Drug Control Policy Reauthorization Act of 1998. Retrieved March 24, 2005, from http://www.whitehousedrugpolicy.gov/about/legislation%5Fc.html.

5. Ibid.

6. Manski, C., Pepper, J., & Petrie, C. (2001). *Informing America's policy on illegal drugs: what we don't know keeps hurting us.* Committee on Data and Research for Policy on Illegal Drugs. Washington, DC: National Academy Press, p. 275.

7. Office of National Drug Control Policy (2002).

8. Ibid., p. 14.

9. Office of National Drug Control Policy (2002). *National drug control strategy of the United States.* Retrieved March 14, 2003, from http://www.whitehousedrugpolicy .gov/publications/policy/03ndcs/index.html, p. 5.

10. Office of National Drug Control Policy (2002). *2002 final report on the 1998 national drug control strategy performance measures of effectiveness.* Retrieved November 30, 2004 from http://www.whitehousedrugpolicy.gov/publications/policy/02pme/index .html, p. 13. All the PME reports can be accessed at http://virlib.ncjrs.org/DrugsAnd Crime.asp.

11. Office of National Drug Control Policy (2002). *National drug control strategy of the United States.* Retrieved March 14, 2003, from http://www.whitehousedrug policy.gov/publications/policy/03ndcs/index.html, p. 6, emphasis added.

12. When 1989 data are unavailable, we use 1990 as the starting point. We do not start our analysis in 1988 because this is the year the ONDCP was created by law, meaning that it was not yet in action.

13. We used 1990 as a beginning point in this figure because the data were not collected in 1989. Data were collected in 1988 but this leaves a two-year gap between 1988 and 1990 in which data were not collected, so we chose to leave out the 1988 data. Since the ONDCP was created in November 1988, any changes in drug use from 1988 to 1989 are unlikely due to anything the ONDCP was doing.

14. We did not include crack cocaine or heroin because the numbers were so small that they could not be sensibly included in the same figure.

15. We did not include PCP or crack cocaine because the numbers were so small that they could not be sensibly included in the figures.

16. The data in this figure for eighth and tenth graders begin in 1991 because the survey did not begin questioning eighth and tenth graders until that year. Data for twelfth graders is available since 1975.

17. See, for example, U.S. Department of Health and Human Services, Substance Abuse and Mental Health Services Administration, Office Applied Statistics (2004). Treatment gap. Retrieved March 2, 2005, from http://www.drugabusestatistics. samhsa.gov/tx.htm#Gap.

18. Boyum & Reuter (2005) report that the percentage of drug users who needed treatment but did not receive it varied between 54% and 64% between 1995 and 1998. See Boyum, D., & P. Reuter (2005). *An analytic assessment of US drug policy.* Washington, DC: AIE Press, p. 63.

19. U.S. Department of Health and Human Services, Substance Abuse and Mental Health Services Administration, Office Applied Statistics (2004). *2003 national survey on drug use and health. Needing and receiving specialty treatment.* Retrieved March 14, 2003, from http://www.drugabusestatistics.samhsa.gov/nhsda/2k3nsduh/2k3Results.htm#7.3

20. Boyum & Reuter (2005), p. 63.

21. See Bennett, B. (2004). Marijuana eradication 1982–2001. Retrieved January 17, 2005, from http://www.briancbennett.com/charts/fed-data/pot-eradication.htm.

22. Sourcebook of Criminal Justice Statistics (2004). Table 4.39. Seizures of illegal drug laboratories by the Drug Enforcement Administration. Retrieved March 10, 2005, from http://www.albany.edu/sourcebook/pdf/t439.pdf.

23. Sourcebook of Criminal Justice Statistics (2004). Table 4.37. Drug removals from the Domestic market by the Drug Enforcement Administration. Retrieved March 10, 2005, from http://www.albany.edu/sourcebook/pdf/t437.pdf.

24. Ibid.

25. Sourcebook of Criminal Justice Statistics (2004). Table 4.43. Drug seizures by the U.S. Customs Service. Retrieved March 10, 2005, from http://www.albany.edu/sourcebook/pdf/t443.pdf.

26. U.S. Customs & Border Protection (2004). Welcome to U.S. Customs and Border Protection. Retrieved March 24, 2005, from http://www.cbp.gov/xp/cgov/tool box/about/mission/cbp.xml.

27. Government agencies also made more arrests for drug offenders, obtained more convictions, and sent more drug offenders to prison during the period of study.

28. Bennett, B. (2004). Consumer drug spending 1988–2000. Retrieved January 17, 2005, from http://www.briancbennett.com/charts/fed-data/consumer-spending.htm.

29. Manski et al. (2001), p. 145.

30. For example, scholars have examined the effects of criminal justice (police, corrections) and noncriminal justice (economic, social) factors on crime. See Blumstein, A., & Wallman, J. (2000). *The crime drop in America.* New York: Cambridge University Press; Conklin, J. (2002). *Why crime rates fell.* Boston: Allyn & Bacon.

31. Blumstein, A., & J. Wallman (2000), p. 2.

32. Ibid., p. 11.

33. Robinson, M. (2005). *Justice blind? Ideals and realities of American criminal justice* (2nd ed.). Upper Saddle River, NJ: Prentice-Hall.

34. See, for example, Reinarman, C., & Levine, H. (1997). *Crack in America: Demon drugs and social justice*. Berkeley: University of California Press; Baum, D. (1997). *Smoke and mirrors: The war on drugs and the politics of failure*. New York: Back Bay Books (Time Warner Book Group); Jensen, E., & Gerber, J. (1997). *The new war on drugs: Symbolic politics and criminal justice policy*. Cincinnati, OH: ACJS/Anderson Monograph Series.

35. Paulsen, D., & Robinson, M. (2004). *Spatial aspects of crime: Theory and practice*. Boston: Allyn & Bacon.

36. See, for example, Miron, J. (2004). *Drug war crimes*. Washington, DC: The Independent Institute.

37. See, for example, Gray, J. (2001). *Why our drug laws have failed and what we can do about it: A judicial indictment of the war on drugs*. Philadelphia: Temple University Press.

38. Miron (2004).

39. Manski et al. (2001), p. 4.

40. Robinson, M. (2005).

41. Gray (2004); MacCoun, R., & Reuter, P. (2001). *Drug war heresies : Learning from other vices, times, and places*. New York: Cambridge University Press.

42. See, for example, Cole, J. (2004). End prohibition now. In B. Masters (Ed.), *The new prohibition: Voices of dissent challenge the drug war*. St Louis, MO: Accurate Press.

43. MacCoun, Reuter, & Wolf (2001).

CHAPTER 8

1. Government Accountability Office (2005). *Office of National Drug Control Policy—video news release, B-303495*, Retrieved March 31, 2005, from http://www.gao.gov/decisions/appro/303495.htm.

2. Ibid.

3. Ibid.

4. Sherman, L., Gottfredson, D., MacKenzie, D., Eck, J., Reuter, P., & Bushway, S. (1998). *Preventing crime: What works, what doesn't, what's promising*. A report to the United States Congress prepared for the National Institute of Justice. Retrieved March 20, 2005, from http://www.ncjrs.org/works/.

5. See, for example, MacCoun, R., Reuter, P., & Wolf, C. (2001). *Drug war heresies: Learning from other vices, times, and places*. New York: Cambridge University Press.

6. See MacCoun et al. (2001) for a thorough evaluation of other strategies.

7. Manski, C., Pepper, J., & Petrie, C. (2001). *Informing America's policy on illegal drugs: What we don't know keeps hurting us*. Committee on Data and Research for Policy on Illegal Drugs. Washington, DC: National Academy Press, p. 127.

8. Ibid., p. 132.

9. Ibid.

10. National Commission on Marijuana and Drug Abuse (1973). Final report. *Drug use in America: Problem in perspective*. Washington, DC: U.S. Government Printing Office.

11. Office of National Drug Control Policy (2005). *President's national drug control strategy*. Retrieved March 5, 2005, from http://www.whitehousedrugpolicy.gov/publications/policy/ndcs05/ndcs05.pdf, p. 8.

12. Manski et al. (2001), p. 11.

13. Ibid., p. 213.

14. Robinson, M. (2004). *Why crime? An integrated systems theory of antisocial behavior*. Upper Saddle River, NJ: Prentice-Hall.

15. Botvin, G. (1990). Substance abuse prevention: Theory, practice, and effectiveness. In M. Tonry & J. Wilson (Eds.), *Drugs and crime*. Chicago: University of Chicago Press.

16. Boyum, D., & P. Reuter (2005). *An analytic assessment of US drug policy*. Washington, DC: AIE Press, p. 89.

17. Ibid., pp. 90-91.

18. Robinson (2004).

19. Office of National Drug Control Policy (2000). *President's national drug control strategy*. Retrieved February 3, 2004, from http://www.ncjrs.org/ondcppubs/publications/policy/ndcs00/strategy2000.pdf, p. 5.

20. Robinson, M. (2005). *Justice blind? Ideals and realities of American criminal justice* (2nd ed.). Upper Saddle River, NJ: Prentice-Hall.

21. Boyum & Reuter (2005), p. 2.

22. Ibid., p. 86.

23. Ibid., p. 61.

24. MacCoun et al. (2001).

25. Nadelmann, E., & Harrison, L. (2000). *Harm reduction: National and international perspectives*. Thousand Oaks, CA: Sage.

26. Office of National Drug Control Policy (2003). *President's national drug control strategy*. Retrieved March 10, 2004, from http://www.whitehousedrugpolicy.gov/publications/pdf/strategy2003.pdf, pp. 40-41.

27. Boyum & Reuter (2005), pp. 93-94.

28. Ibid., p. 102.

Postscript

1. Office of National Drug Control Policy (2006). *The President's national drug control strategy*. Retrieved June 17, 2006, from http://www.whitehousedrugpolicy.gov/publications/policy/ndcs06/ndcs06.pdf, p. 2.

2. Office of National Drug Control Policy (2006). Drug control funding tables. Retrieved June 17, 2006, from http://www.ondcp.gov/publications/policy/07budget/partii_funding_tables.pdf.

3. Office of National Drug Control Policy (2006), p. 7.

4. Ibid., p. 6.

5. Ibid., p. 1, emphasis added.

6. Monitoring the Future (2006). Table 1—Trends in lifetime prevalence of use of various drugs of eighth, tenth, and twelfth graders. [Online]. Available: http://www.monitoringthefuture.org/pubs/monographs/overview2005.pdf.

7. U.S. Department of Health and Human Services (2005). Substance Abuse and Mental Health Services Administration. *2004 national survey on drug use and health*. Retrieved June 18, 2006, from http://oas.samhsa.gov/nsduh/2k4nsduh/2k4Results/2k4Results.htm#1of).

8. Office of National Drug Control Policy (2006), p. 2.

9. Ibid.

10. Ibid., p. 1.

11. Ibid.

12. Ibid., p. 2.

13. Ibid.

14. Monitoring the Future (2006). Table 3—Trends in 30-day prevalence of use of various drugs of eighth, tenth, and twelfth graders. [Online]. Available: http://www.monitoringthefuture.org/pubs/monographs/overview2005.pdf.

15. Office of National Drug Control Policy (2006), p. 5.

16. Ibid., p. 28.

17. Ibid., p. 28.

18. Ibid., pp. 5-6.

19. Ibid., p. 3.

20. Ibid., p. 6.

21. Ibid., p. 8.

22. Ibid., p. 10.

23. Ibid., pp. 8, 10.

24. Ibid., p. 14.

25. Ibid., p. 23.

26. Ibid.

27. Ibid., p. 17.

28. Ibid.

29. Ibid., p. 18.

30. Ibid., p. 19, emphasis added.

31. Ibid.

32. Ibid.

33. Ibid.

34. Ibid., p. 18.

35. Ibid., pp. 18–19.

36. Ibid., p. 20.

37. Ibid., p. 24.

38. Ibid., p. 19.

39. Ibid., p. 3.

40. O'Driscoll, P. (2005). Denver votes to legalize marijuana possession. *USA TODAY* November 3, 2005. [Online]. Available: http://www.usatoday.com/news/nation/2005-11-03-pot_x.htm.

41. Office of National Drug Control Policy (2006), p. 12.

42. Office of National Drug Control Policy (2006), p. 13.

43. Ibid., p. 23.

44. Ibid., p. 8.

45. Ibid., p. 30.

46. Ibid., p. 31.

47. Ibid., p. 32.

48. Ibid., p. 33.

49. Ibid., p. 35.

50. Ibid., p. 37.

51. Ibid., p. 38.

52. Ibid.

53. Ibid.

Index

259